MURDER BALLADS

BY GABE SORIA, PAUL REINWAND & CHRIS HUNT

PROLOGUE & EPILOGUE BY RUSS BADGETT

MUSIC BY ROBERT FINLEY & DAN AUERBACH

COLORING BY KENDRA WELLS & FRED STRESING

PART 4 FLATS BY M. CODY WILEY

LETTERING BY FRED STRESING

DESIGN BY TYLER BOSS

MURDER BALLADS

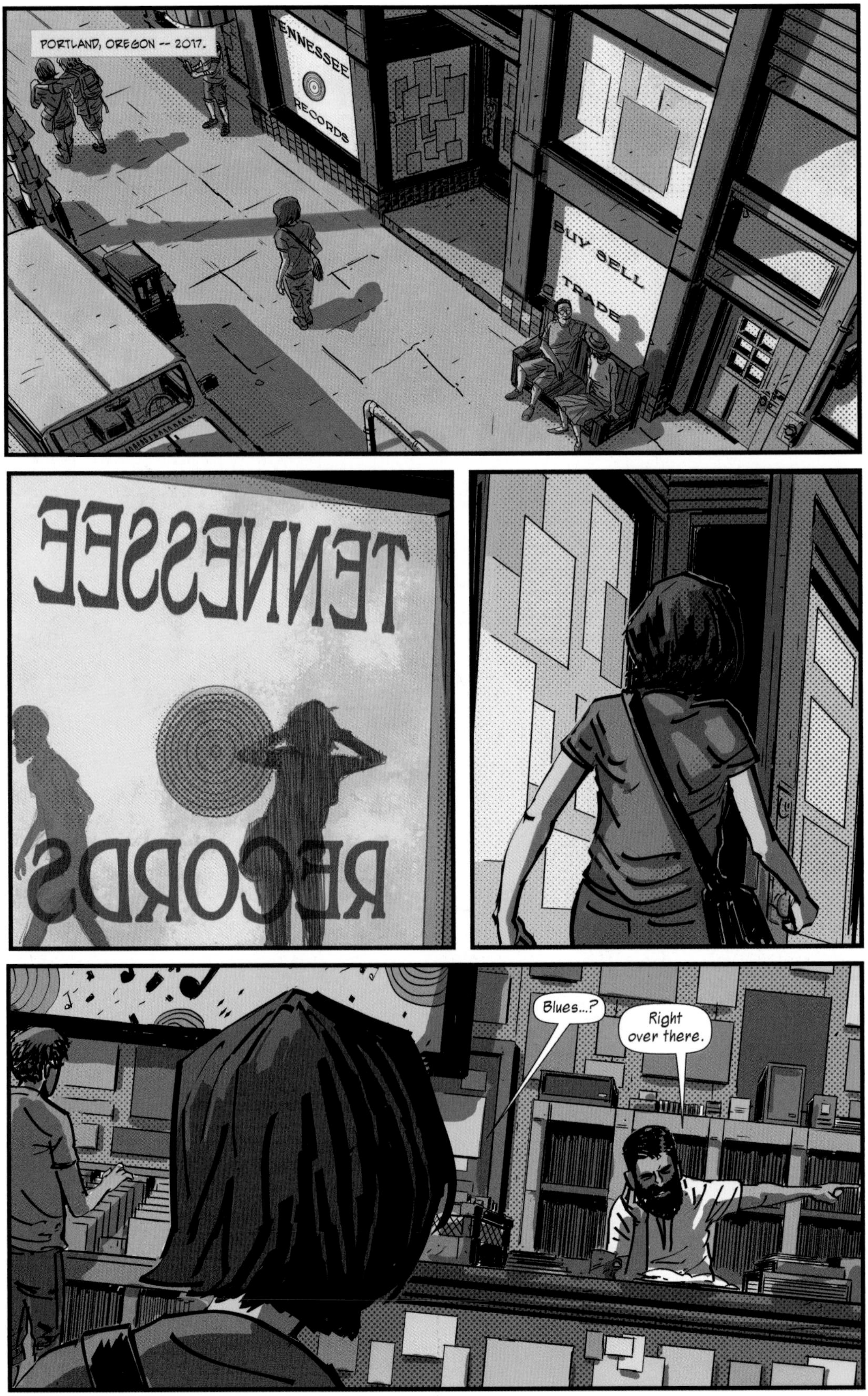
PORTLAND, OREGON -- 2017.
TENNESSEE RECORDS
BUY SELL TRADE
TENNESSEE RECORDS
Blues...?
Right over there.

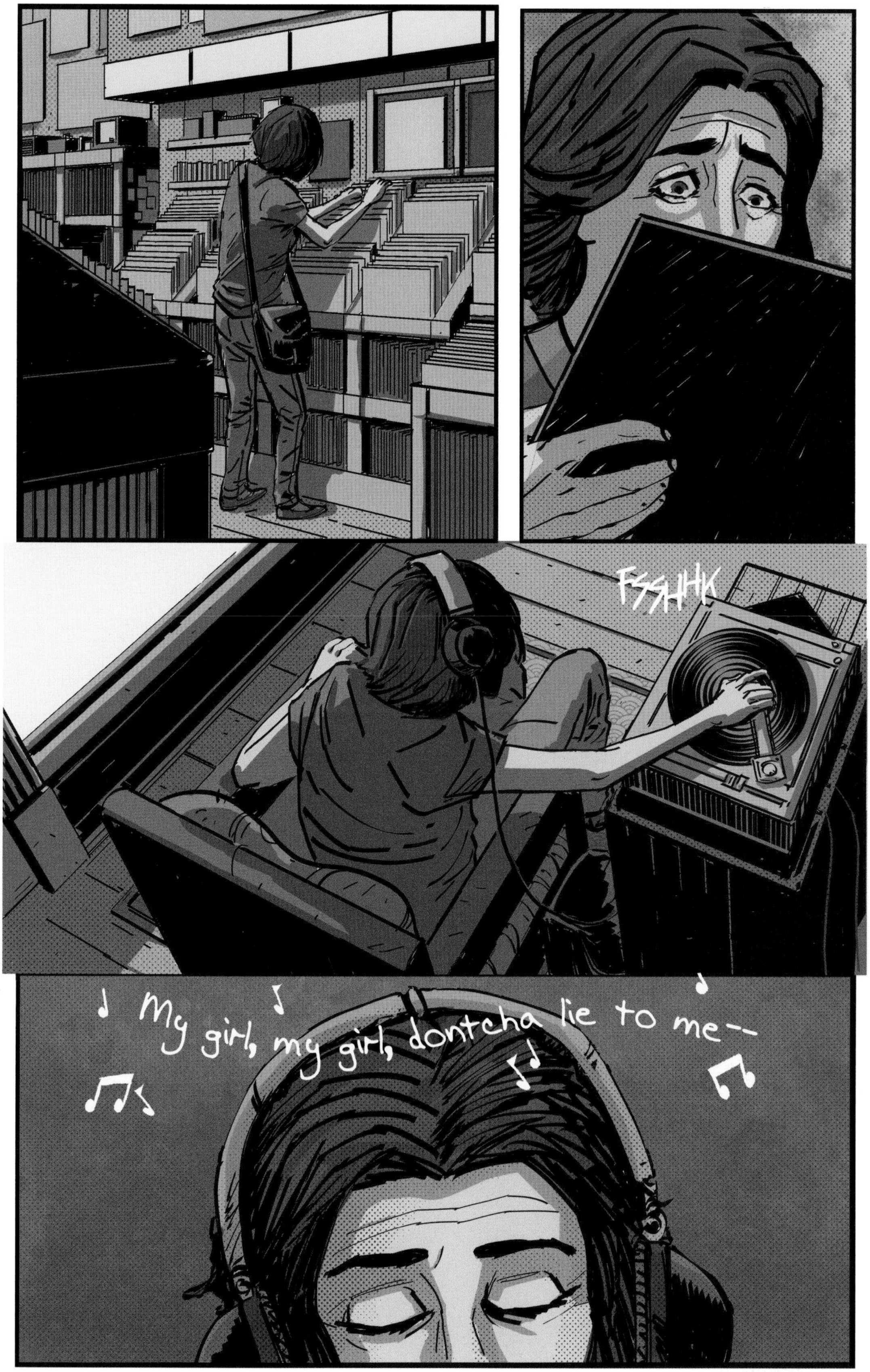
FSSHHK
My girl, my girl, dontcha lie to me--

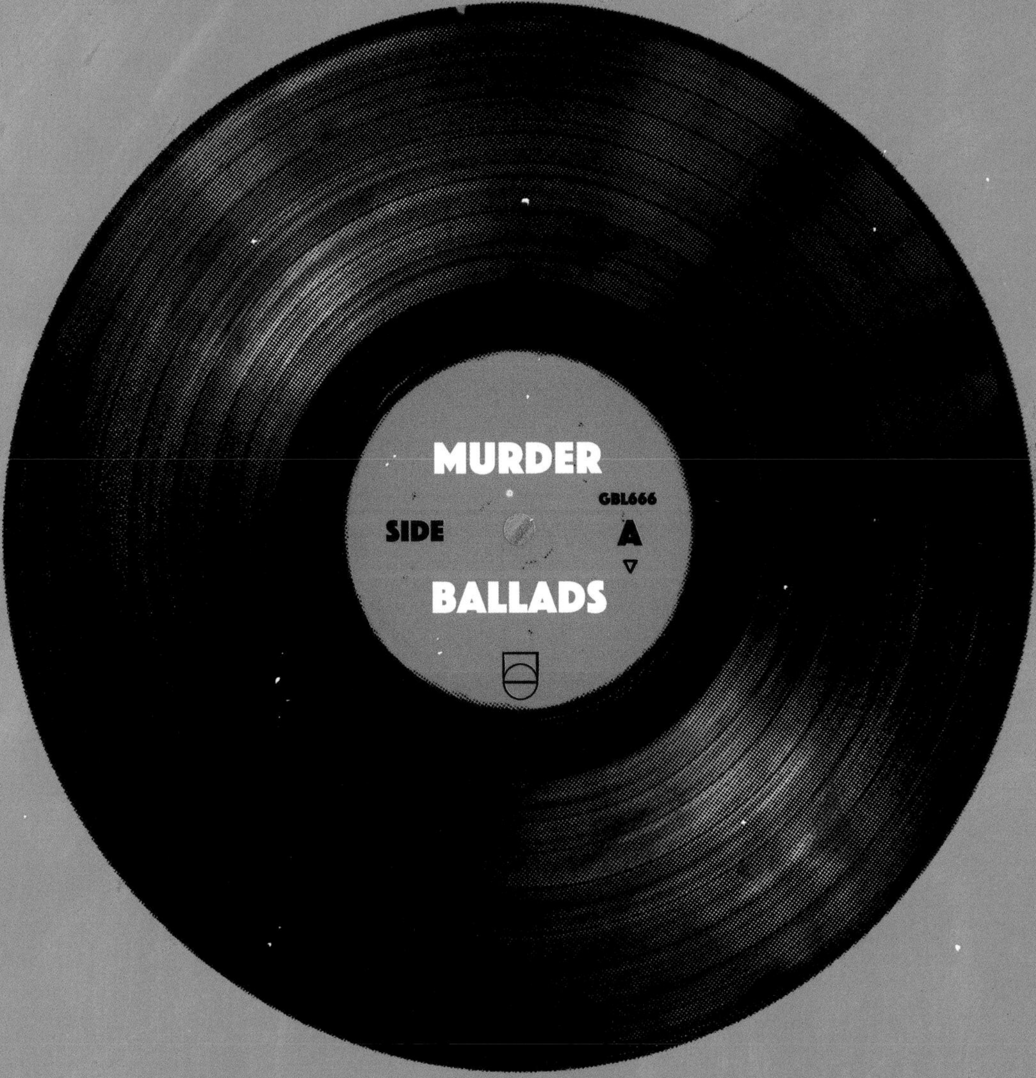
MURDER
GBL666
SIDE
A
BALLADS

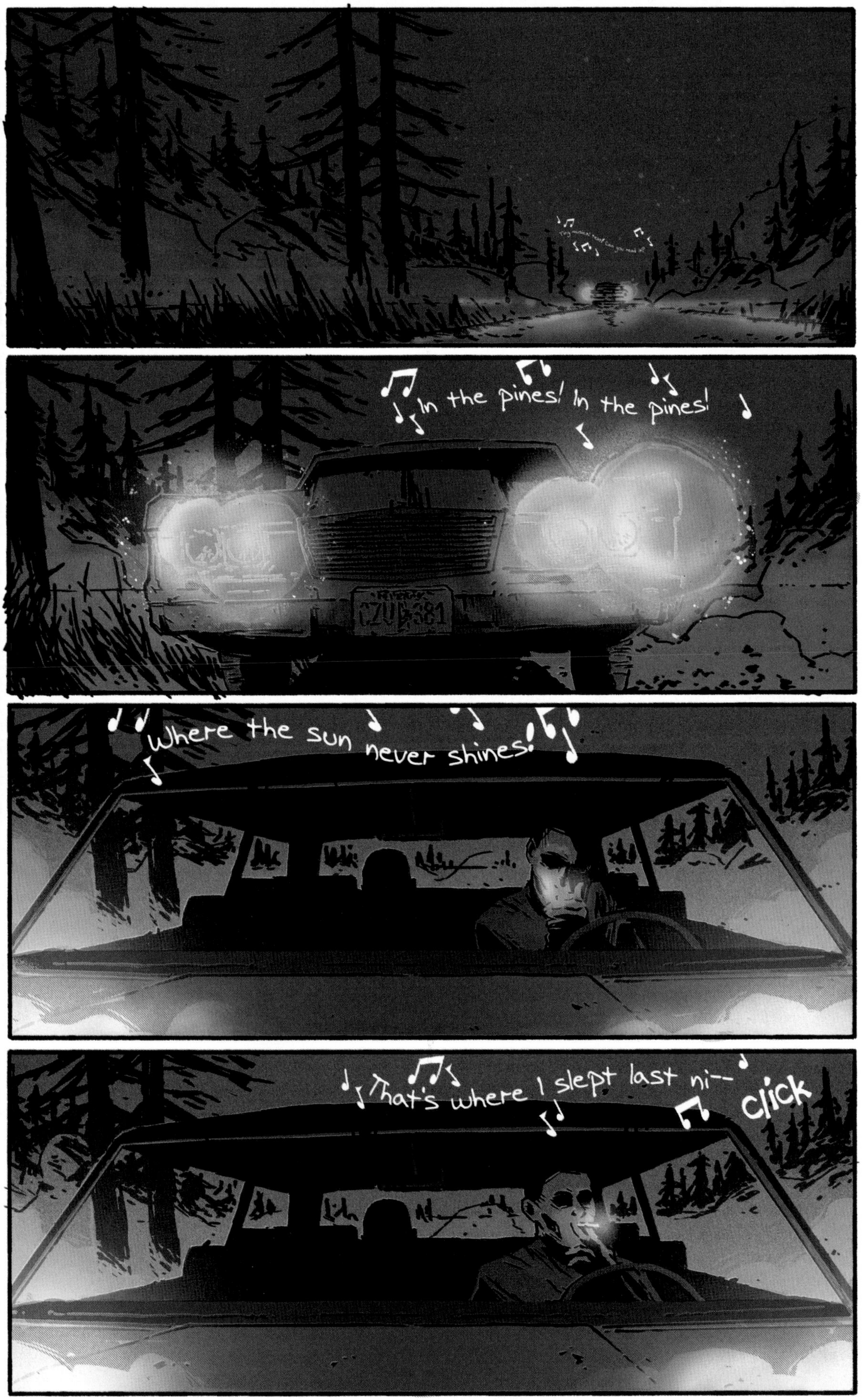
In the pines! In the pines!
Where the sun never shines!
That's where I slept last ni--
CLICK

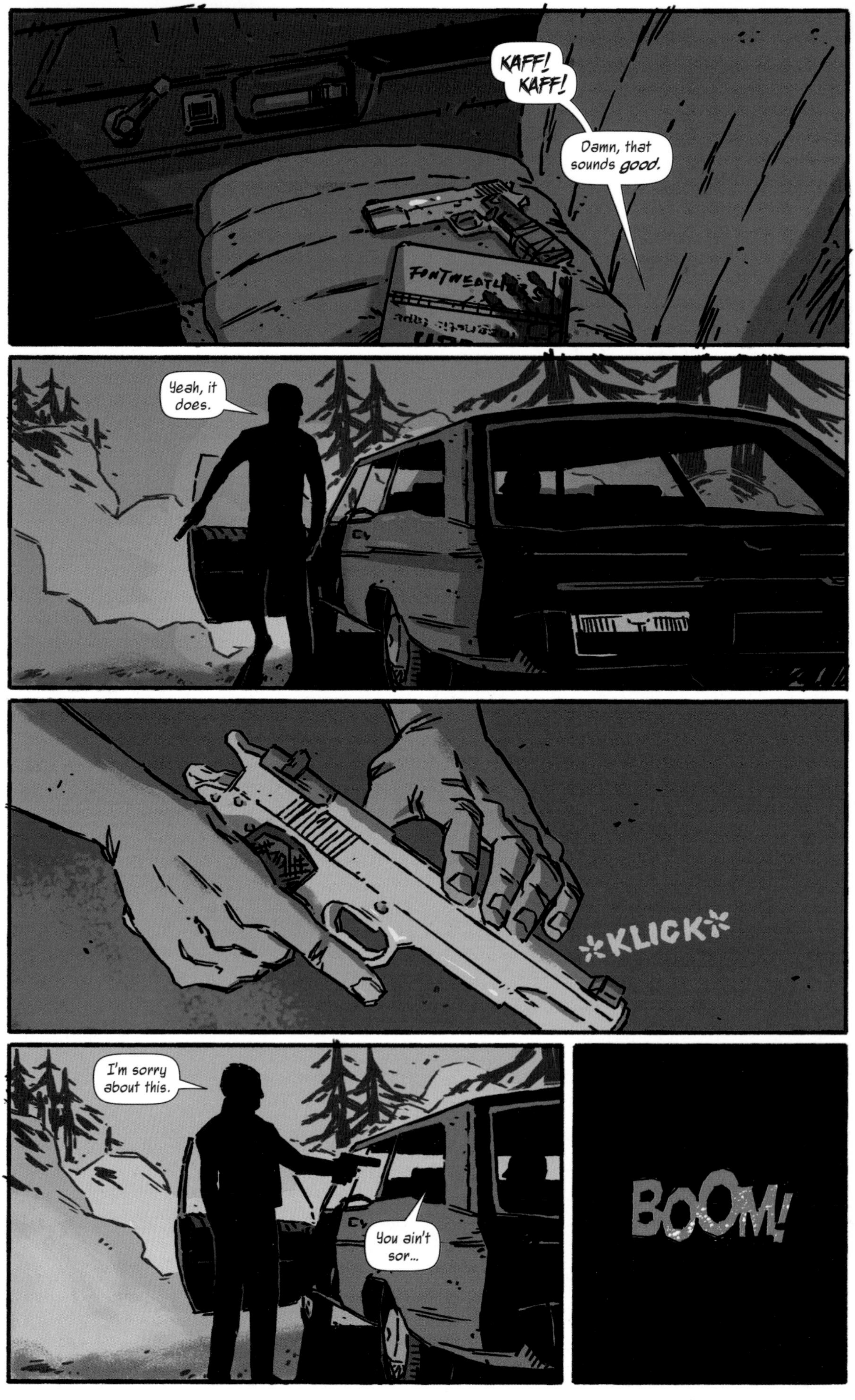
KAFF! KAFF!
Damn, that sounds good.
FONTWEATHERS
Yeah, it does.
KLICK
I'm sorry about this.
You ain't sor...
BOOM!

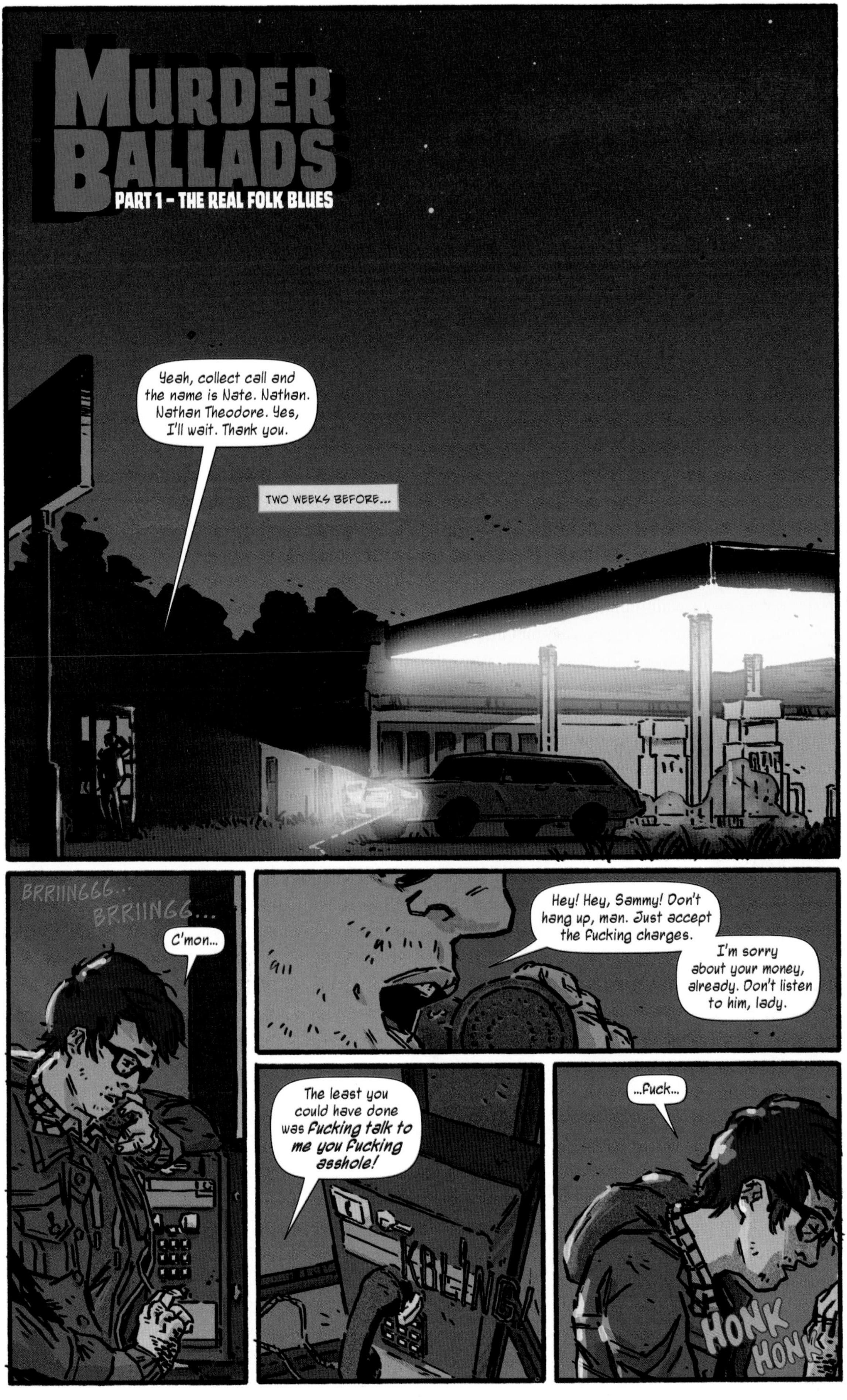
MURDER BALLADS
PART 1 - THE REAL FOLK BLUES
Yeah, collect call and the name is Nate. Nathan. Nathan Theodore. Yes, I'll wait. Thank you.
TWO WEEKS BEFORE...
BRRIINGGG... BRRIINGG...
C'mon...
Hey! Hey, Sammy! Don't hang up, man. Just accept the fucking charges.
I'm sorry about your money, already. Don't listen to him, lady.
The least you could have done was fucking talk to me you fucking asshole!
KRLING!
...Fuck...
HONK HONK

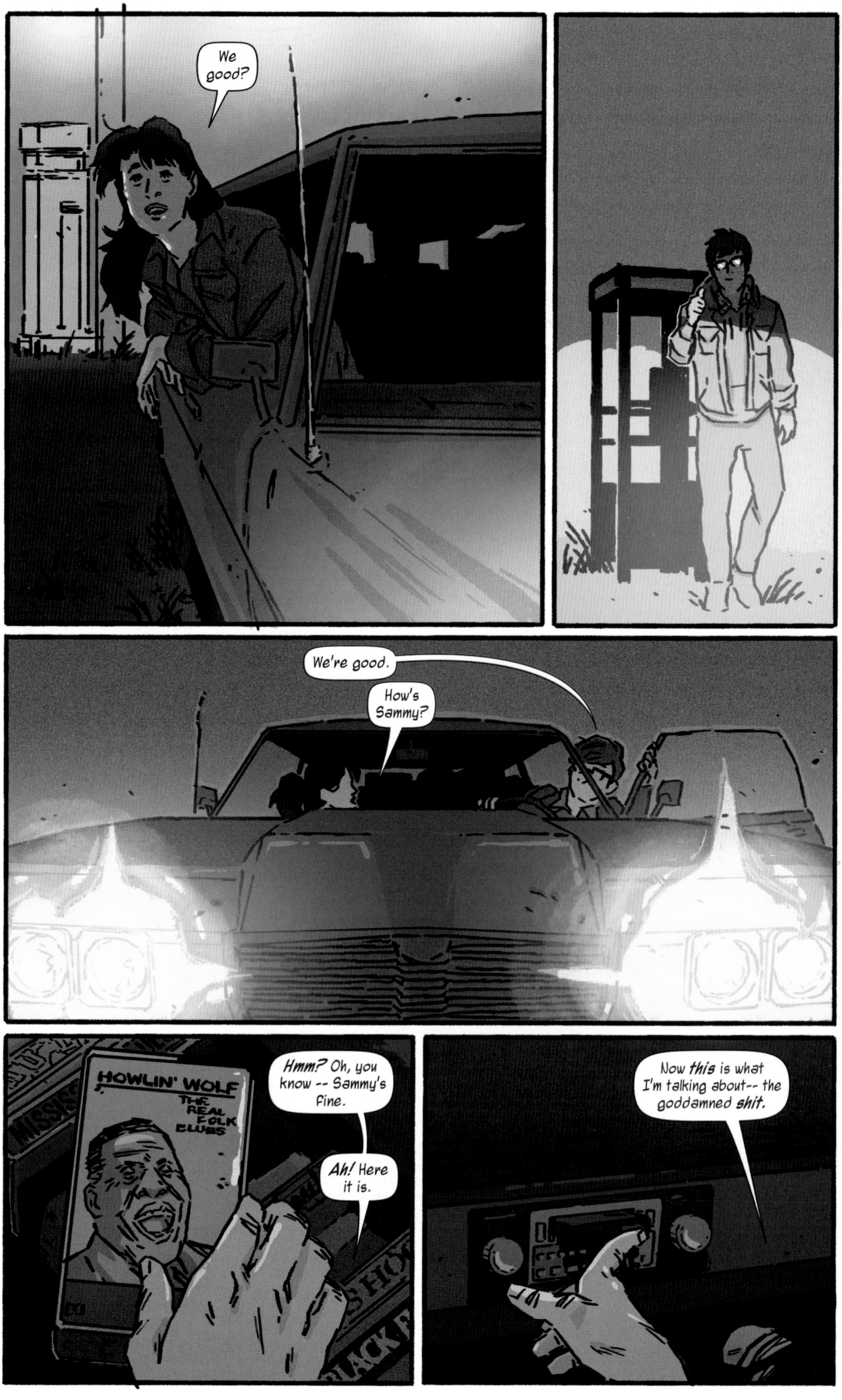
We good?
We're good.
How's Sammy?
HOWLIN' WOLF
THE REAL FOLK BLUES
Hmm? Oh, you know -- Sammy's fine.
Ah! Here it is.
Now this is what I'm talking about-- the goddamned shit.

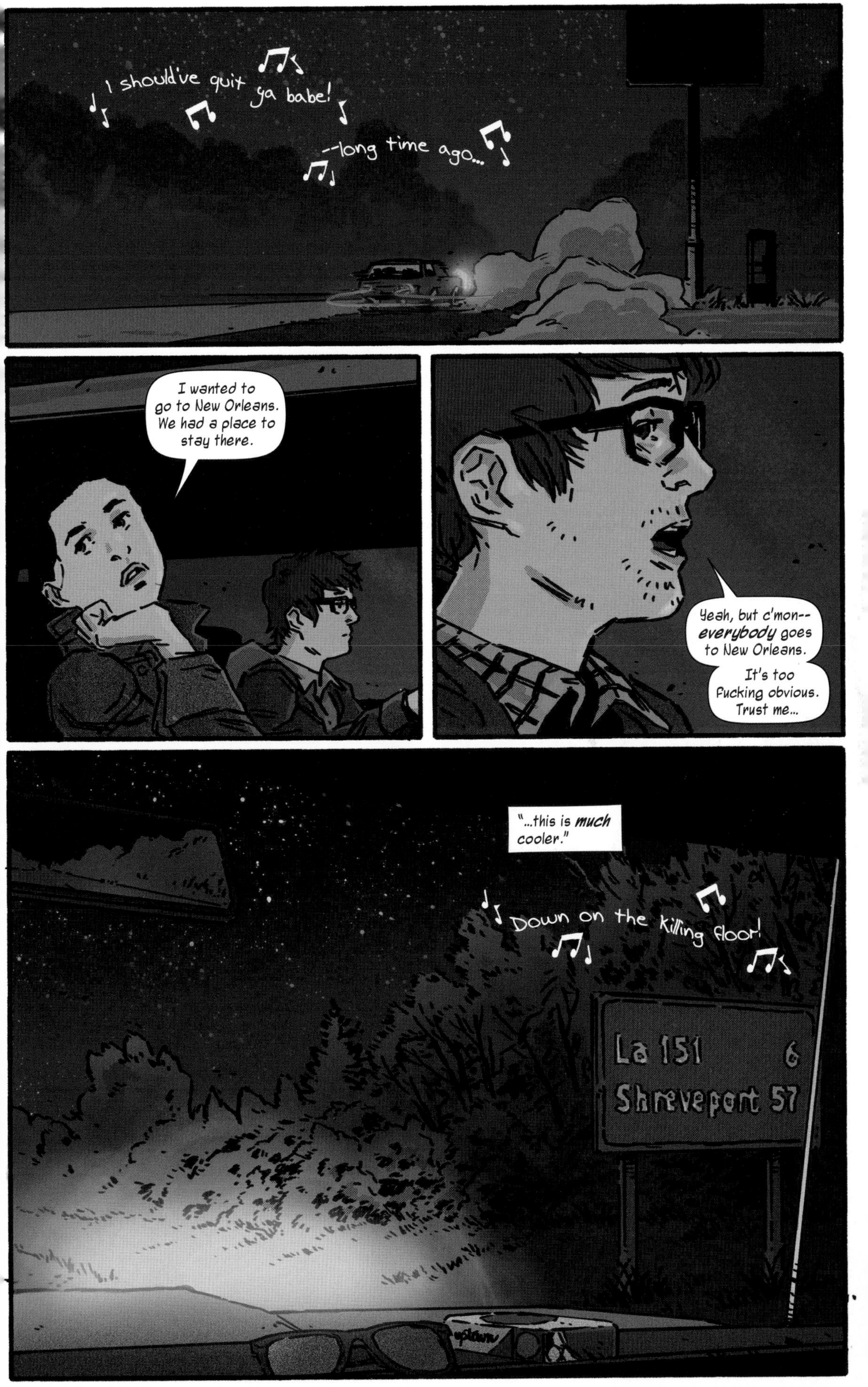
I should've quit ya babe!
--long time ago...
I wanted to go to New Orleans. We had a place to stay there.
Yeah, but c'mon-- *everybody* goes to New Orleans.
It's too fucking obvious. Trust me...
"...this is *much* cooler."
Down on the killing floor!
La 151 6
Shreveport 57

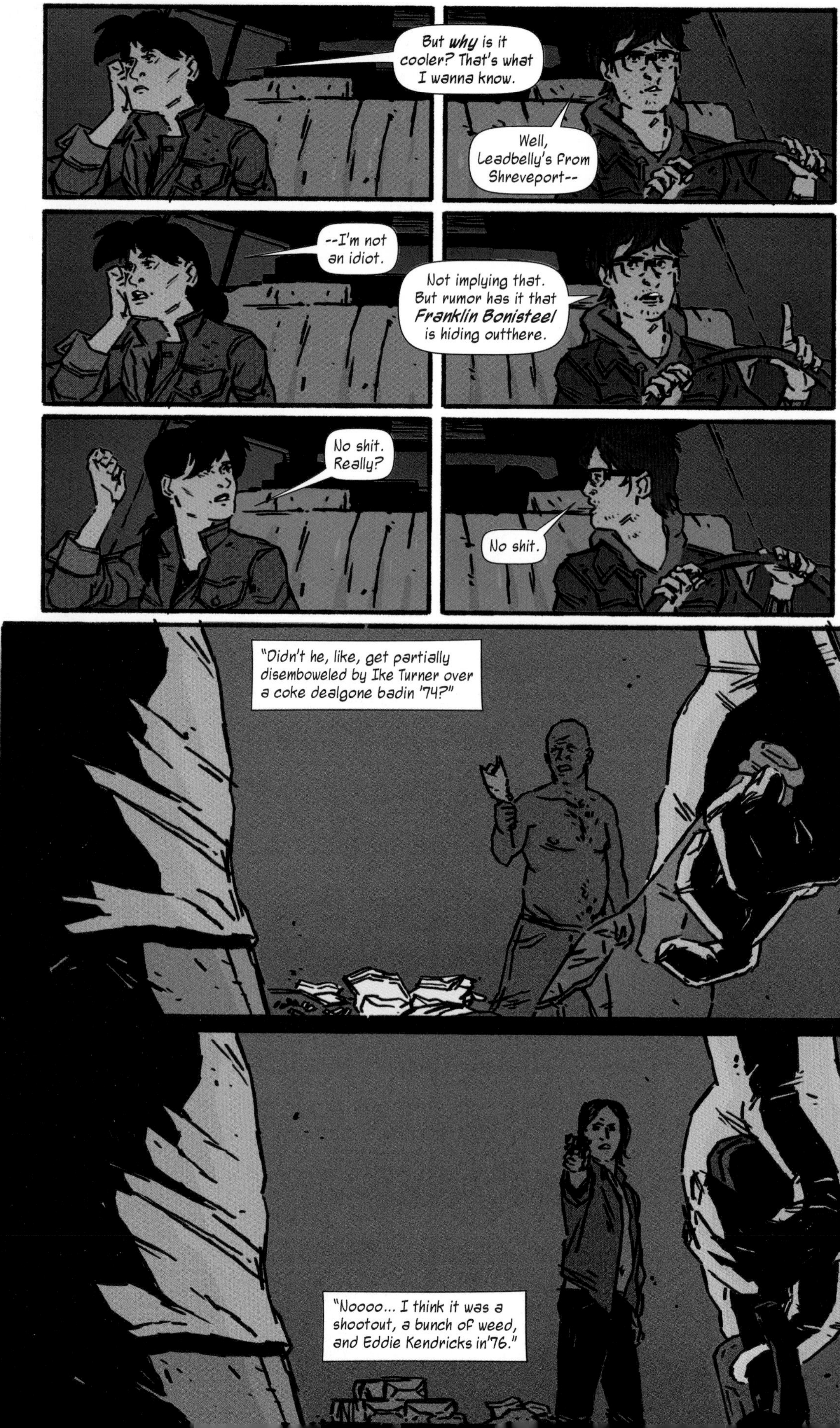
But why is it cooler? That's what I wanna know.
Well, Leadbelly's from Shreveport--
--I'm not an idiot.
Not implying that. But rumor has it that Franklin Bonisteel is hiding outthere.
No shit. Really?
No shit.
"Didn't he, like, get partially disemboweled by Ike Turner over a coke dealgone badin '74?"
"Noooo... I think it was a shootout, a bunch of weed, and Eddie Kendricks in'76."

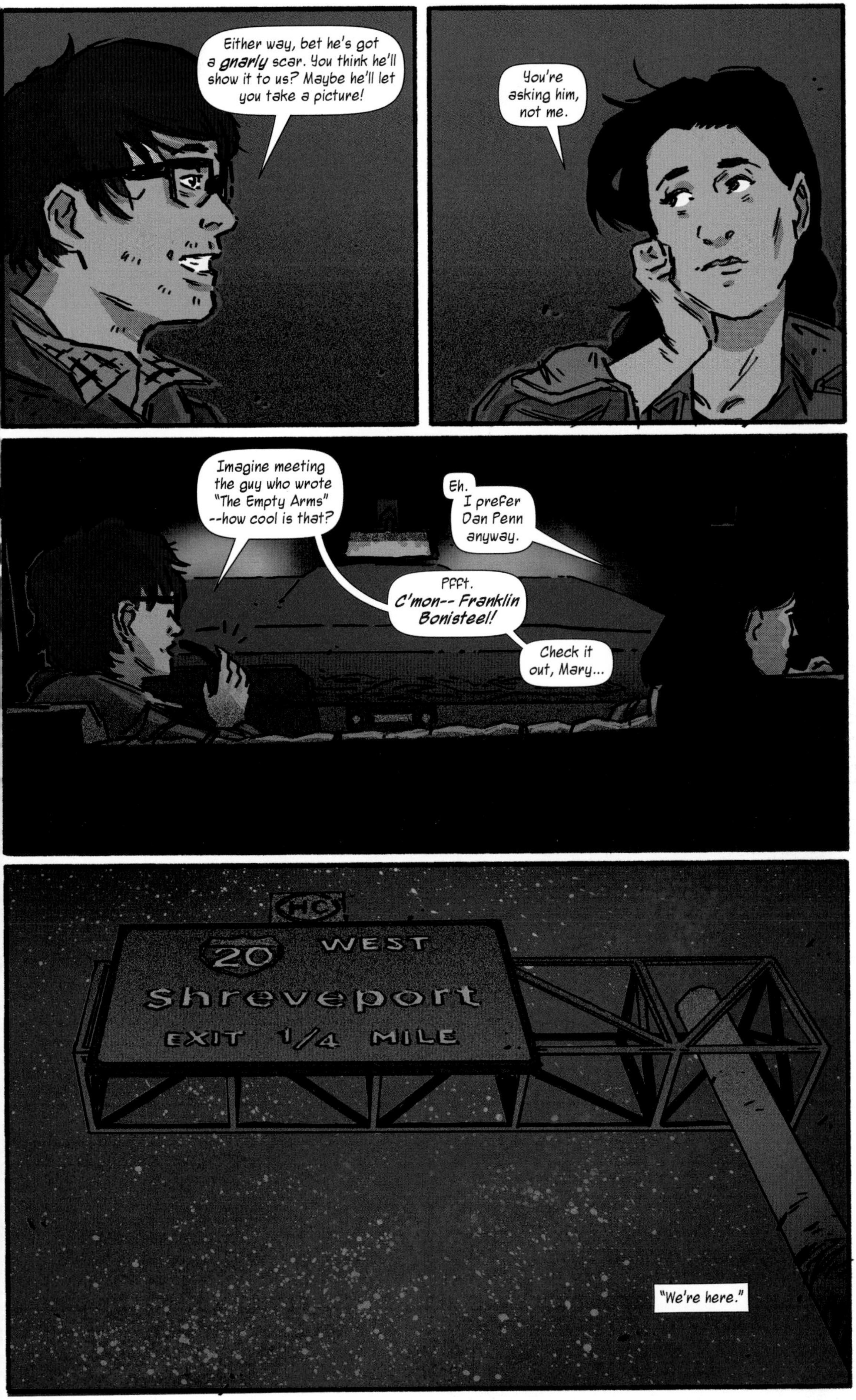

Either way, bet he's got a gnarly scar. You think he'll show it to us? Maybe he'll let you take a picture!
You're asking him, not me.
Imagine meeting the guy who wrote "The Empty Arms" --how cool is that?
Eh. I prefer Dan Penn anyway.
Pfft. C'mon-- Franklin Bonisteel!
Check it out, Mary...
HC
20 WEST
Shreveport
EXIT 1/4 MILE
"We're here."

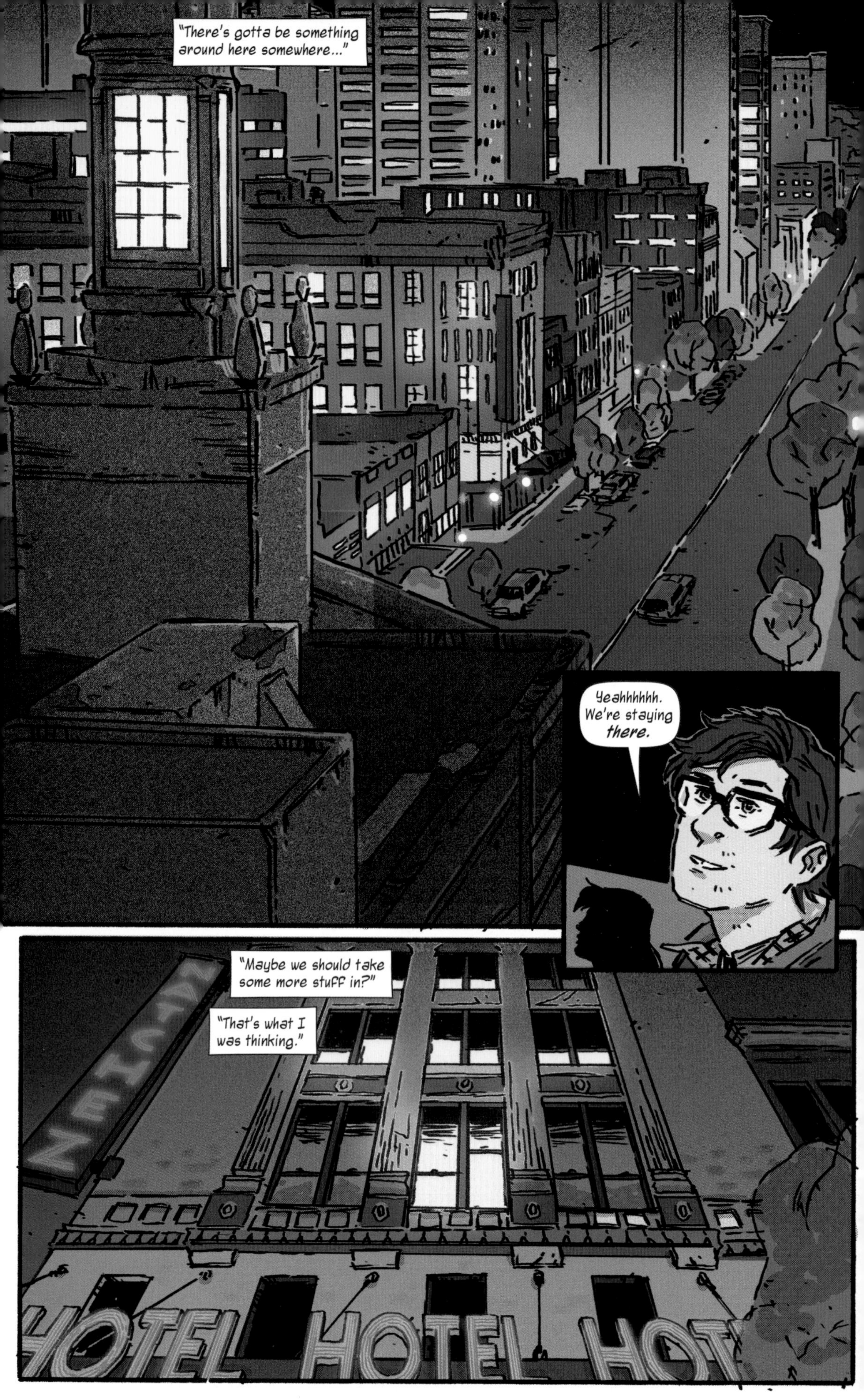
"There's gotta be something around here somewhere..."
Yeahhhhhh. We're staying *there.*
"Maybe we should take some more stuff in?"
"That's what I was thinking."
HOTEL HOTEL HOT

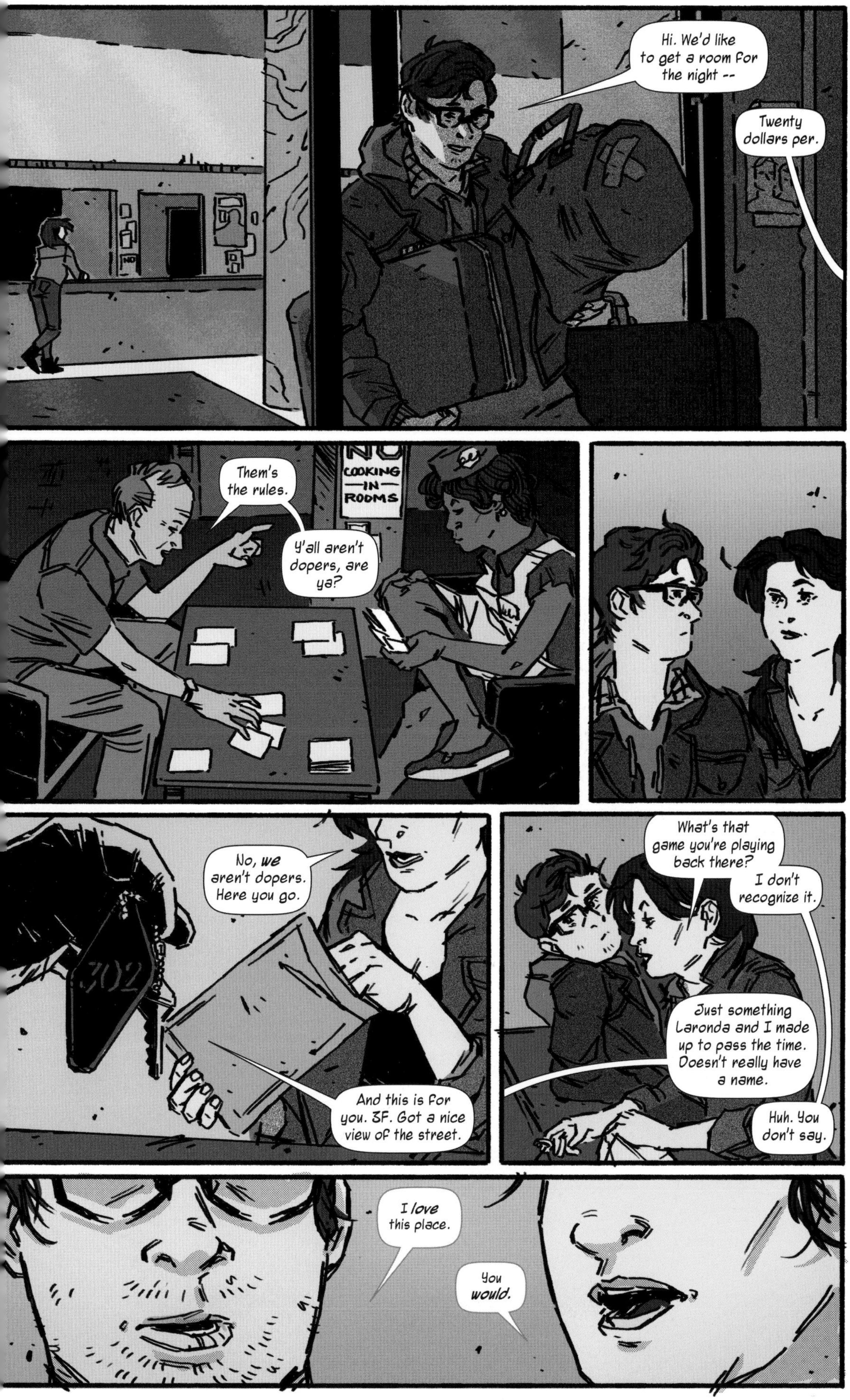
Hi. We'd like to get a room for the night --
Twenty dollars per.
Them's the rules.
Y'all aren't dopers, are ya?
COOKING IN ROOMS
No, we aren't dopers. Here you go.
302
And this is for you. 3F. Got a nice view of the street.
What's that game you're playing back there?
I don't recognize it.
Just something Laronda and I made up to pass the time. Doesn't really have a name.
Huh. You don't say.
I love this place.
You would.

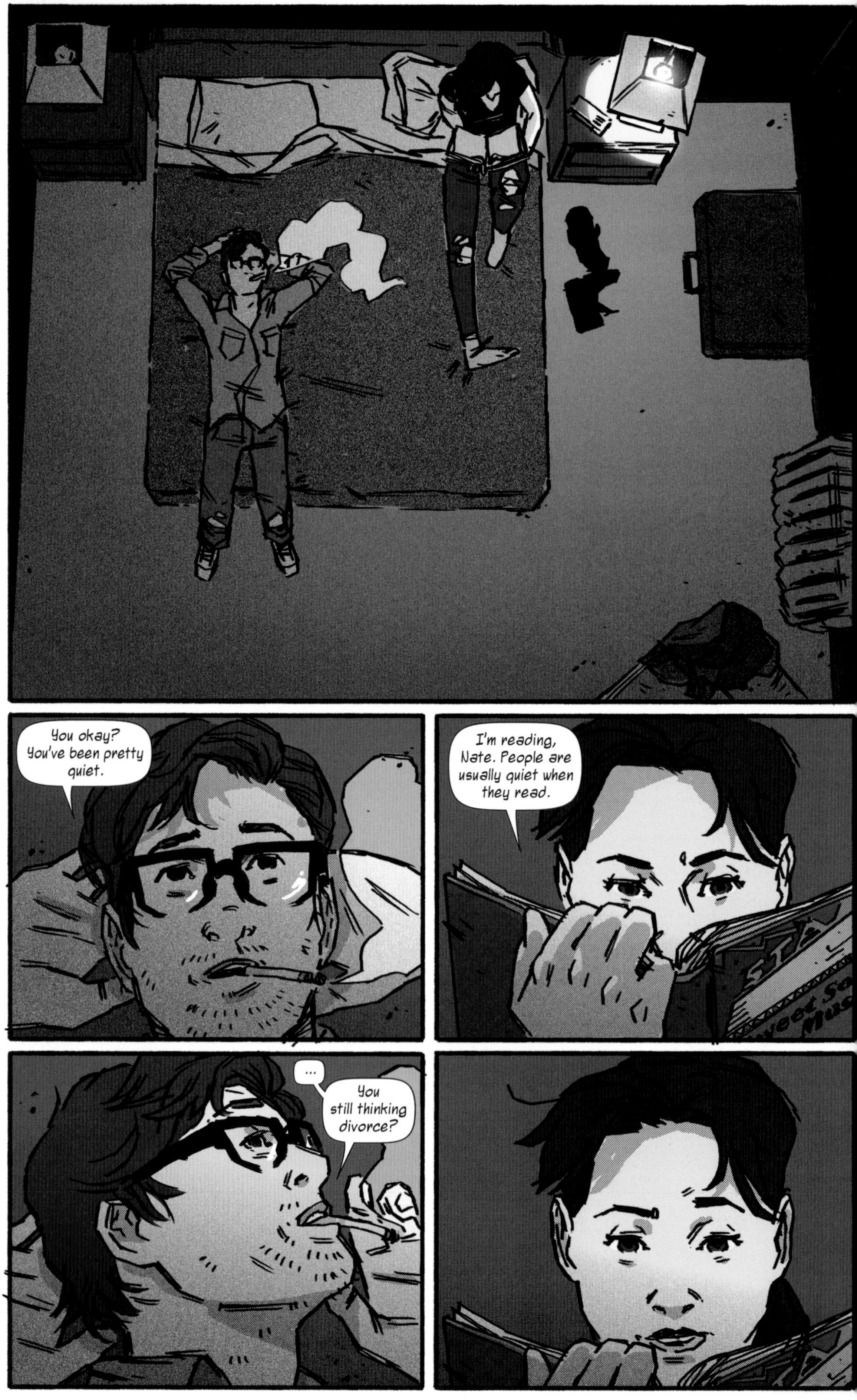
You okay? You've been pretty quiet.
I'm reading, Nate. People are usually quiet when they read.
...
You still thinking divorce?

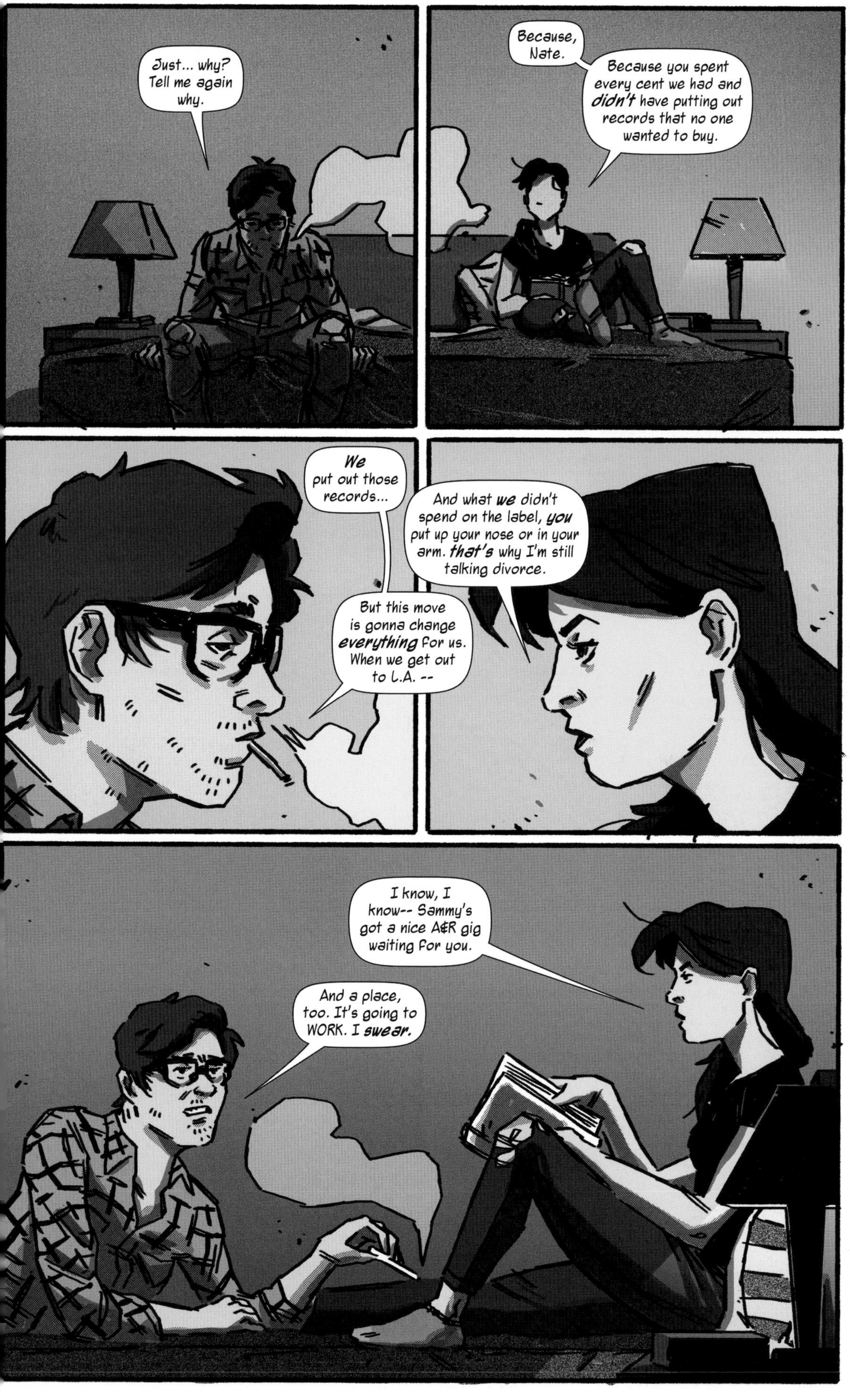
Just... why? Tell me again why.
Because, Nate.
Because you spent every cent we had and didn't have putting out records that no one wanted to buy.
We put out those records...
But this move is gonna change everything for us. When we get out to L.A. --
And what we didn't spend on the label, you put up your nose or in your arm. that's why I'm still talking divorce.
I know, I know-- Sammy's got a nice A&R gig waiting for you.
And a place, too. It's going to WORK. I swear.

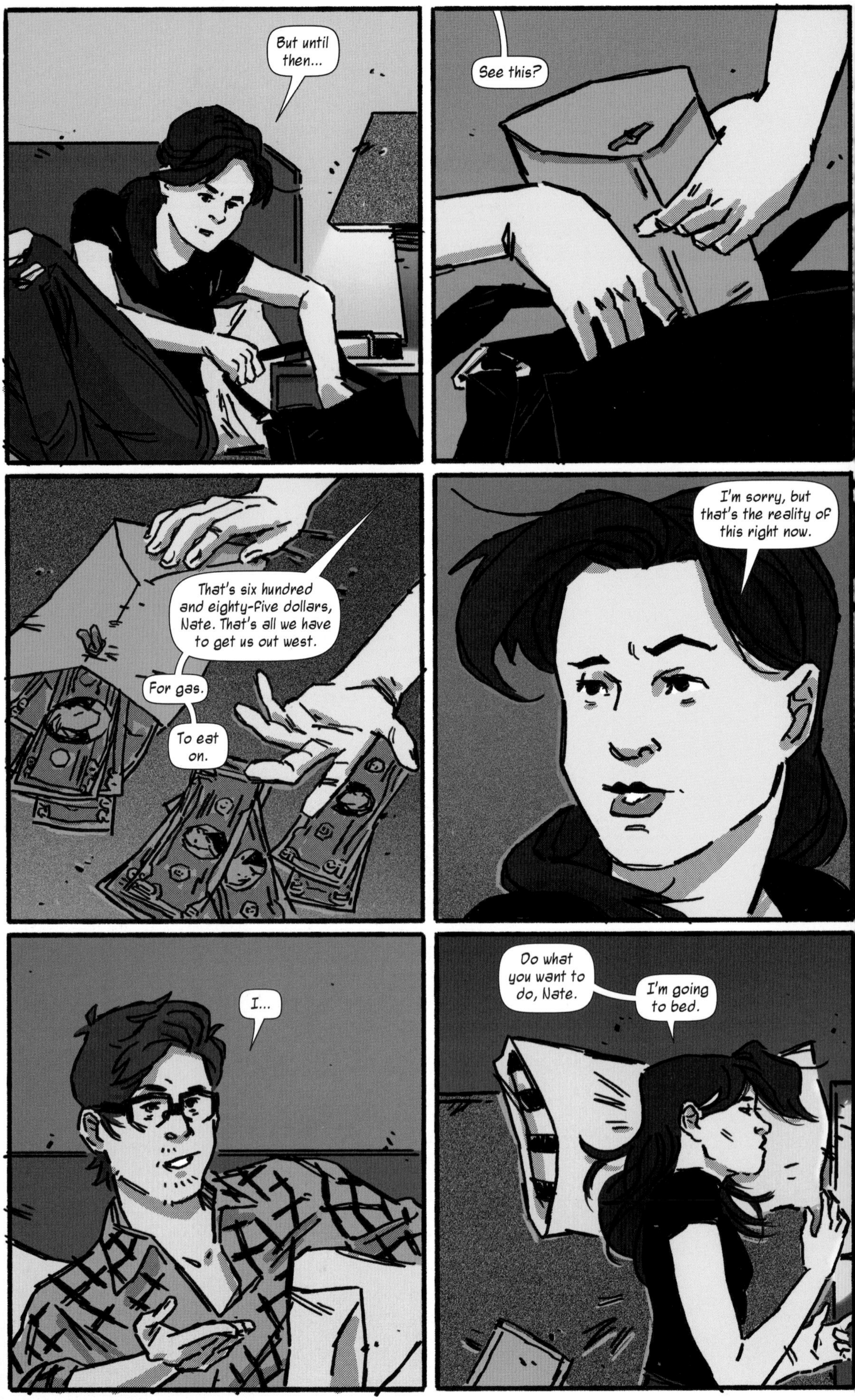
But until then...
See this?
That's six hundred and eighty-five dollars, Nate. That's all we have to get us out west.
For gas.
To eat on.
I'm sorry, but that's the reality of this right now.
I...
Do what you want to do, Nate.
I'm going to bed.

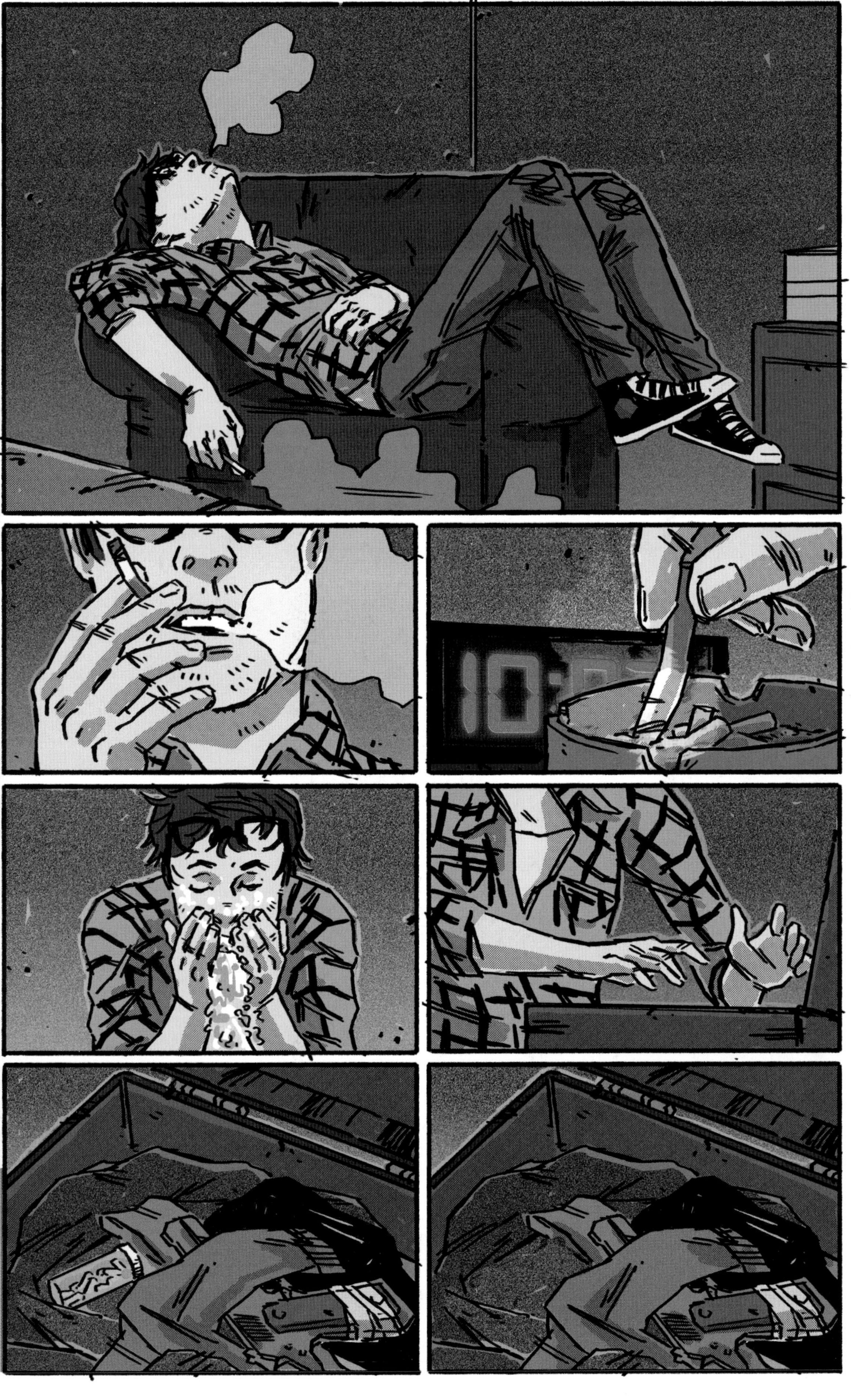

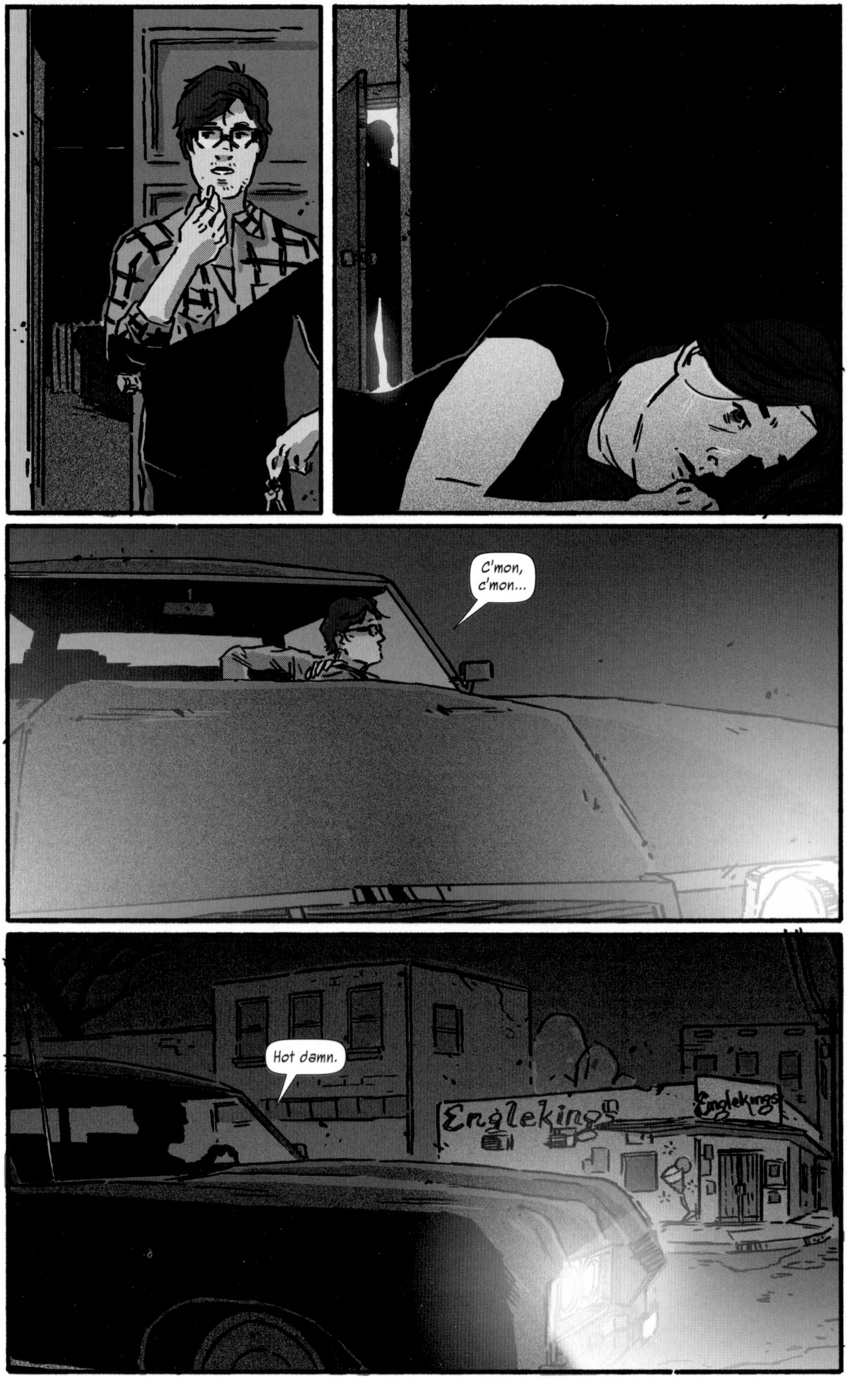

C'mon, c'mon...
Hot damn.
Englekings
Englekings

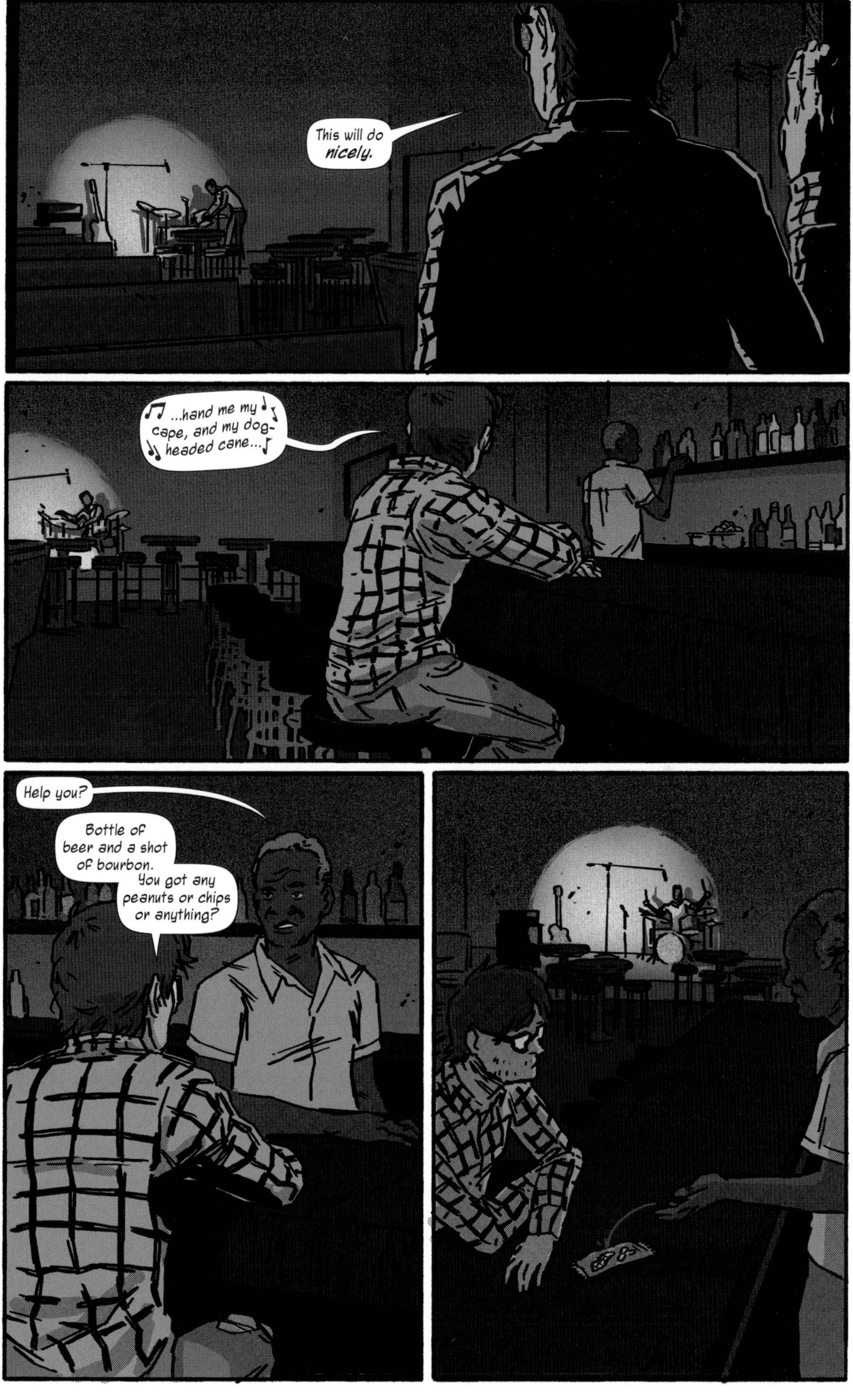
This will do *nicely.*
♫ ...hand me my cape, and my dog-headed cane...♪
Help you?
Bottle of beer and a shot of bourbon.
You got any peanuts or chips or anything?

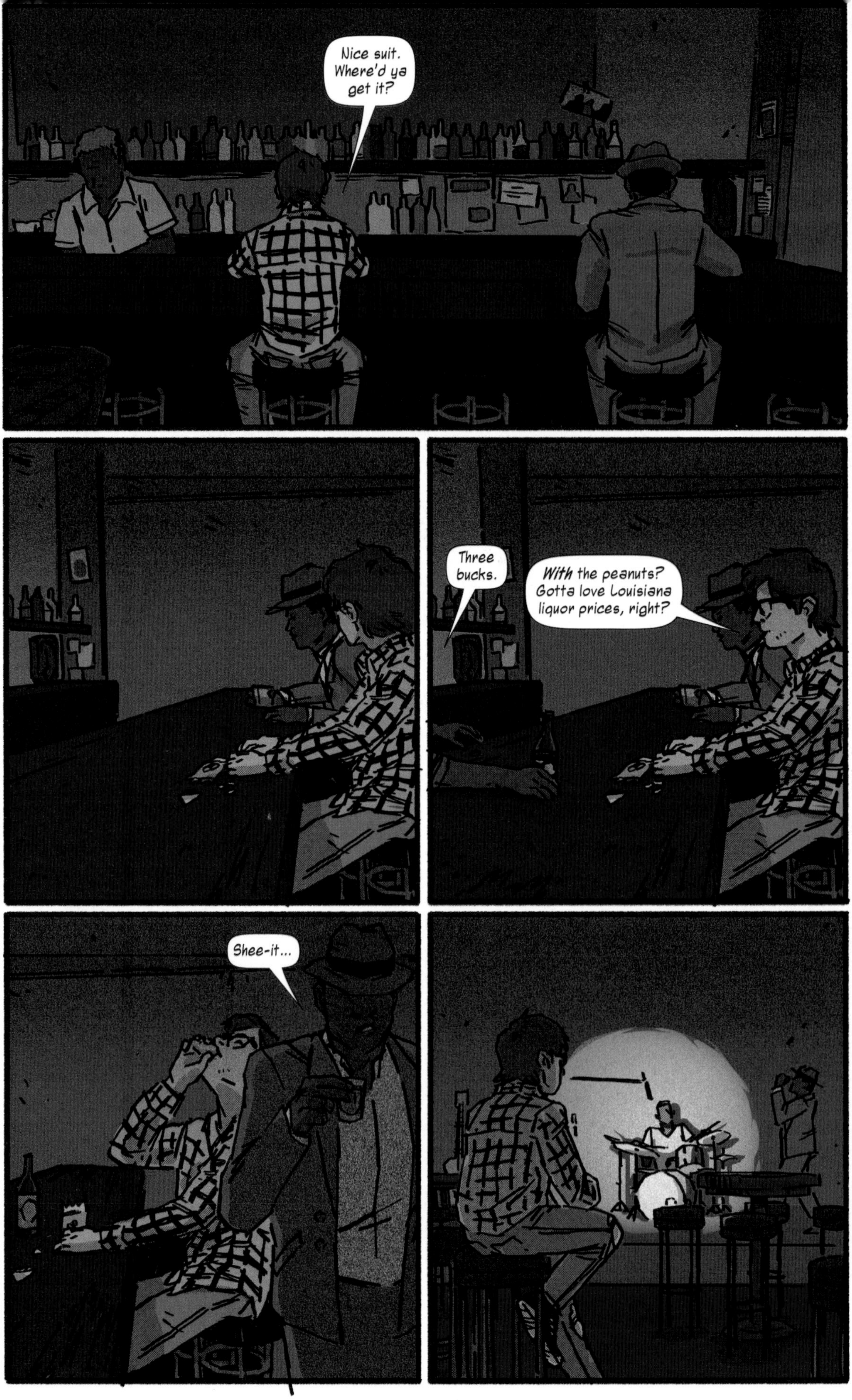
Nice suit. Where'd ya get it?
Three bucks.
With the peanuts? Gotta love Louisiana liquor prices, right?
Shee-it...

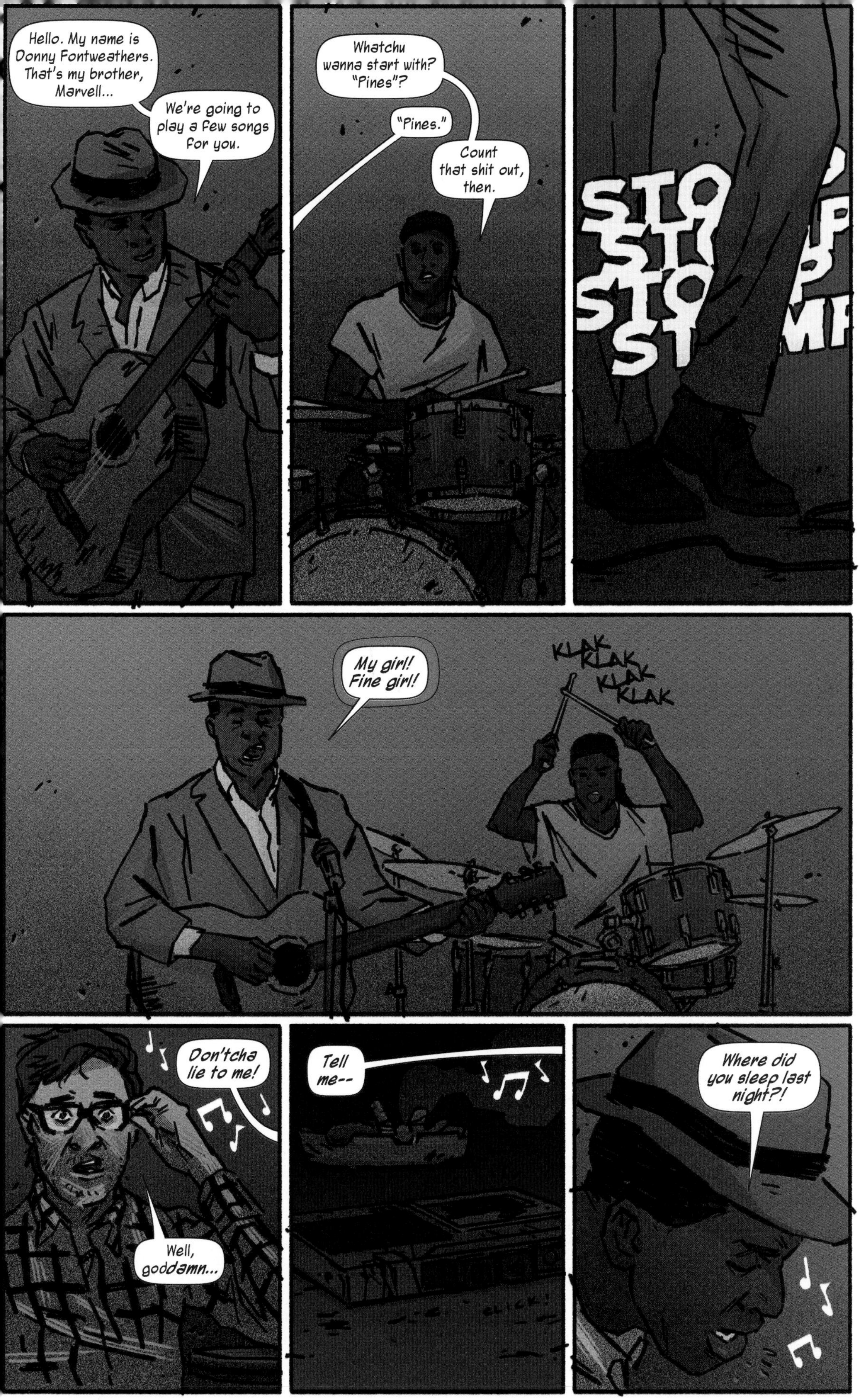
Hello. My name is Donny Fontweathers. That's my brother, Marvell...
We're going to play a few songs for you.
Whatchu wanna start with? "Pines"?
"Pines."
Count that shit out, then.
My girl! Fine girl!
KLAK KLAK KLAK KLAK
Don'tcha lie to me!
Well, goddamn...
Tell me--
Where did you sleep last night?!

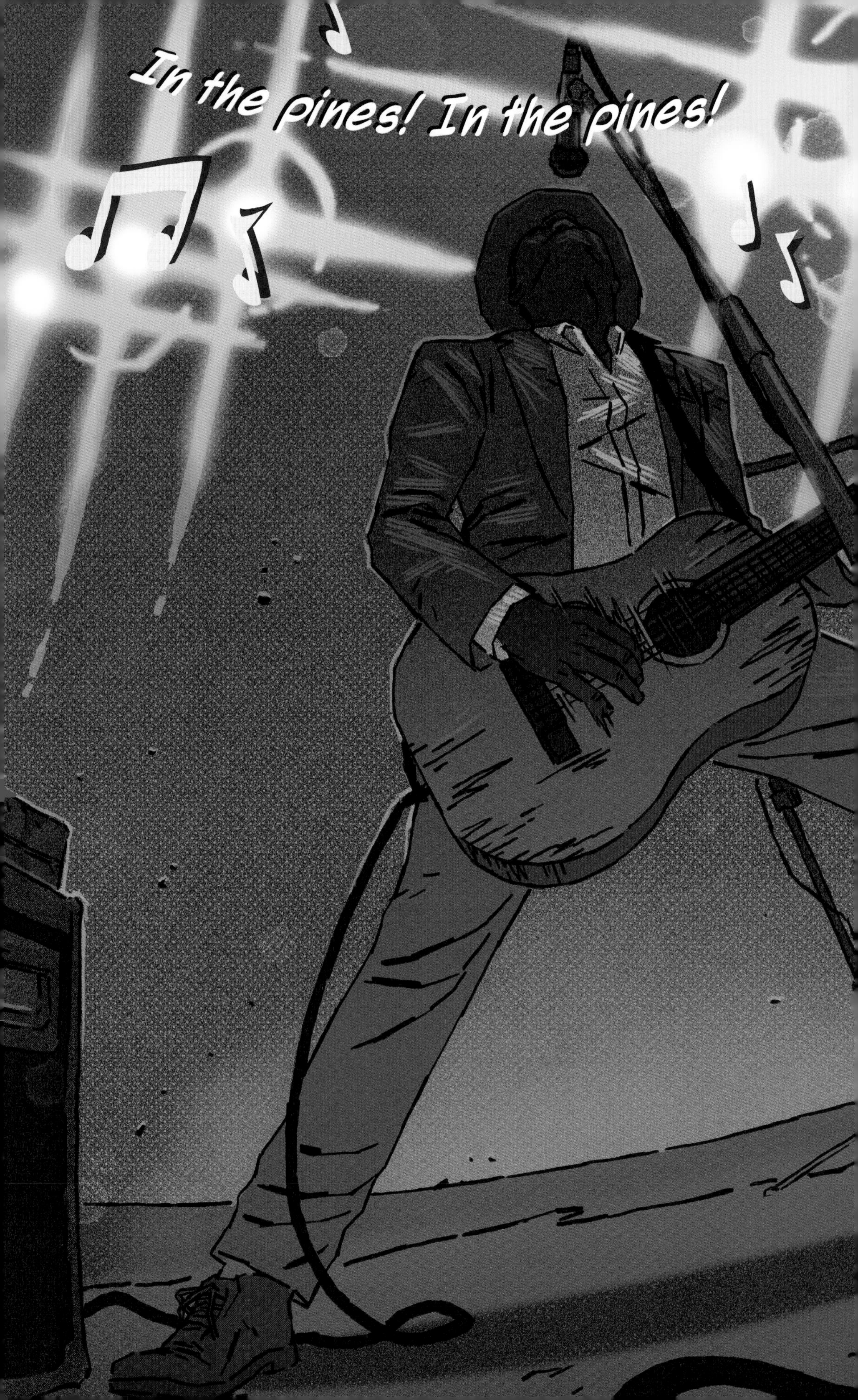
In the pines! In the pines!

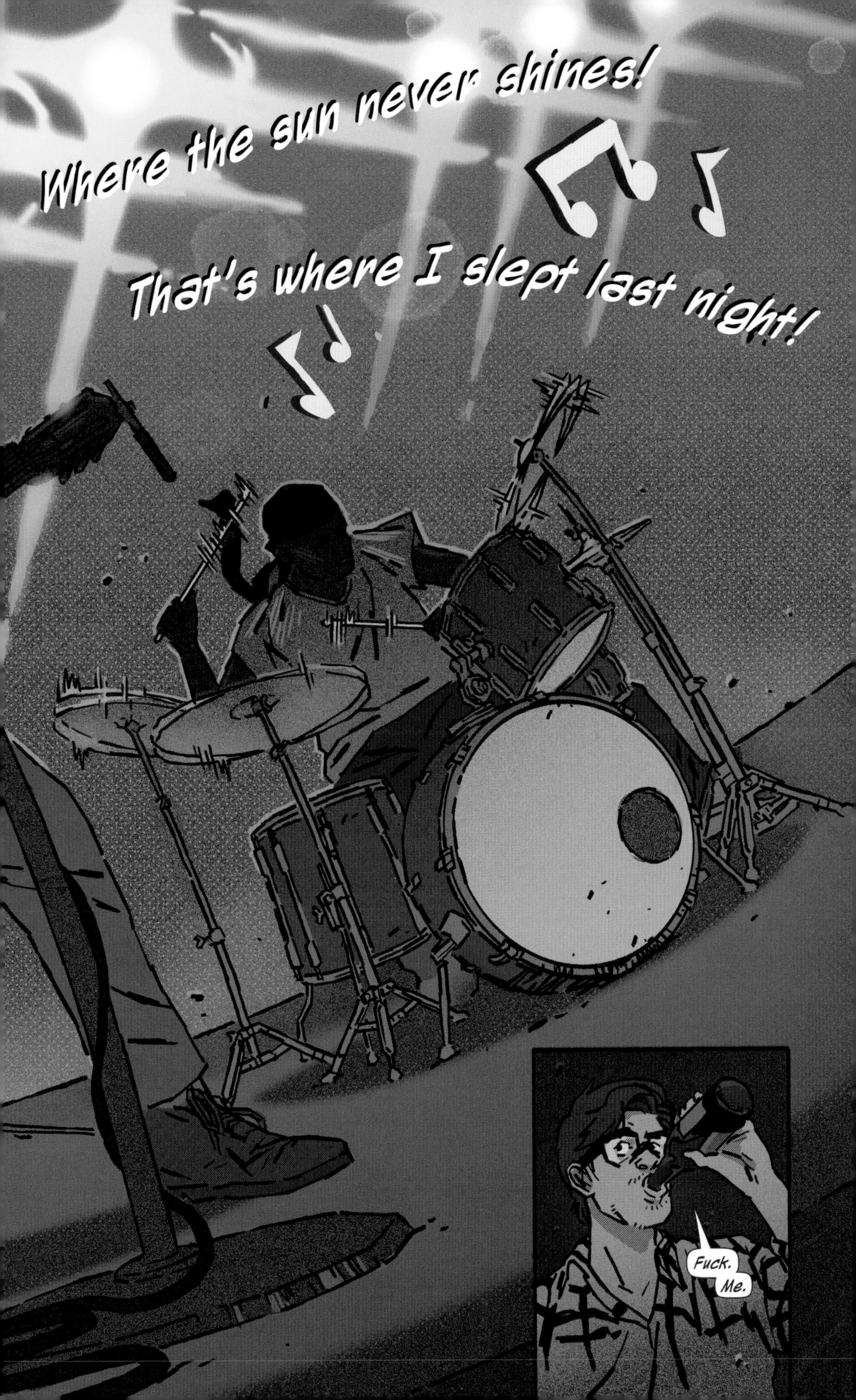
Where the sun never shines!
That's where I slept last night!
Fuck.
Me.

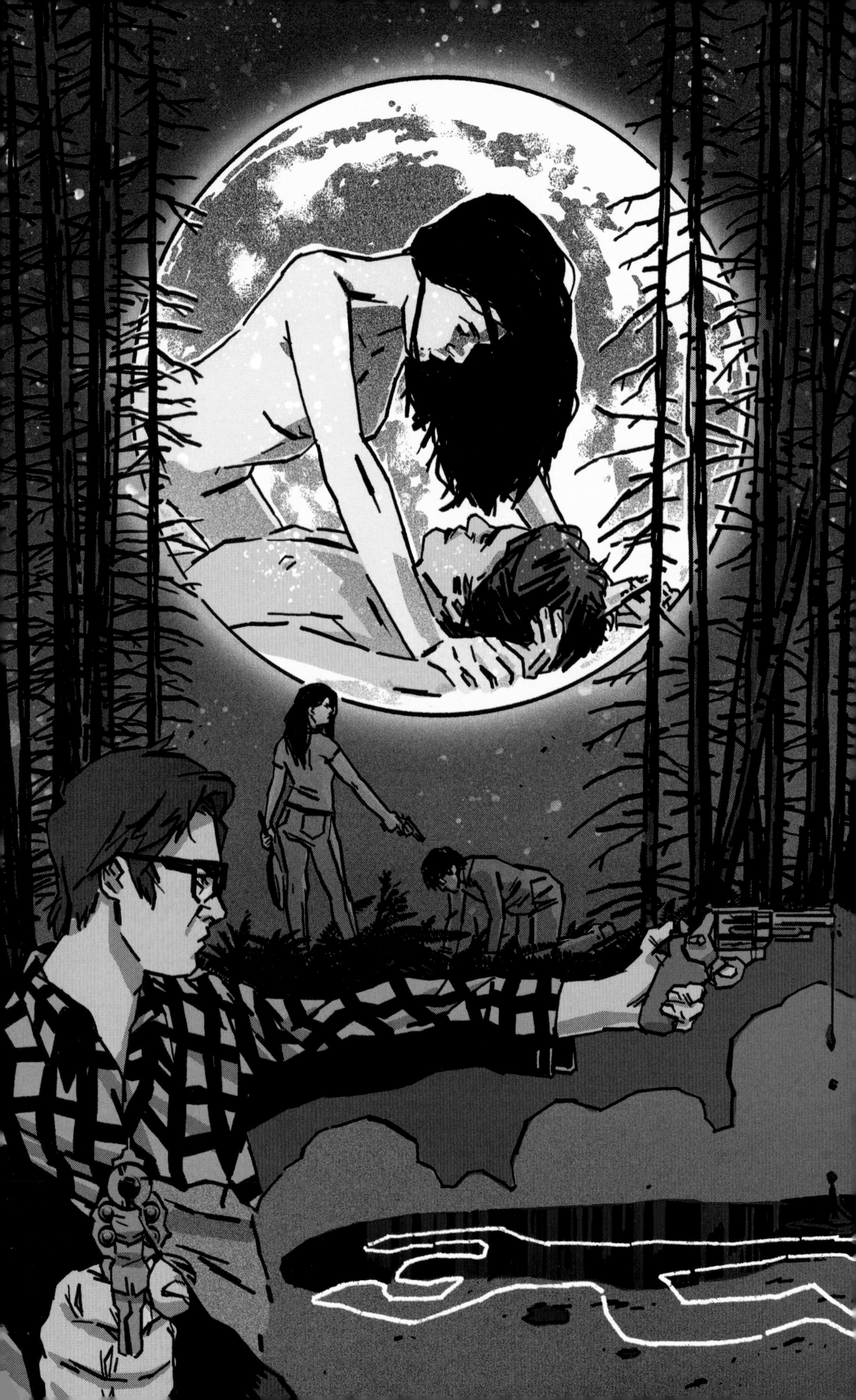

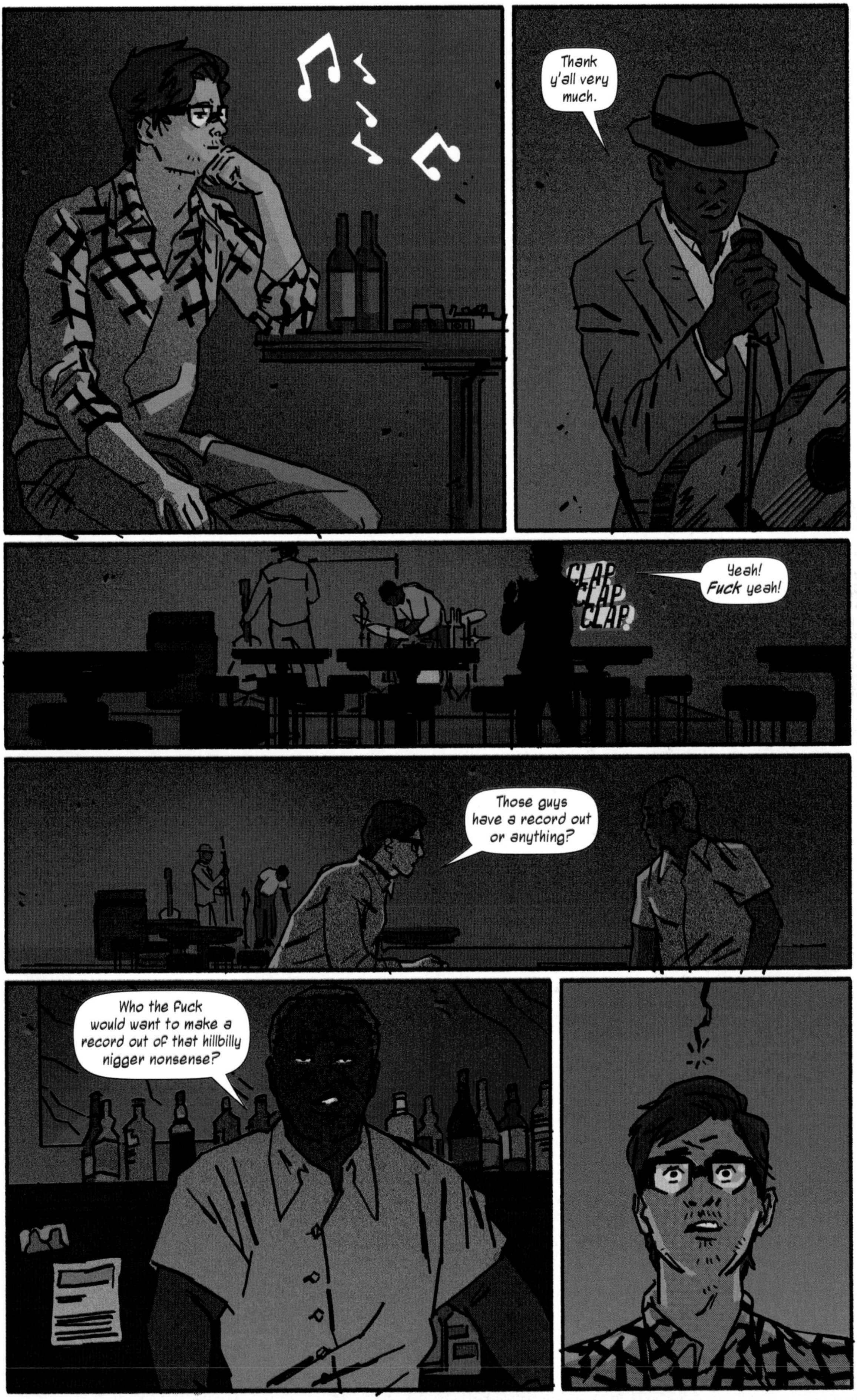
Thank y'all very much.
CLAP CLAP CLAP
Yeah! Fuck yeah!
Those guys have a record out or anything?
Who the fuck would want to make a record out of that hillbilly nigger nonsense?

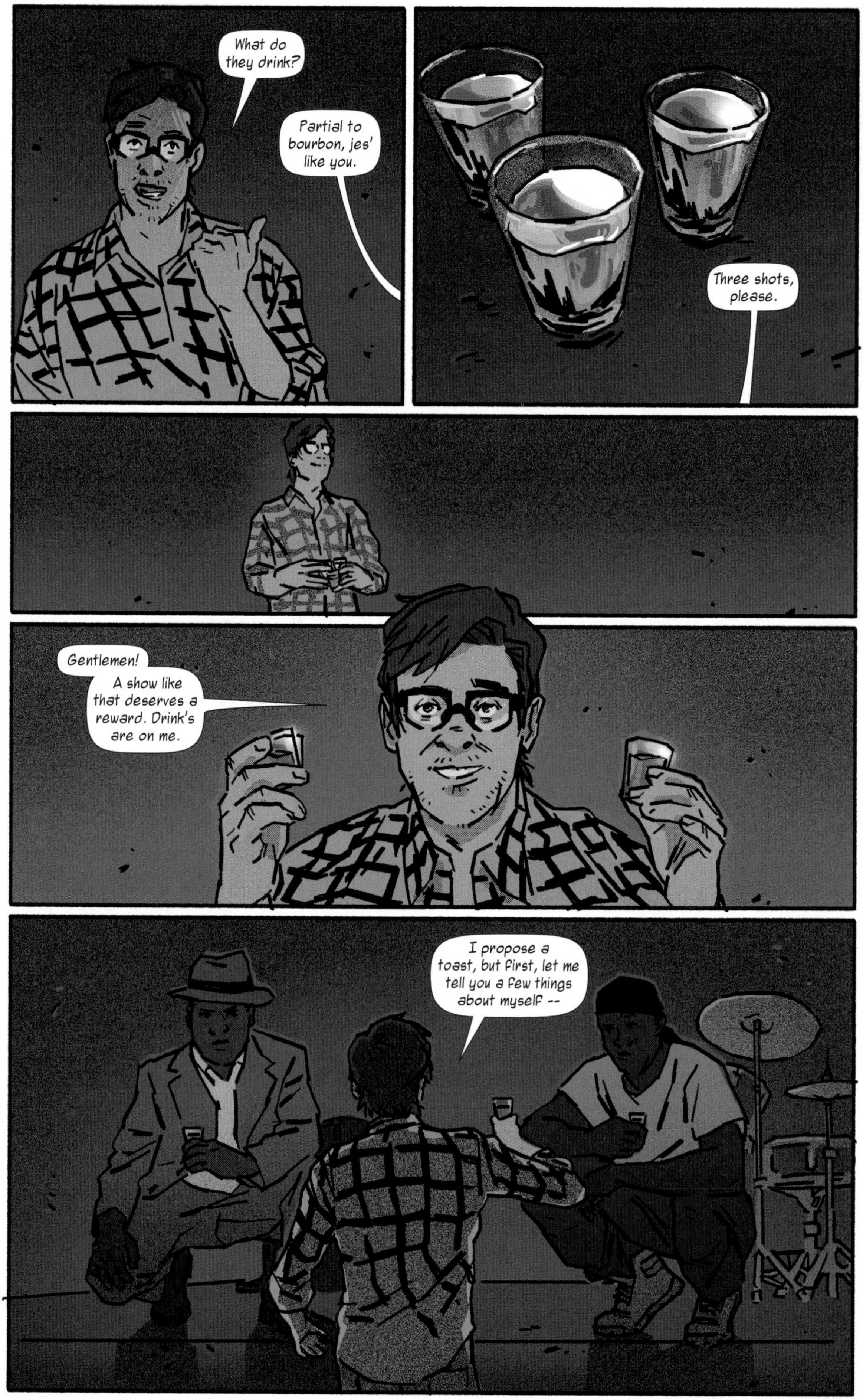
What do they drink?
Partial to bourbon, jes' like you.
Three shots, please.
Gentlemen!
A show like that deserves a reward. Drink's are on me.
I propose a toast, but first, let me tell you a few things about myself --

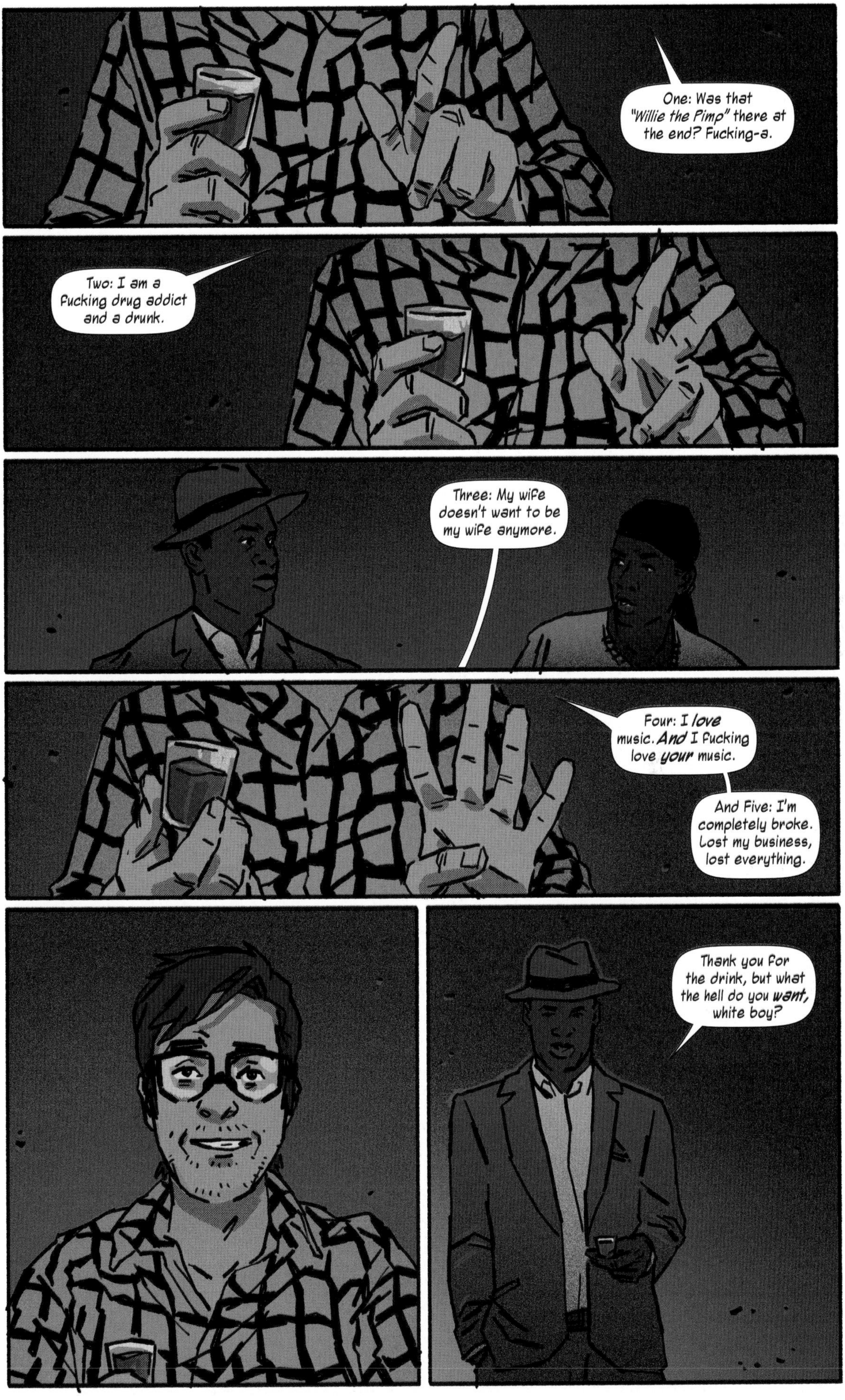
One: Was that "Willie the Pimp" there at the end? Fucking-a.
Two: I am a fucking drug addict and a drunk.
Three: My wife doesn't want to be my wife anymore.
Four: I love music. And I fucking love your music.
And Five: I'm completely broke. Lost my business, lost everything.
Thank you for the drink, but what the hell do you want, white boy?

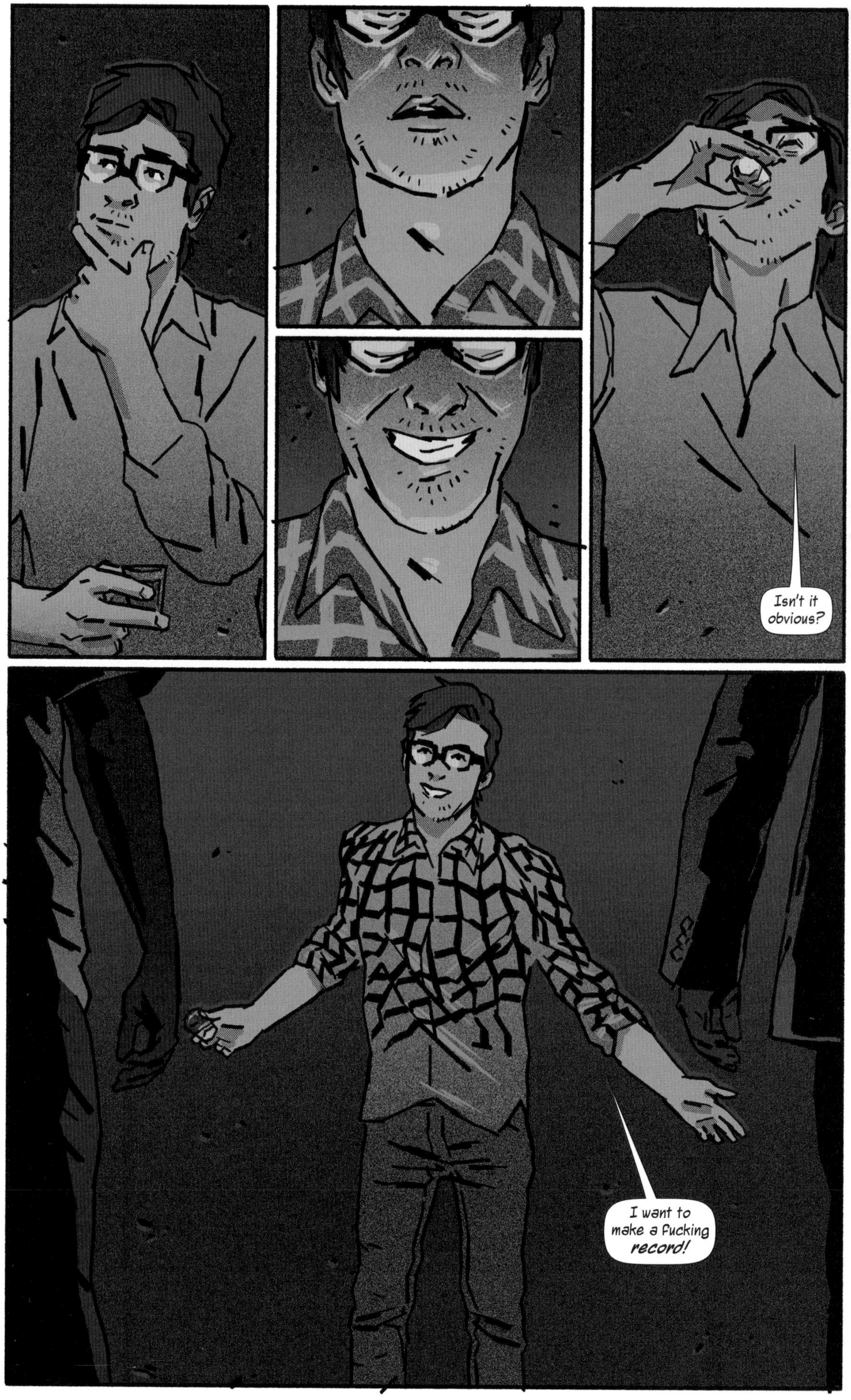
Isn't it obvious?
I want to make a fucking record!

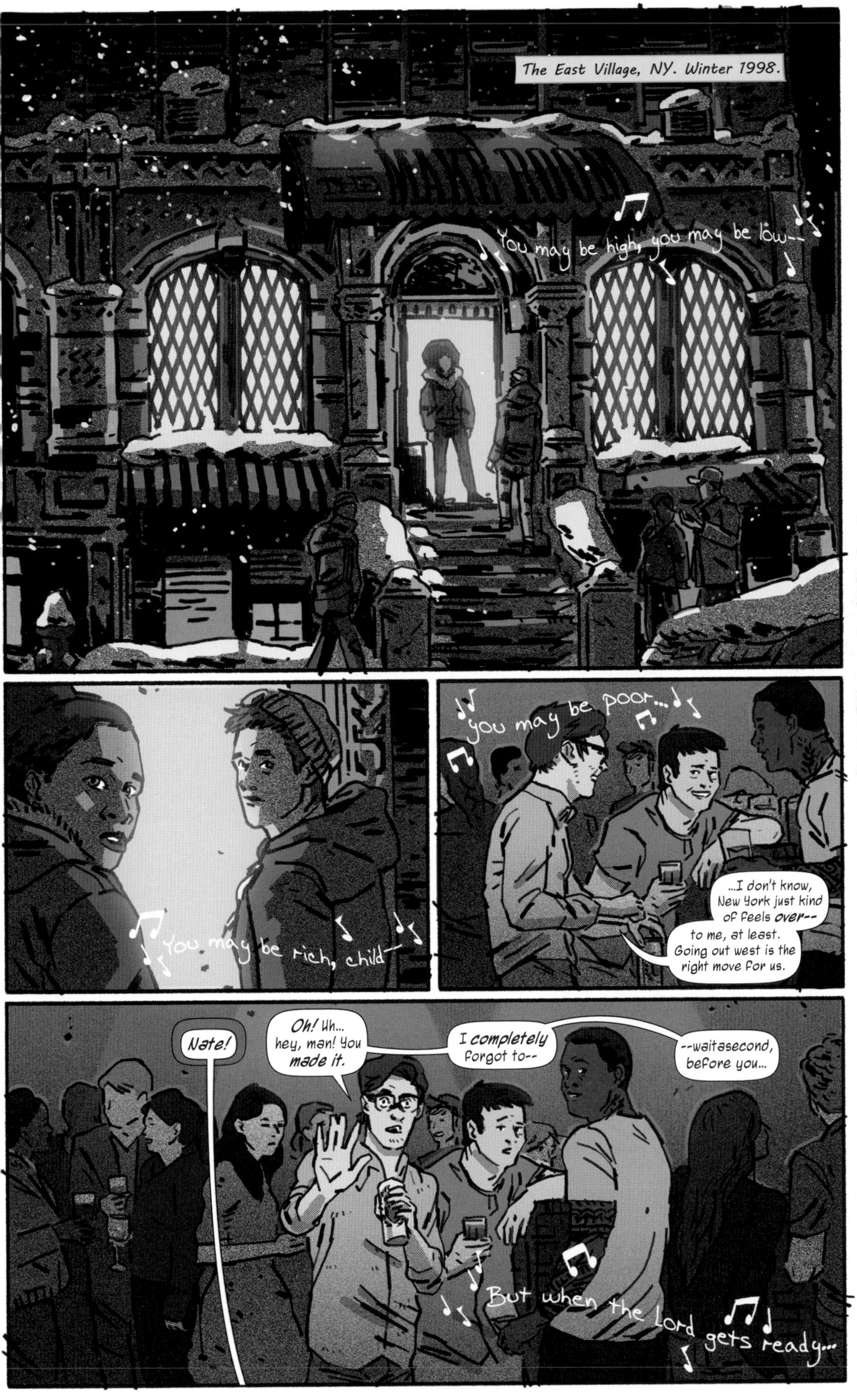
The East Village, NY. Winter 1998.
You may be high, you may be low--
You may be rich, child--
you may be poor...
...I don't know, New York just kind of feels over-- to me, at least. Going out west is the right move for us.
Nate!
Oh! Uh... hey, man! You made it.
I completely forgot to--
--waitasecond, before you...
But when the Lord gets ready...

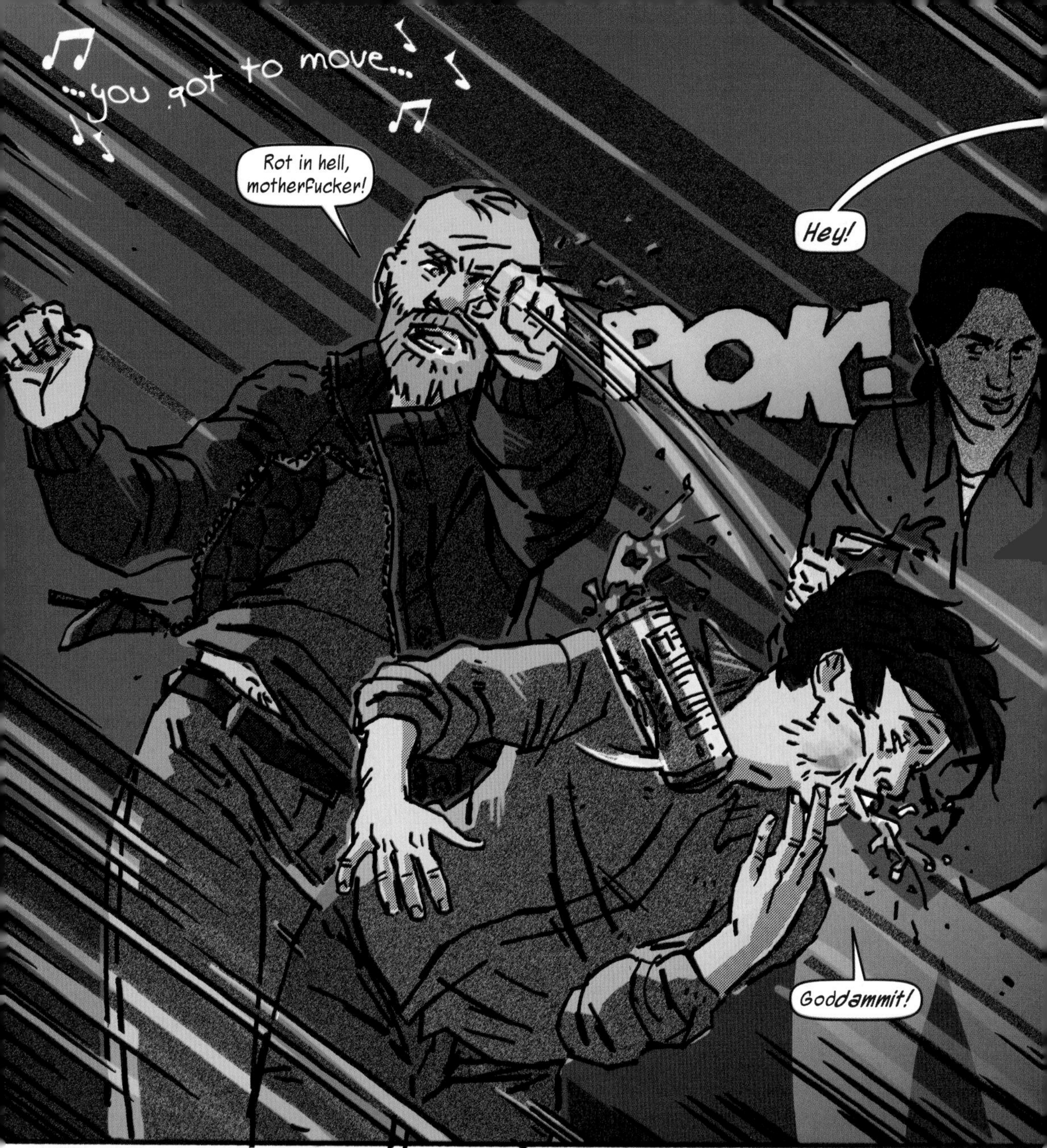
...you got to move...
Rot in hell, motherfucker!
Hey!
POK!
Goddammit!

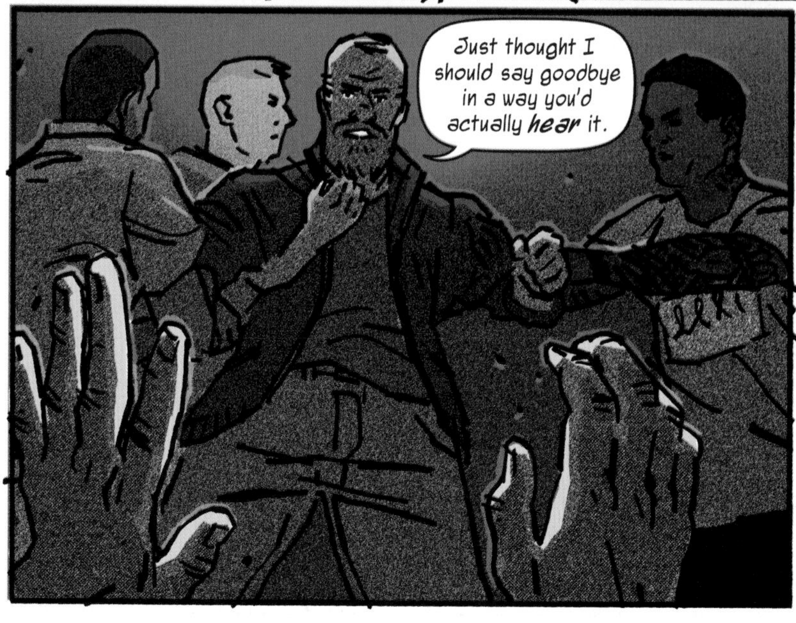
Just thought I should say goodbye in a way you'd actually ***hear*** it.

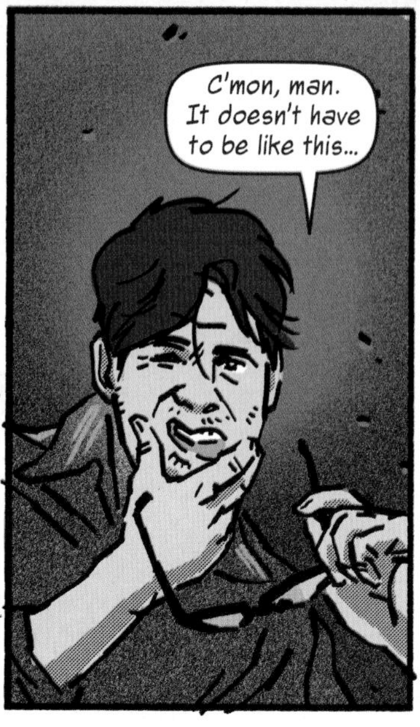
C'mon, man. It doesn't have to be like this...

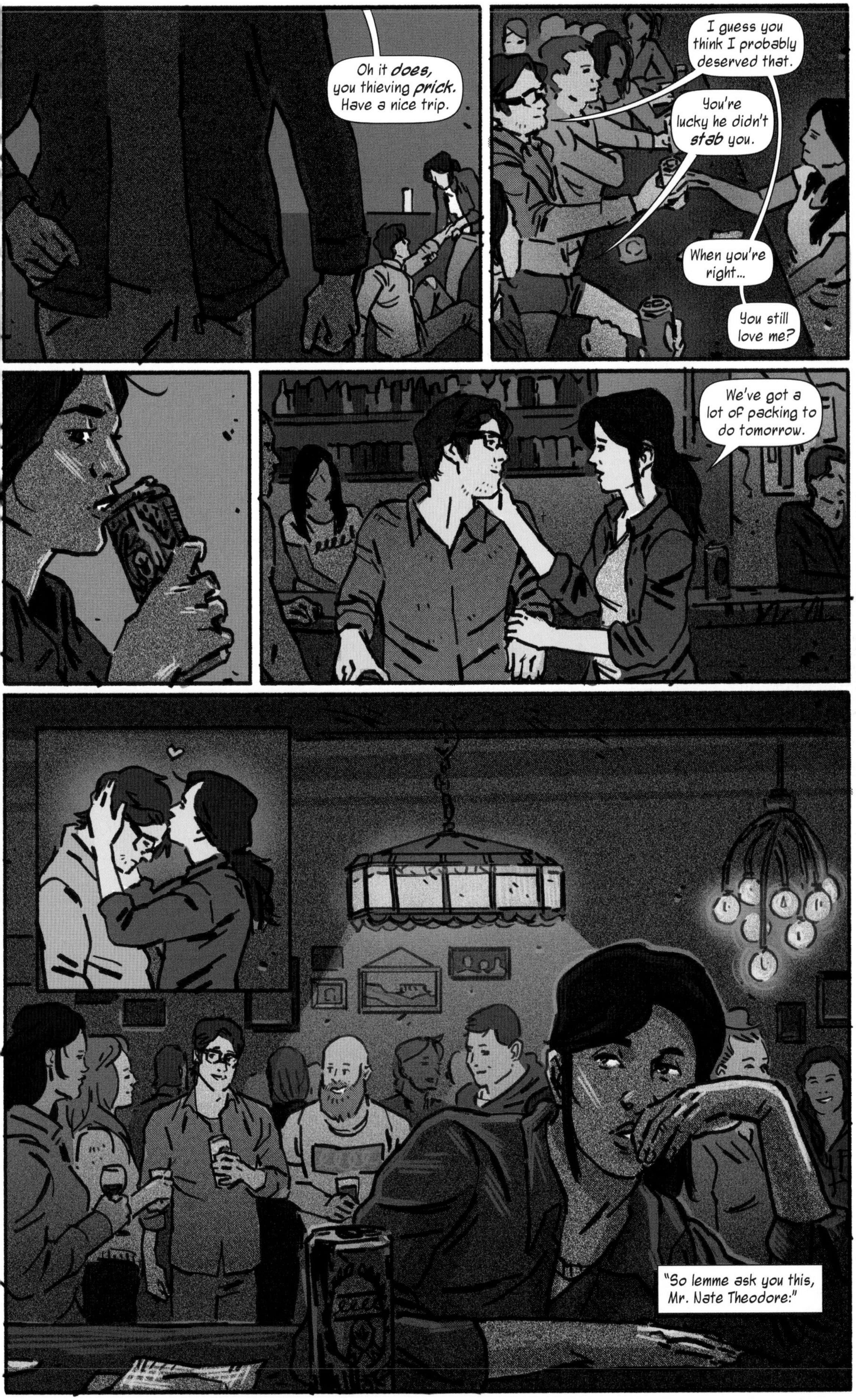
Oh it does, you thieving prick. Have a nice trip.
I guess you think I probably deserved that.
You're lucky he didn't stab you.
When you're right...
You still love me?
We've got a lot of packing to do tomorrow.
"So lemme ask you this, Mr. Nate Theodore:"

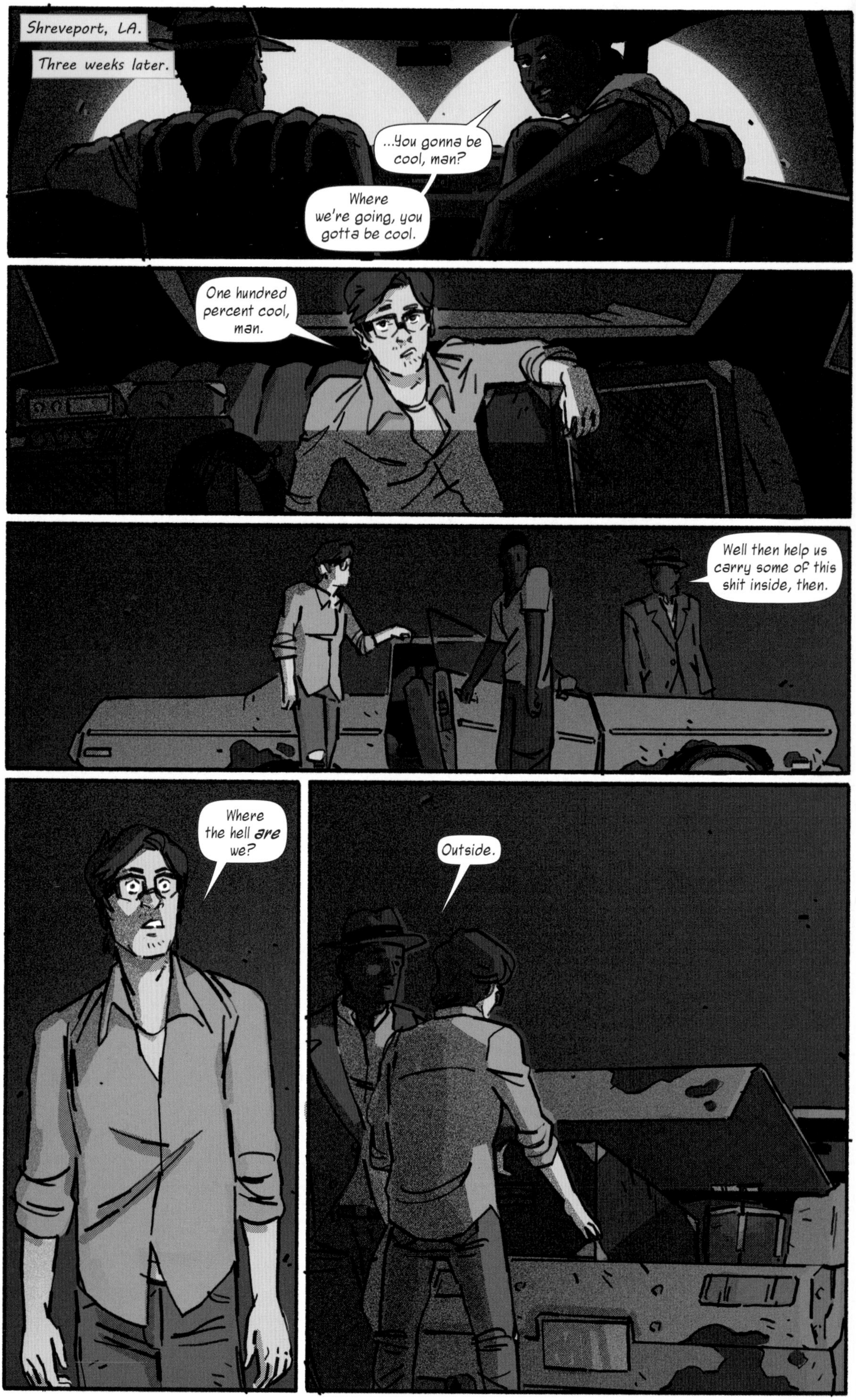
Shreveport, LA.
Three weeks later.
...You gonna be cool, man?
Where we're going, you gotta be cool.
One hundred percent cool, man.
Well then help us carry some of this shit inside, then.
Where the hell *are* we?
Outside.

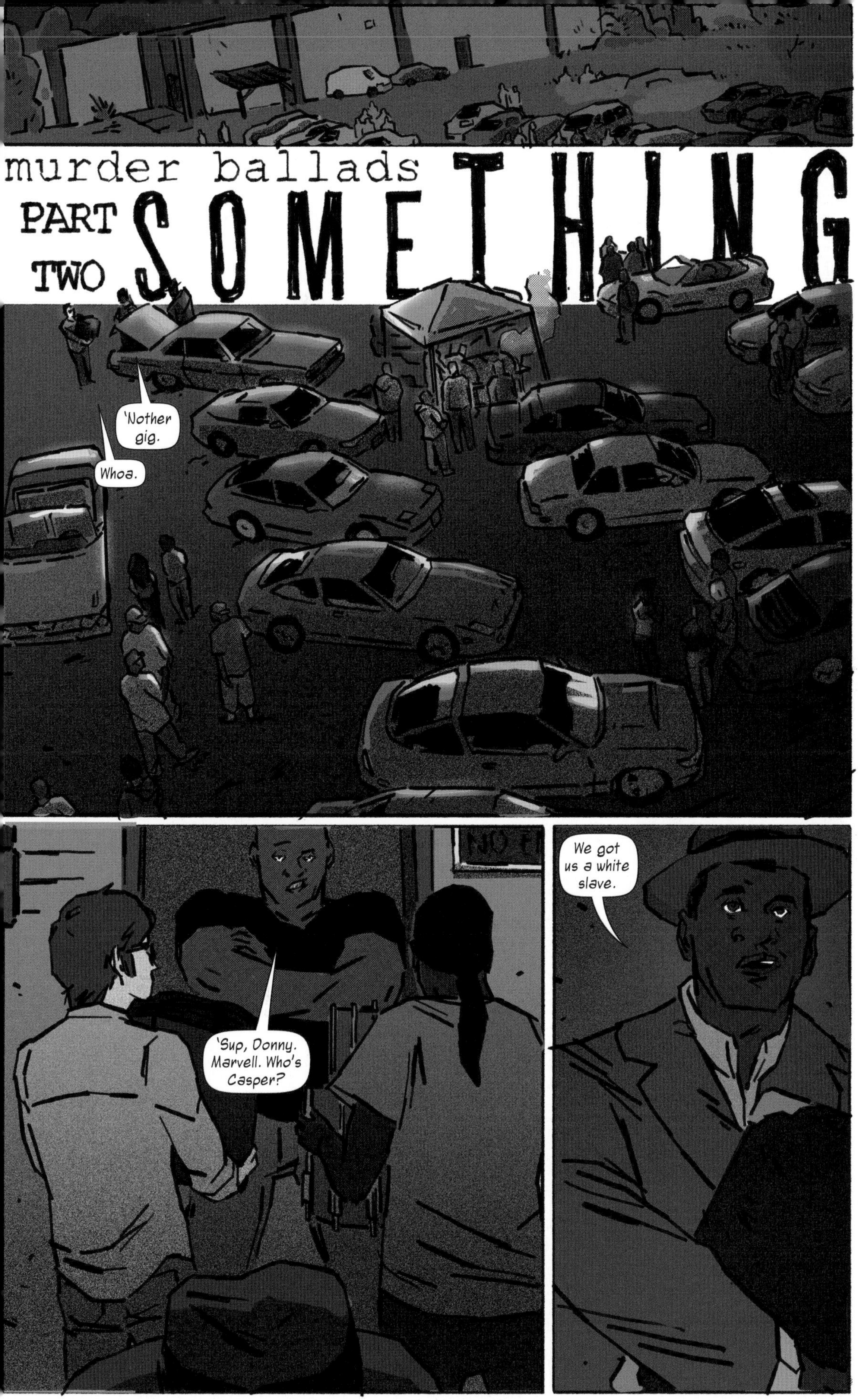
murder ballads
PART TWO
SOMETHING
'Nother gig.
Whoa.
'Sup, Donny. Marvell. Who's Casper?
We got us a white slave.

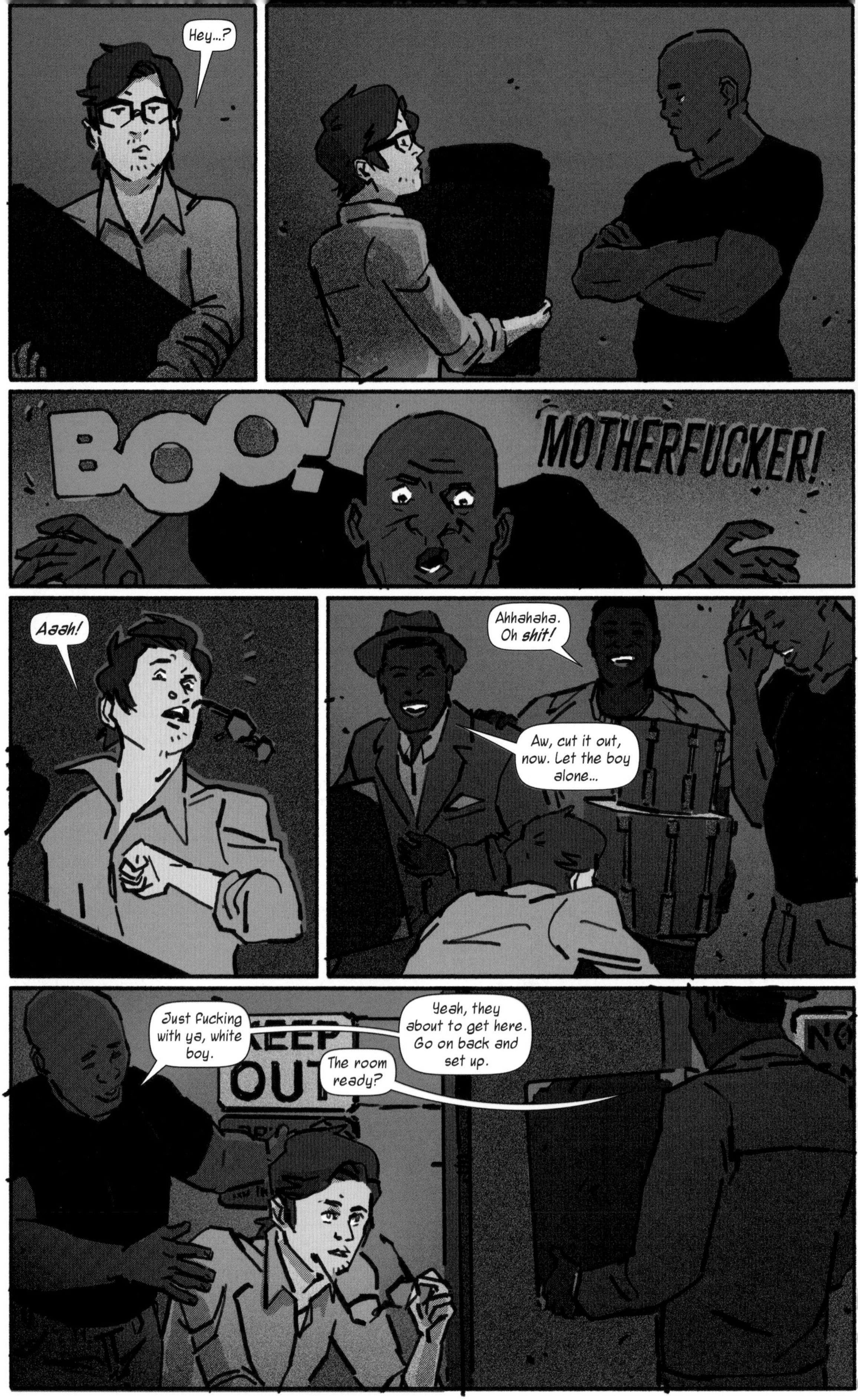
Hey...?
BOO!
MOTHERFUCKER!
Aaah!
Ahhahaha. Oh shit!
Aw, cut it out, now. Let the boy alone...
Just fucking with ya, white boy.
Yeah, they about to get here. Go on back and set up.
The room ready?
KEEP OUT

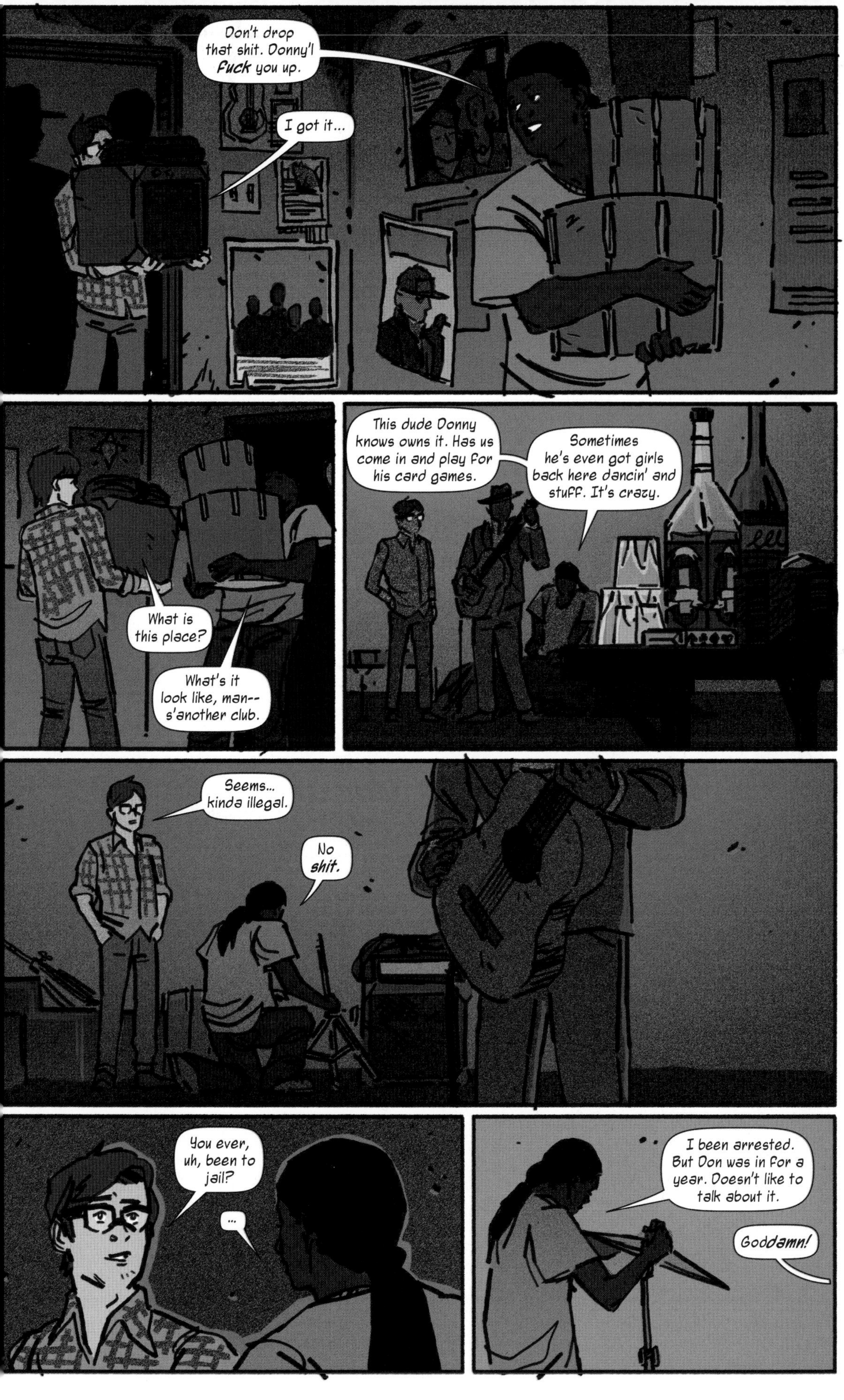

Don't drop that shit. Donny'l *Fuck* you up.
I got it...
What is this place?
What's it look like, man--s'another club.
This dude Donny knows owns it. Has us come in and play for his card games.
Sometimes he's even got girls back here dancin' and stuff. It's crazy.
Seems... kinda illegal.
No *shit.*
You ever, uh, been to jail?
...
I been arrested. But Don was in for a year. Doesn't like to talk about it.
God*damn!*

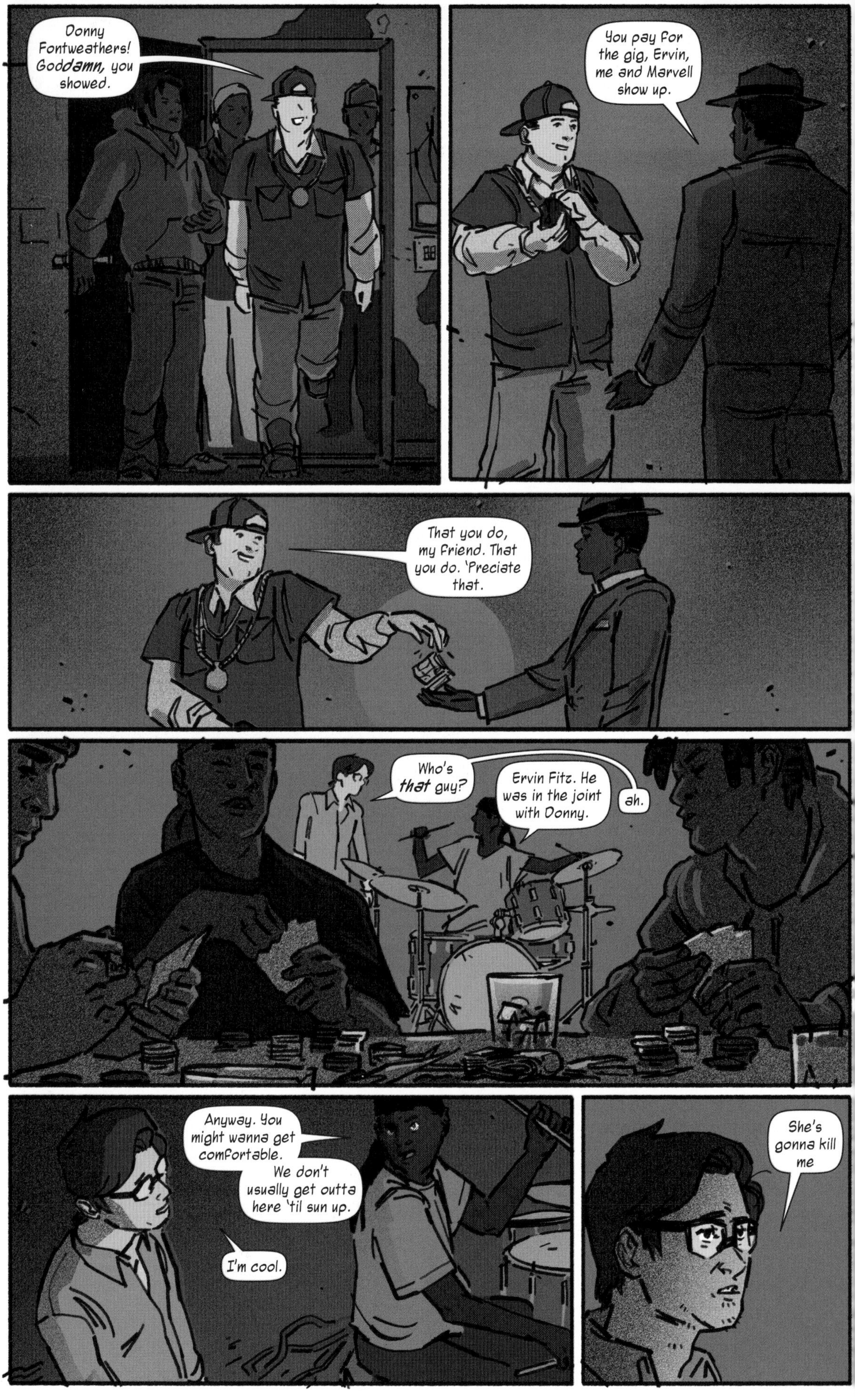
Donny Fontweathers! Goddamn, you showed.
You pay for the gig, Ervin, me and Marvell show up.
That you do, my friend. That you do. 'Preciate that.
Who's that guy?
Ervin Fitz. He was in the joint with Donny.
ah.
Anyway. You might wanna get comfortable.
We don't usually get outta here 'til sun up.
I'm cool.
She's gonna kill me

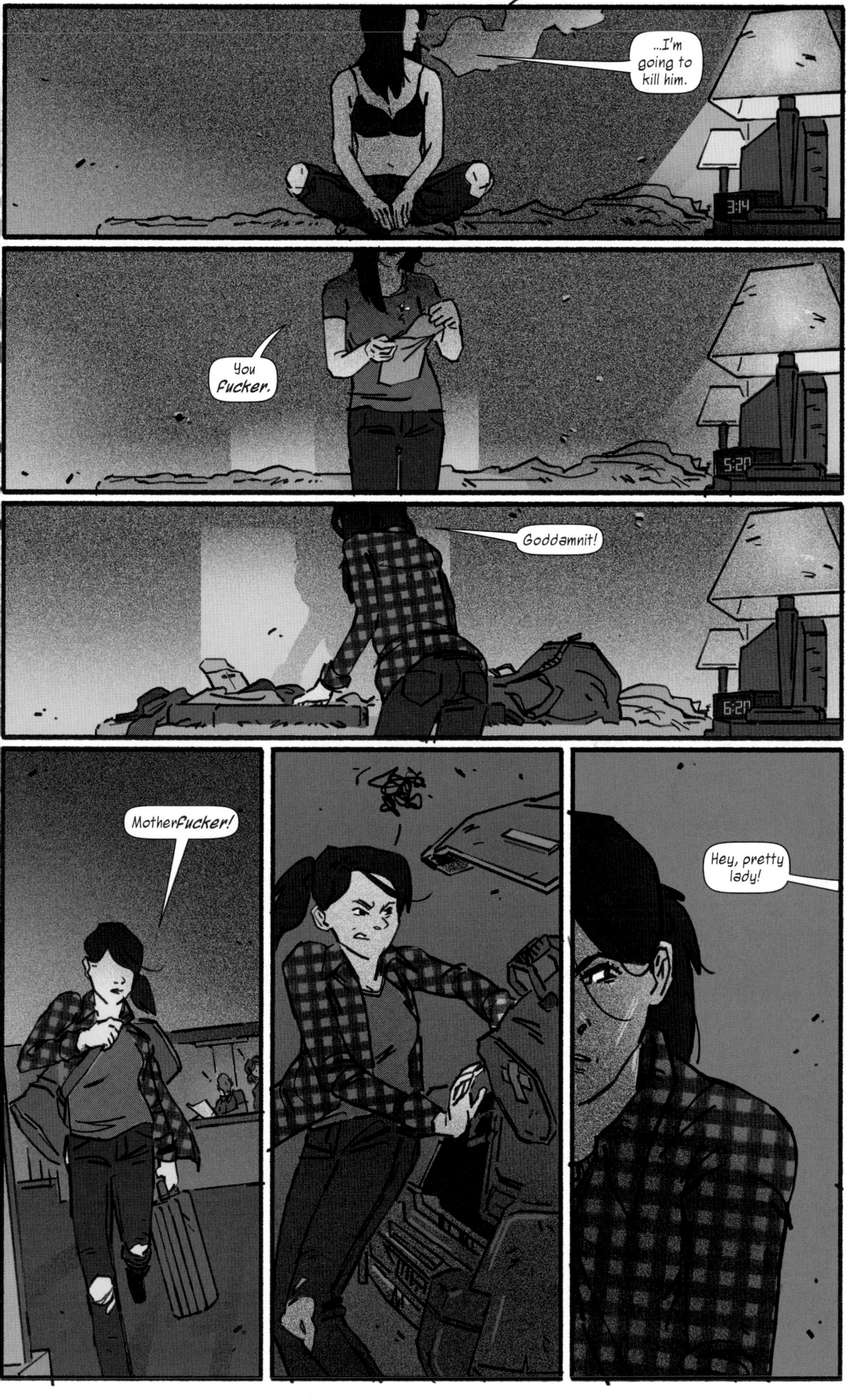
...I'm going to kill him.
3:14
You Fucker.
5:20
Goddamnit!
6:20
MotherFucker!
Hey, pretty lady!

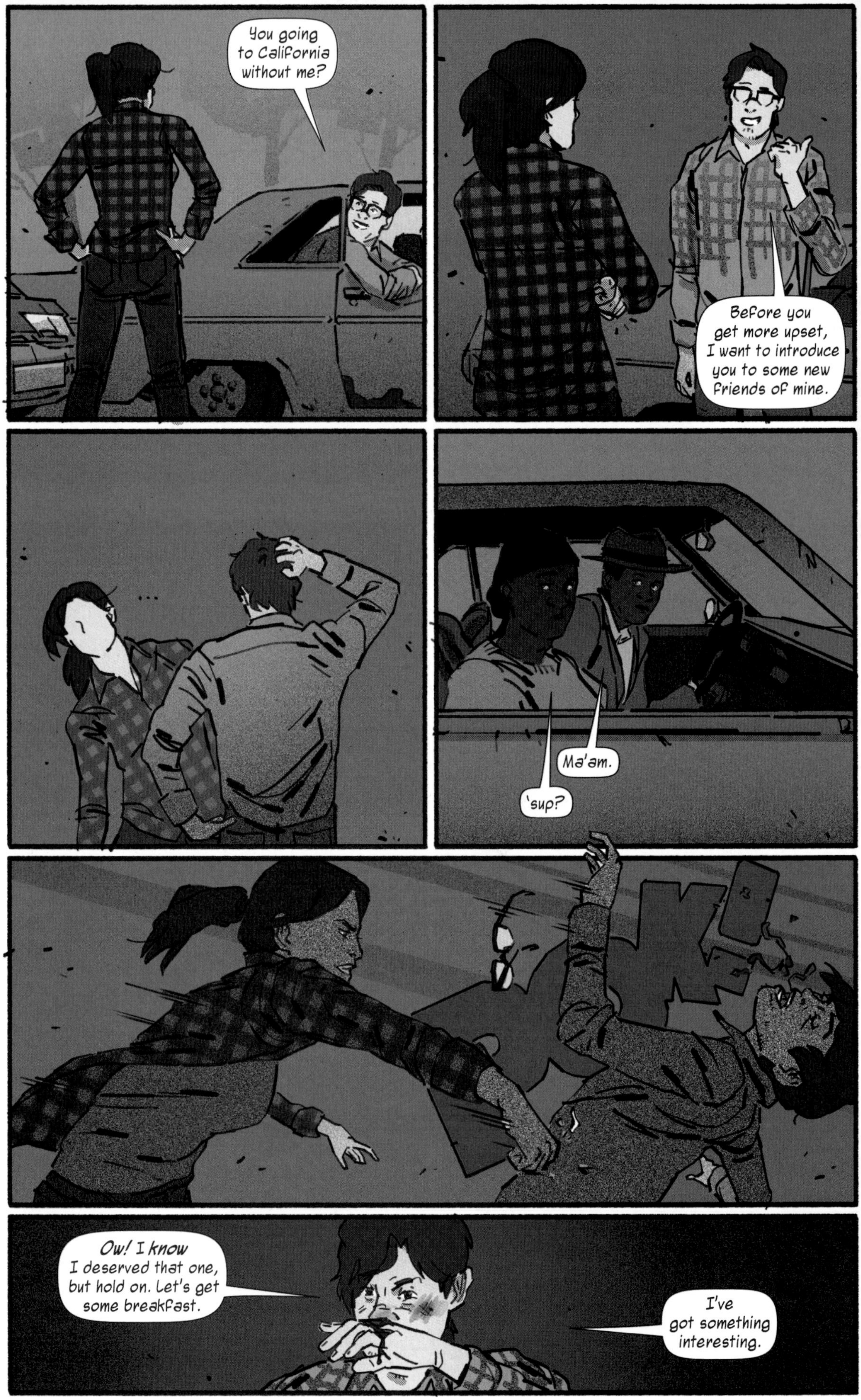
You going to California without me?
Before you get more upset, I want to introduce you to some new friends of mine.
...
Ma'am.
'sup?
Ow! I know I deserved that one, but hold on. Let's get some breakfast.
I've got something interesting.

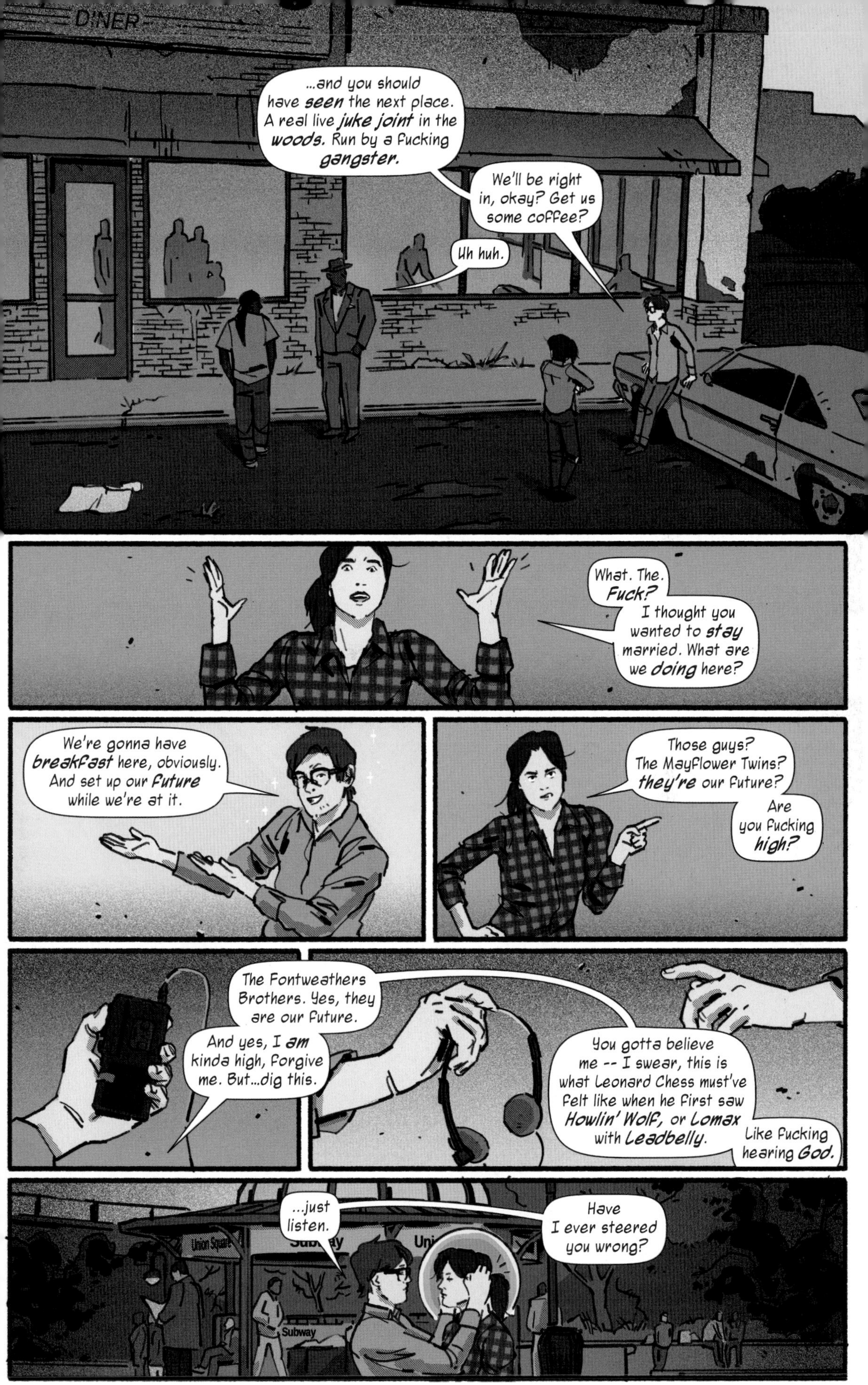
DINER
...and you should have seen the next place. A real live juke joint in the woods. Run by a fucking gangster.
We'll be right in, okay? Get us some coffee?
Uh huh.
What. The. Fuck?
I thought you wanted to stay married. What are we doing here?
We're gonna have breakfast here, obviously. And set up our future while we're at it.
Those guys? The Mayflower Twins? they're our future?
Are you fucking high?
The Fontweathers Brothers. Yes, they are our future.
And yes, I am kinda high, forgive me. But...dig this.
You gotta believe me -- I swear, this is what Leonard Chess must've felt like when he first saw Howlin' Wolf, or Lomax with Leadbelly.
Like fucking hearing God.
Union Square
Subway
...just listen.
Have I ever steered you wrong?

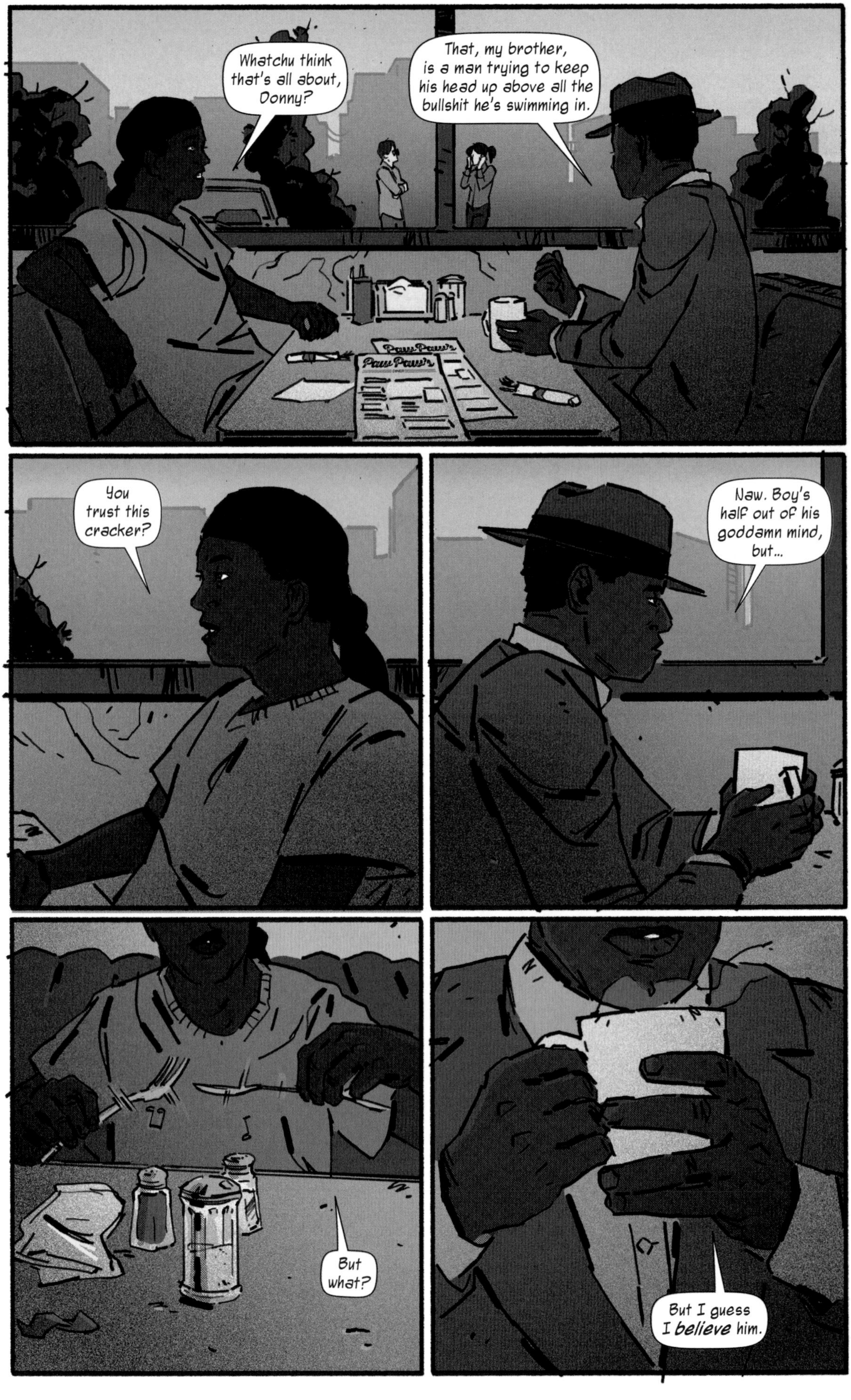
Whatchu think that's all about, Donny?
That, my brother, is a man trying to keep his head up above all the bullshit he's swimming in.
You trust this cracker?
Naw. Boy's half out of his goddamn mind, but...
Paw Paw's
But what?
But I guess I *believe* him.

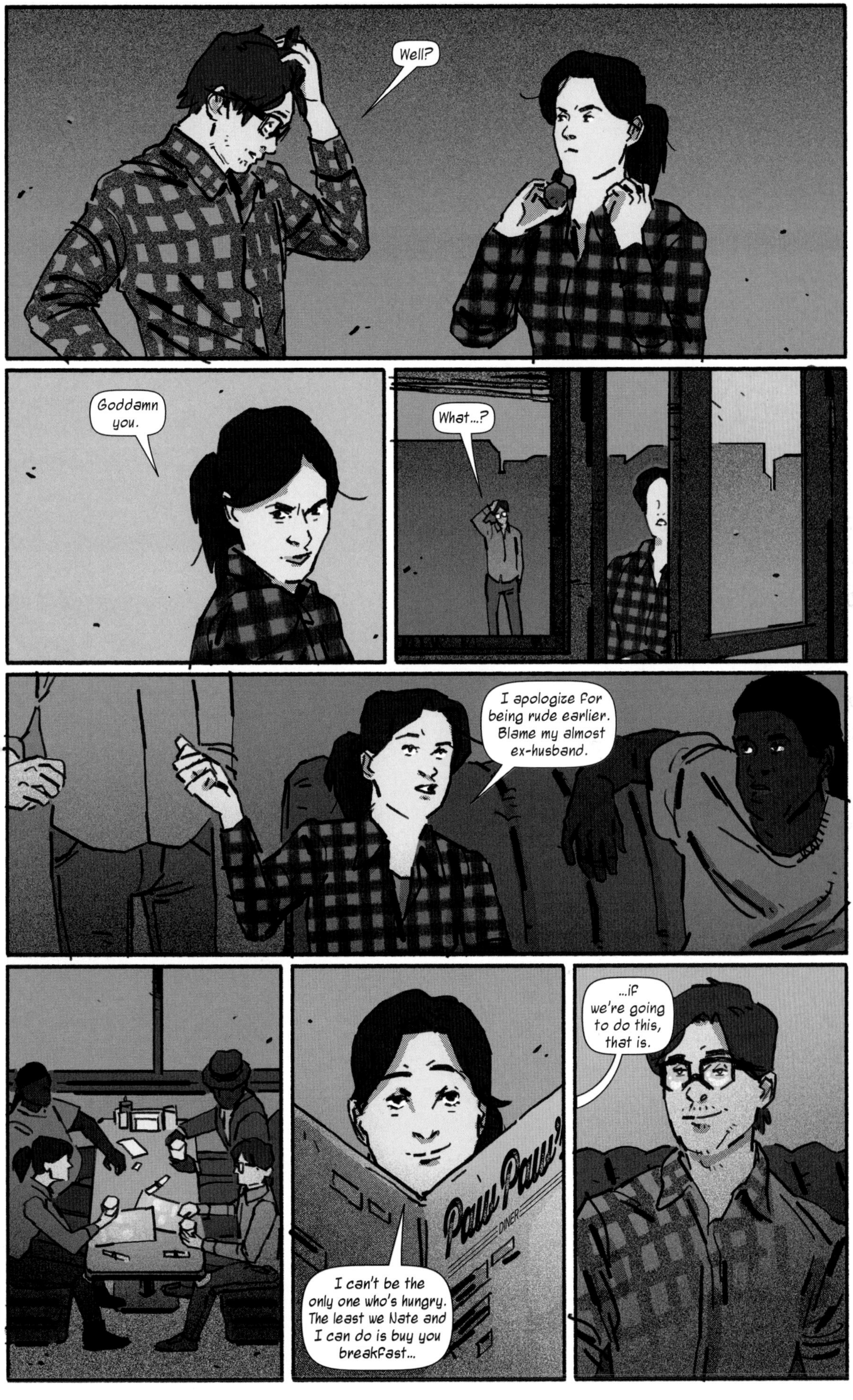
Well?
Goddamn you.
What...?
I apologize for being rude earlier. Blame my almost ex-husband.
I can't be the only one who's hungry. The least we Nate and I can do is buy you breakfast...
...if we're going to do this, that is.
Paw Paw's
DINER

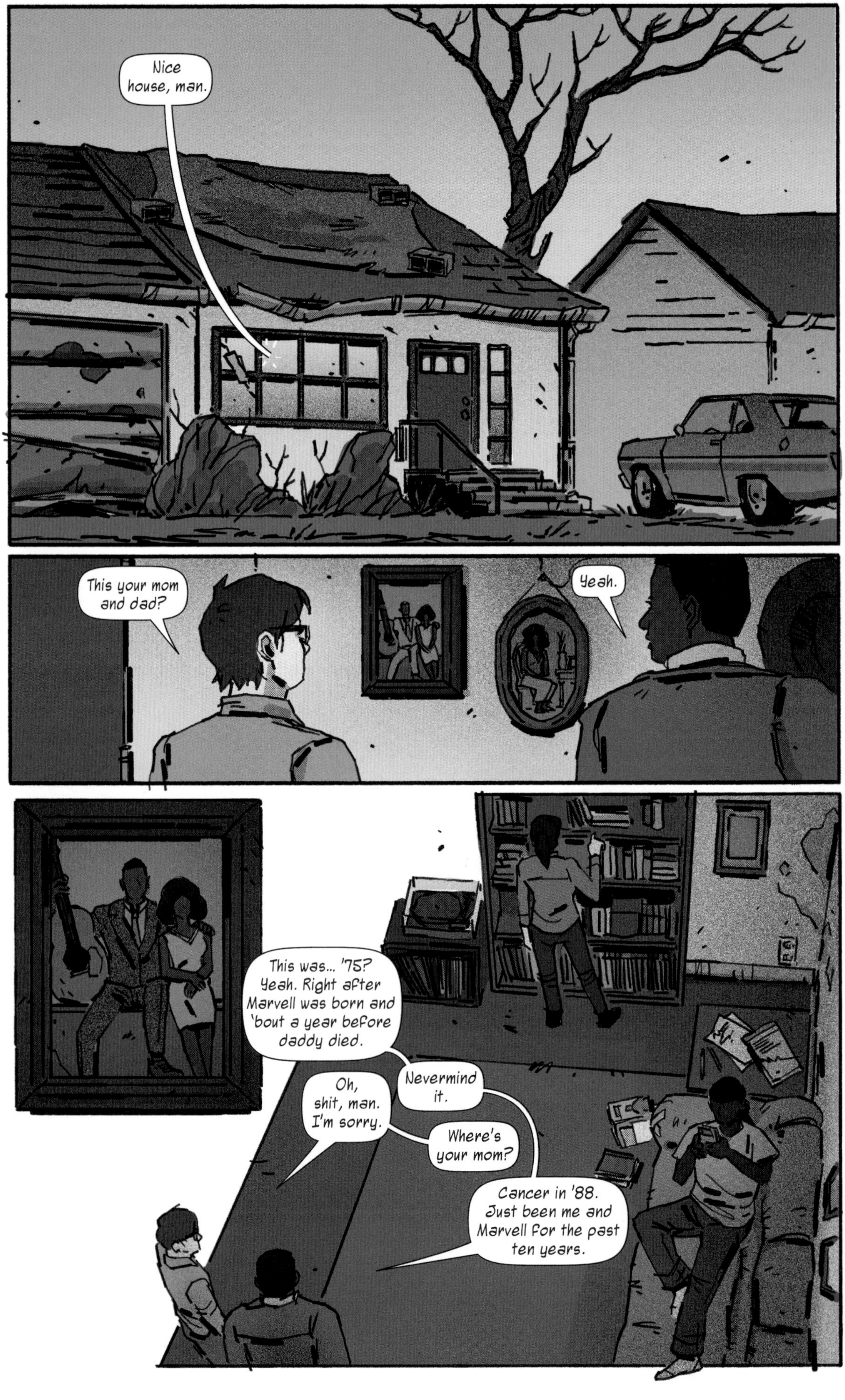
Nice house, man.
This your mom and dad?
Yeah.
This was... '75? Yeah. Right after Marvell was born and 'bout a year before daddy died.
Nevermind it.
Oh, shit, man. I'm sorry.
Where's your mom?
Cancer in '88. Just been me and Marvell for the past ten years.

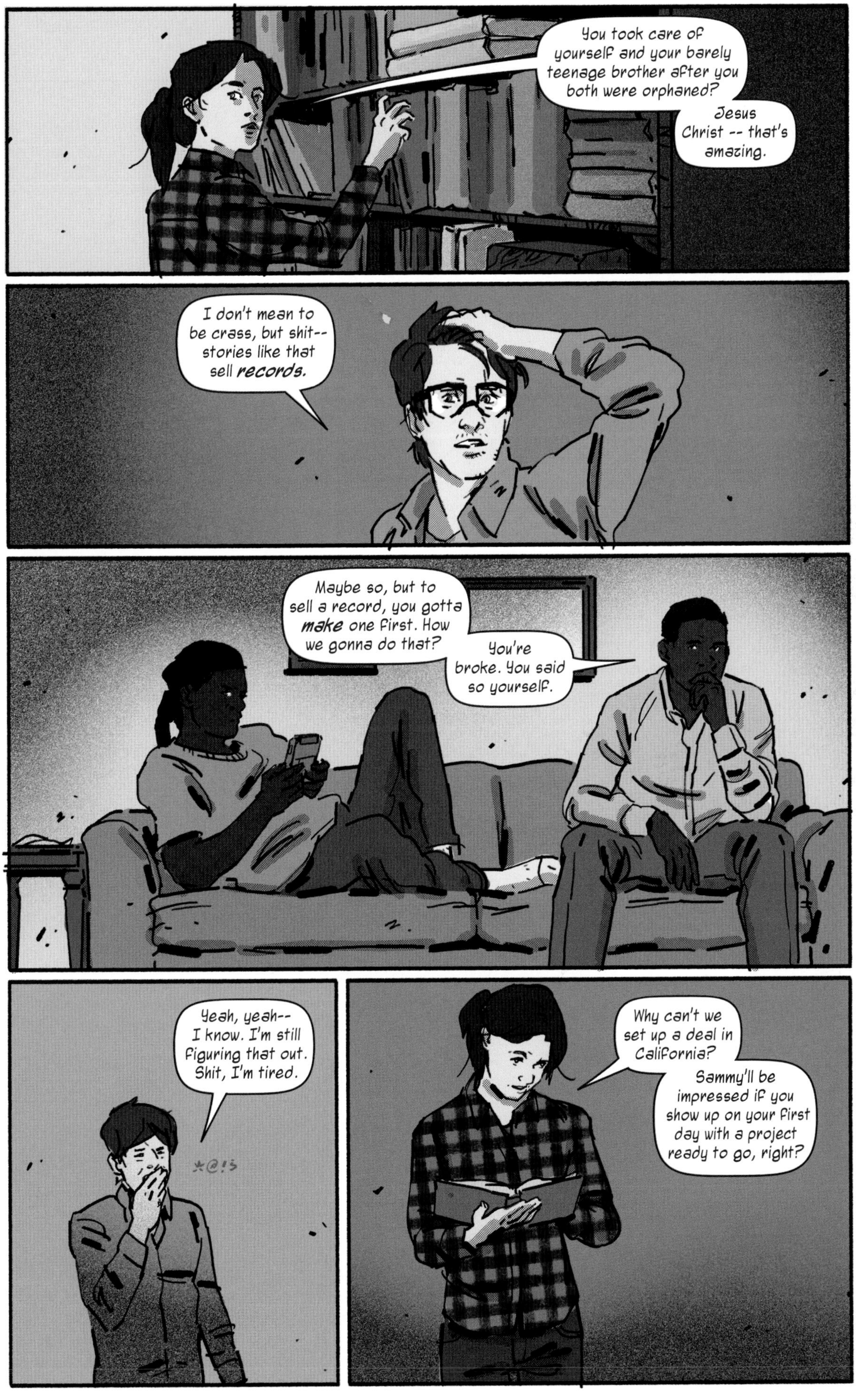
You took care of yourself and your barely teenage brother after you both were orphaned?
Jesus Christ -- that's amazing.
I don't mean to be crass, but shit-- stories like that sell *records.*
Maybe so, but to sell a record, you gotta *make* one first. How we gonna do that?
You're broke. You said so yourself.
Yeah, yeah-- I know. I'm still figuring that out. Shit, I'm tired.
Why can't we set up a deal in California?
Sammy'll be impressed if you show up on your first day with a project ready to go, right?

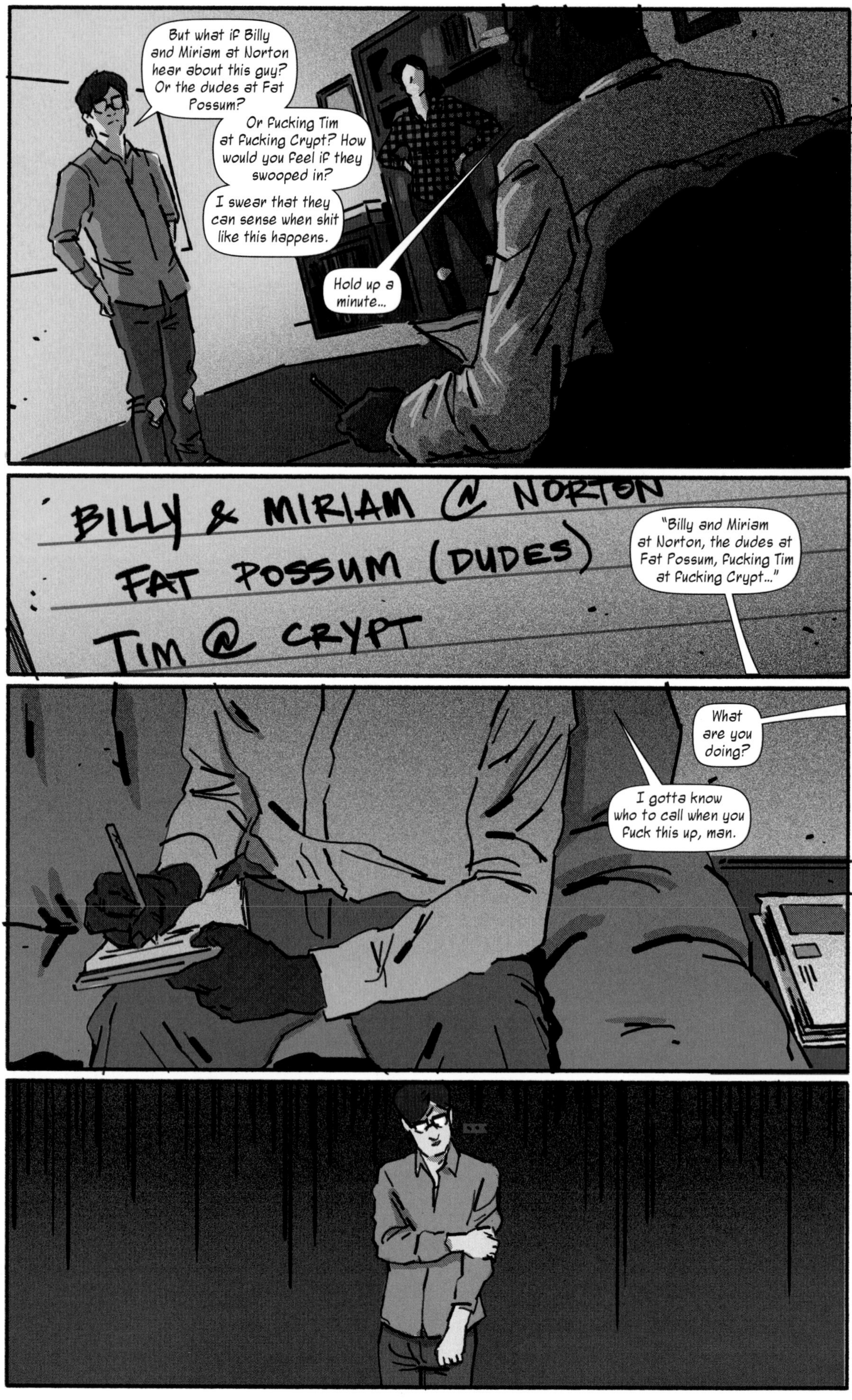
But what if Billy and Miriam at Norton hear about this guy? Or the dudes at Fat Possum?
Or fucking Tim at fucking Crypt? How would you feel if they swooped in?
I swear that they can sense when shit like this happens.
Hold up a minute...
BILLY & MIRIAM @ NORTON
FAT POSSUM (DUDES)
TIM @ CRYPT
"Billy and Miriam at Norton, the dudes at Fat Possum, fucking Tim at fucking Crypt..."
What are you doing?
I gotta know who to call when you fuck this up, man.

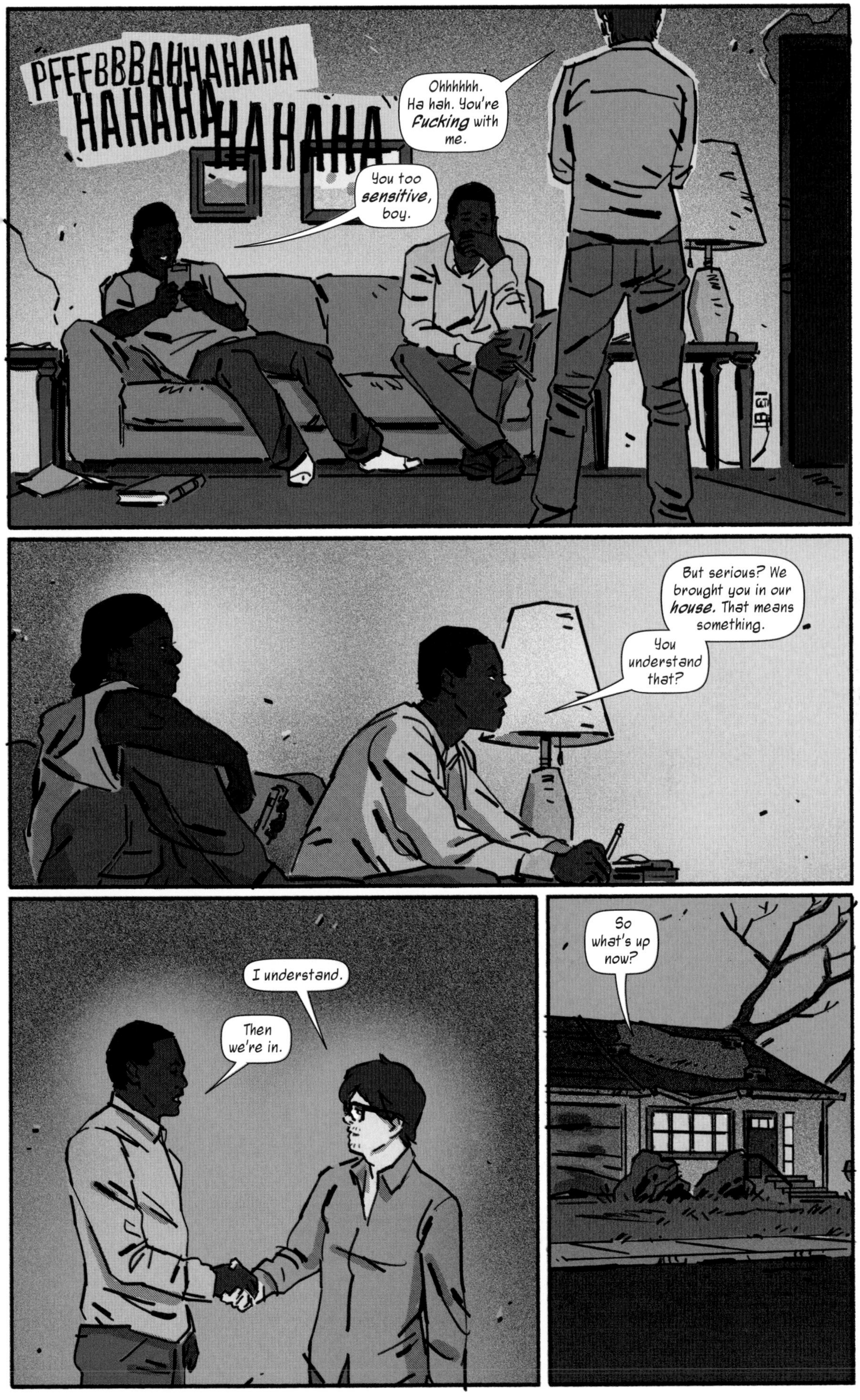
PFFFBBBAHHAHAHA
HAHAHAHAHAHA
Ohhhhhh. Ha hah. You're *fucking* with me.
You too *sensitive*, boy.
But serious? We brought you in our *house.* That means something.
You understand that?
I understand.
Then we're in.
So what's up now?

I've got a Tascam in the car and a couple of mics.
I figure I can record your guys' next few gigs and cobble *something* together.
Something raw, like a real field recording.
Field recording? This ain't no sharecropper shack. You want us to put on some overalls, too?
White boy, if we make a record I want us to make a *record.*
I didn't mean it *that* way. I mean...
I meant that I just can't leave town without something that *captures* last night.
huh...
I think I've got an idea.

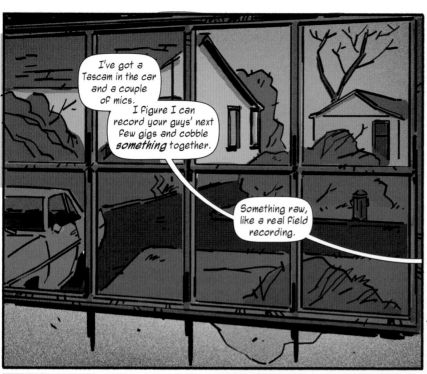

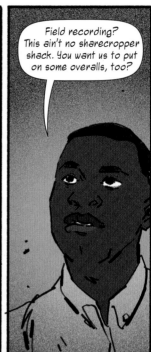

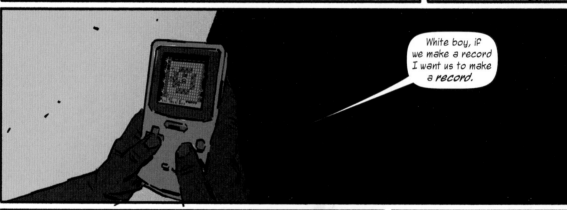

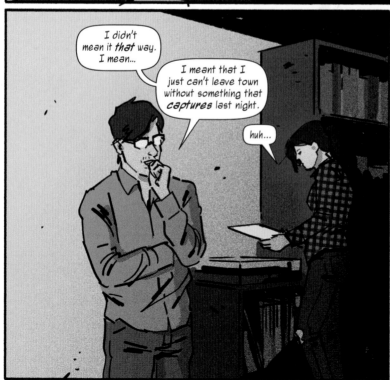

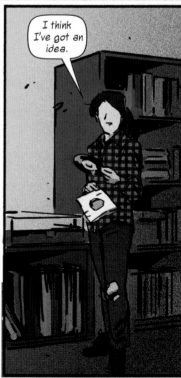

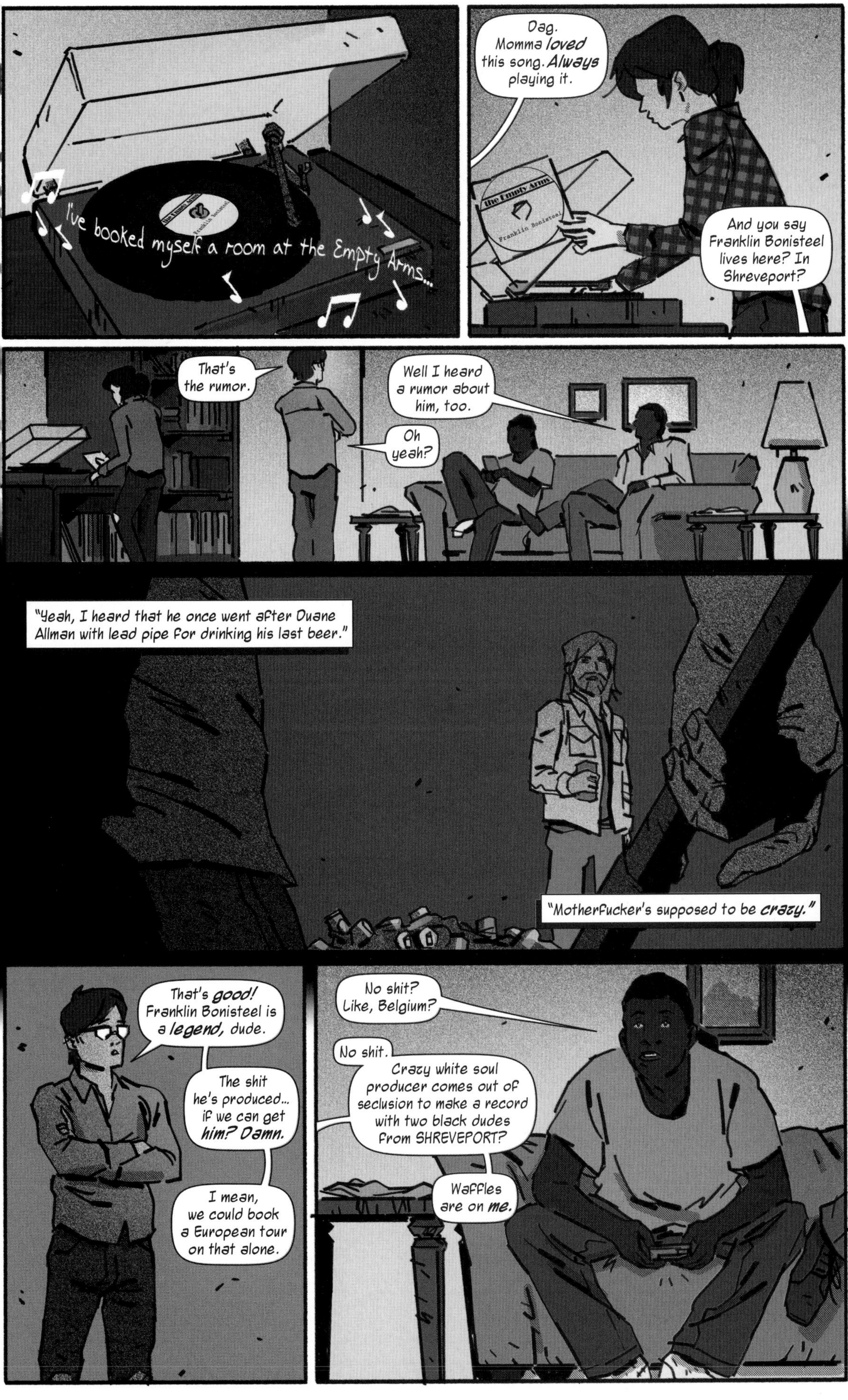

I've booked myself a room at the Empty Arms...
The Empty Arms
Franklin Bonisteel
Dag. Momma *loved* this song. *Always* playing it.
And you say Franklin Bonisteel lives here? In Shreveport?
That's the rumor.
Well I heard a rumor about him, too.
Oh yeah?
"Yeah, I heard that he once went after Duane Allman with lead pipe for drinking his last beer."
"Motherfucker's supposed to be *crazy.*"
That's *good!* Franklin Bonisteel is a *legend,* dude.
The shit he's produced... if we can get *him? Damn.*
I mean, we could book a European tour on that alone.
No shit? Like, Belgium?
No shit.
Crazy white soul producer comes out of seclusion to make a record with two black dudes from SHREVEPORT?
Waffles are on *me.*

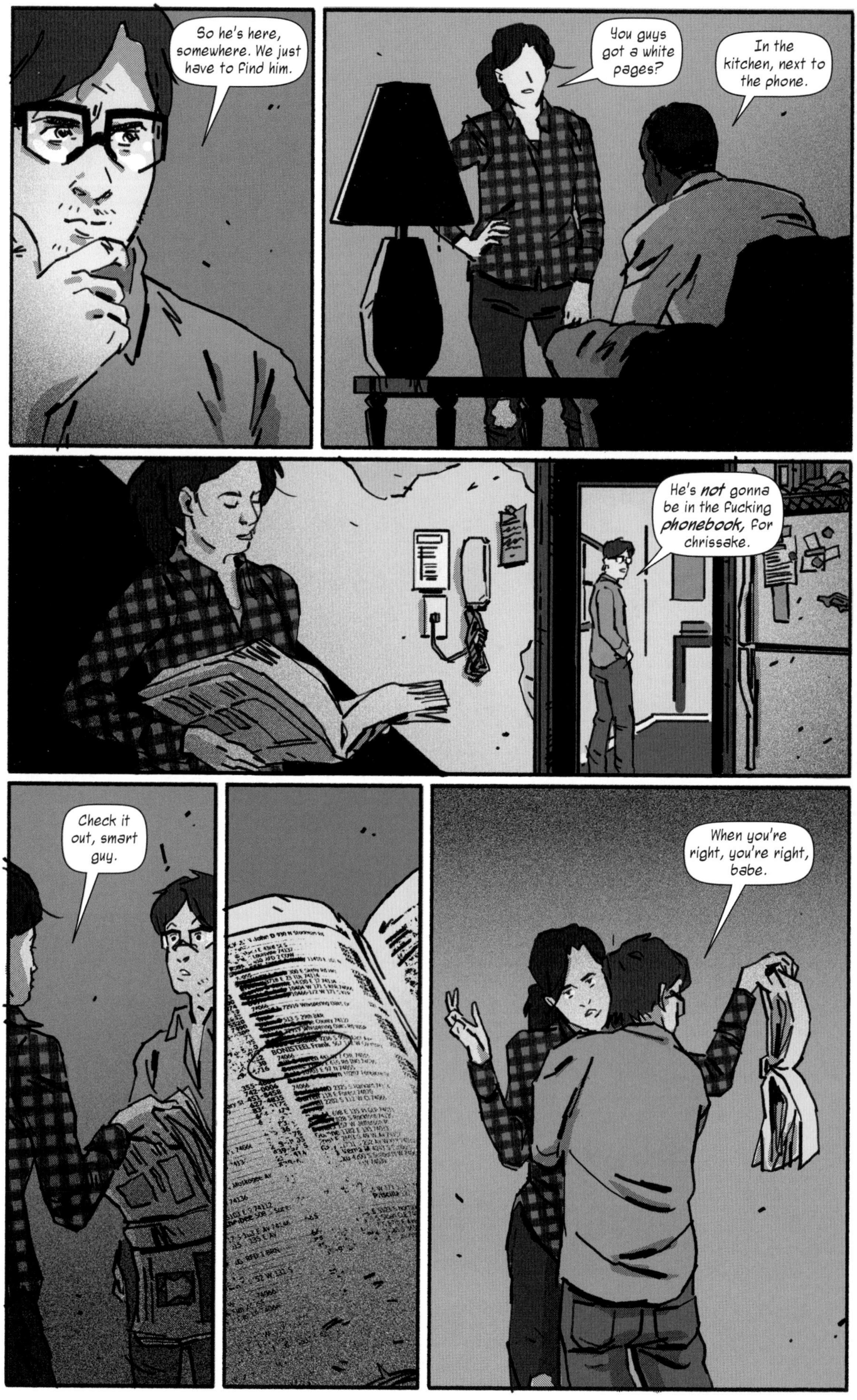
So he's here, somewhere. We just have to find him.
You guys got a white pages?
In the kitchen, next to the phone.
He's *not* gonna be in the fucking *phonebook,* for chrissake.
Check it out, smart guy.
When you're right, you're right, babe.

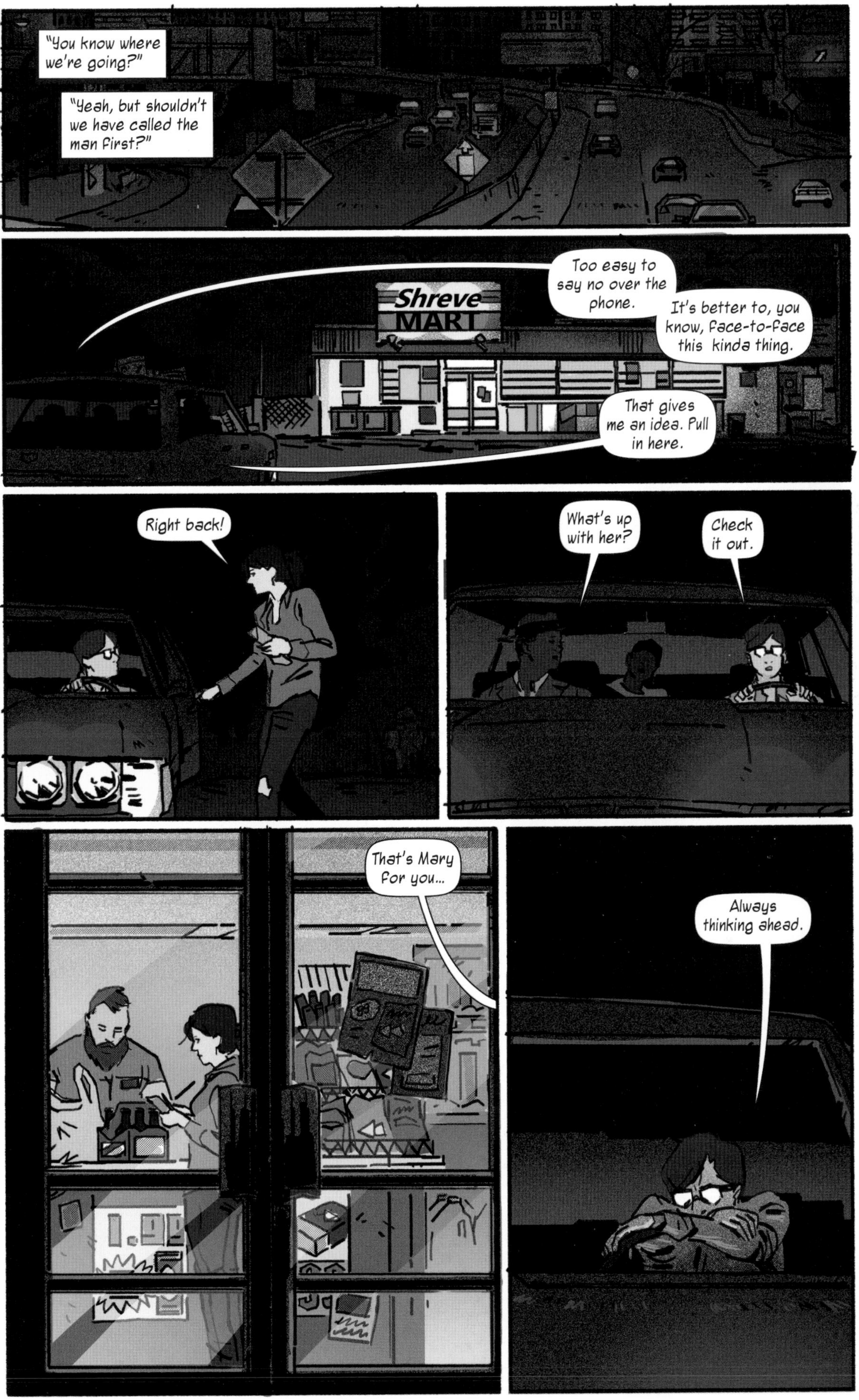
"You know where we're going?"
"Yeah, but shouldn't we have called the man first?"
Shreve MART
Too easy to say no over the phone.
It's better to, you know, face-to-face this kinda thing.
That gives me an idea. Pull in here.
Right back!
What's up with her?
Check it out.
That's Mary for you...
Always thinking ahead.

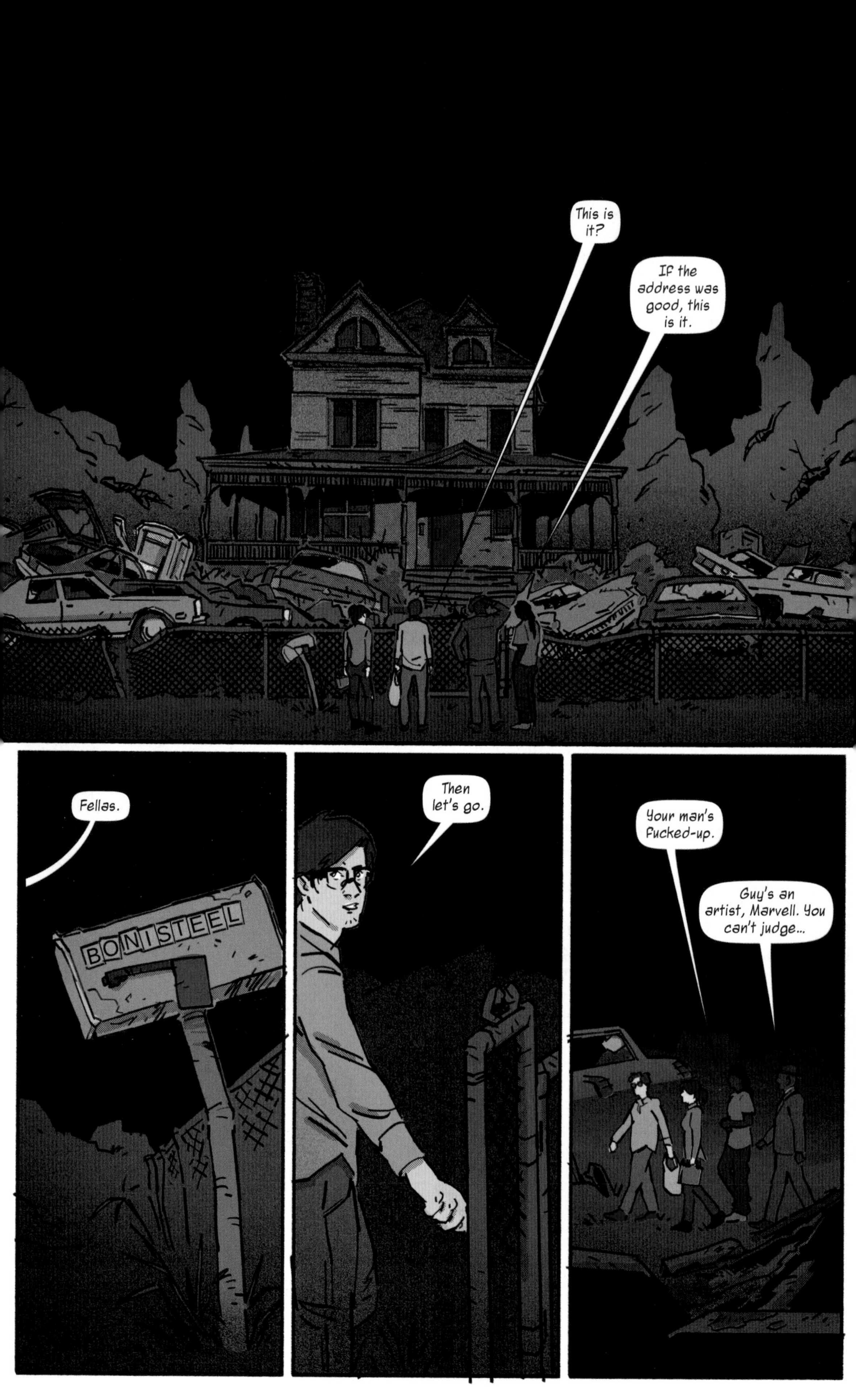
This is it?
If the address was good, this is it.
Fellas.
BONISTEEL
Then let's go.
Your man's fucked-up.
Guy's an artist, Marvell. You can't judge...

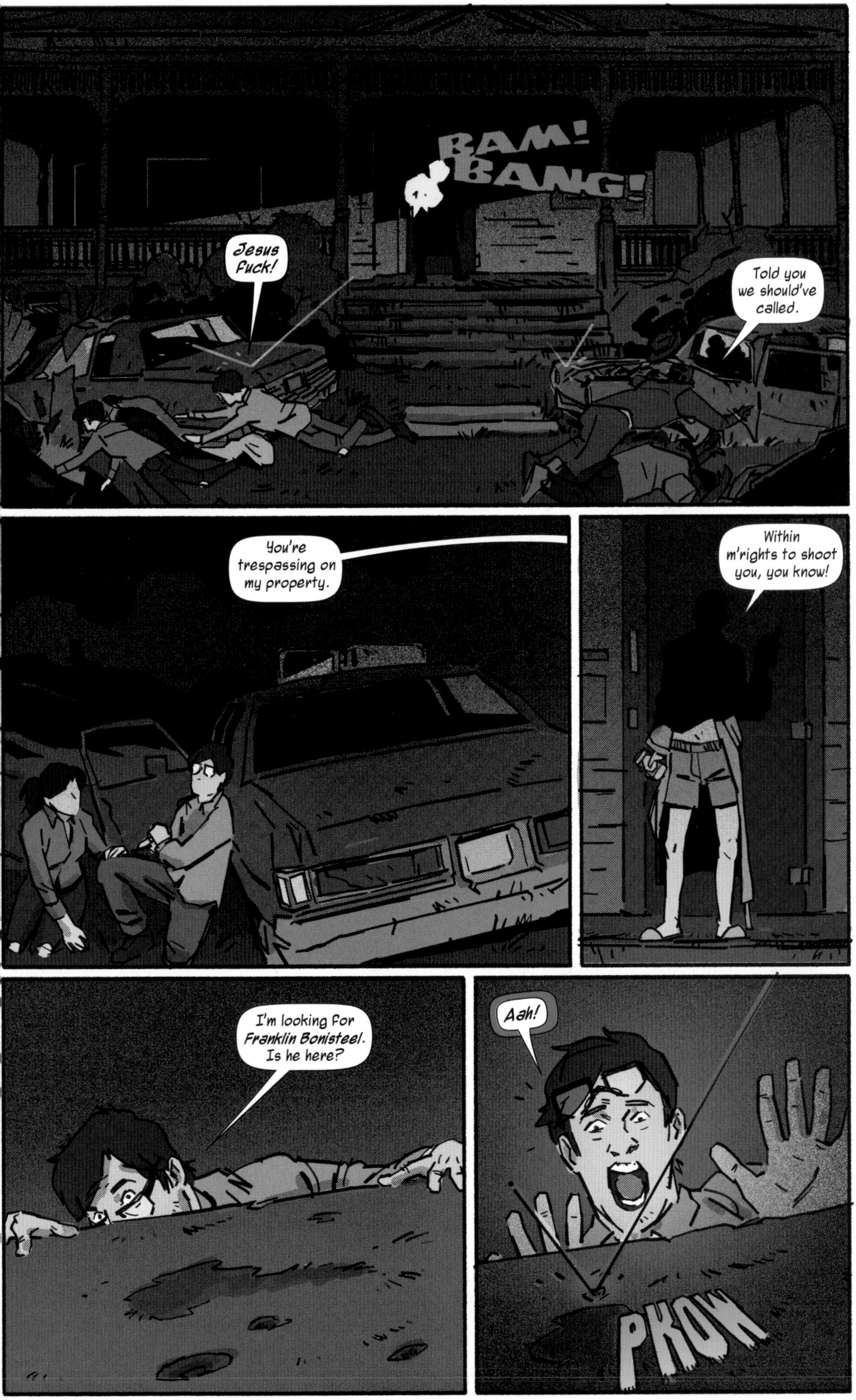
BAM!
BANG!
Jesus Fuck!
Told you we should've called.
You're trespassing on my property.
Within m'rights to shoot you, you know!
I'm looking for Franklin Bonisteel. Is he here?
Aah!
PKOW

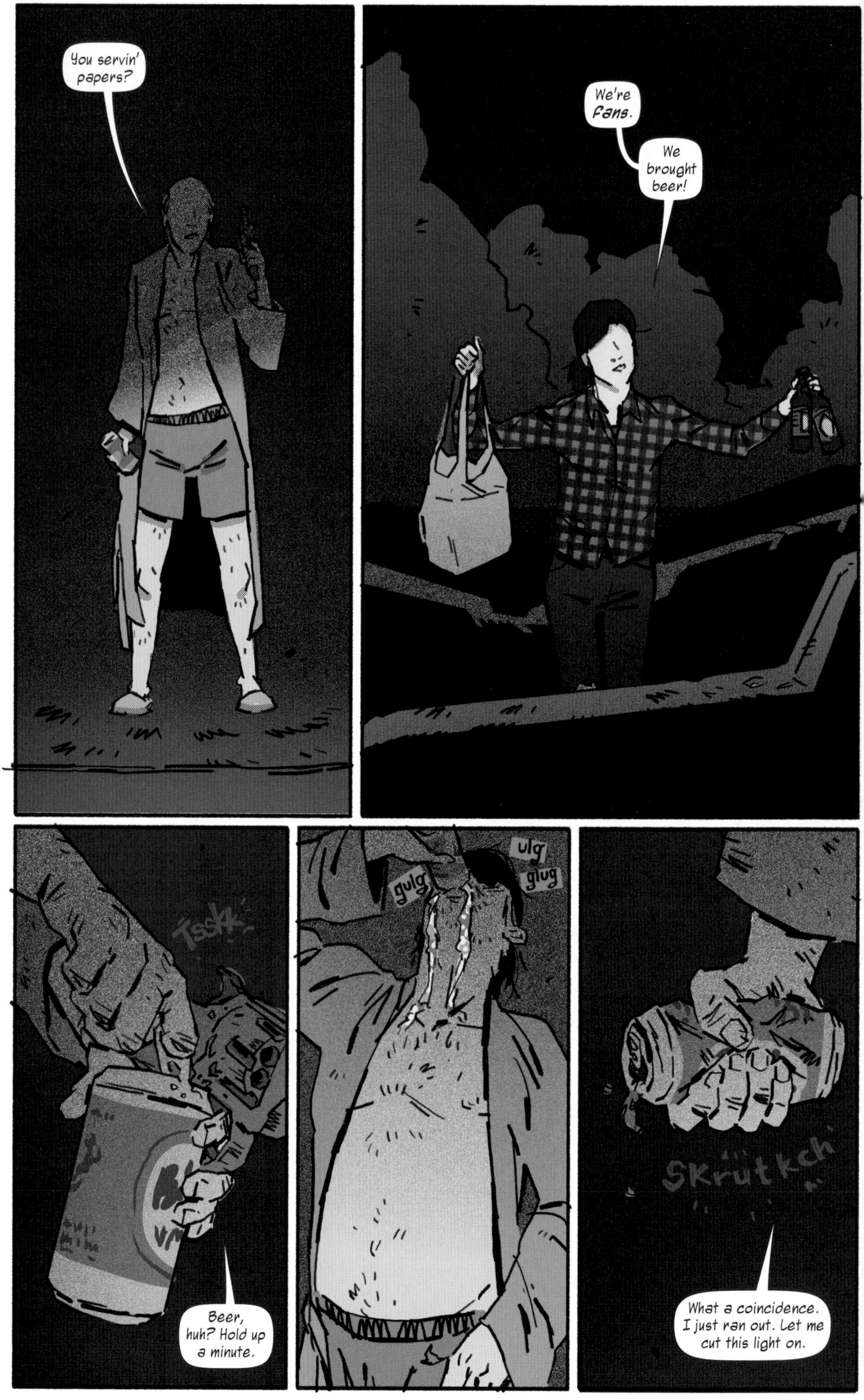
You servin' papers?
We're fans.
We brought beer!
Tssk
Beer, huh? Hold up a minute.
gulg
ulg
glug
Skrutkch
What a coincidence. I just ran out. Let me cut this light on.

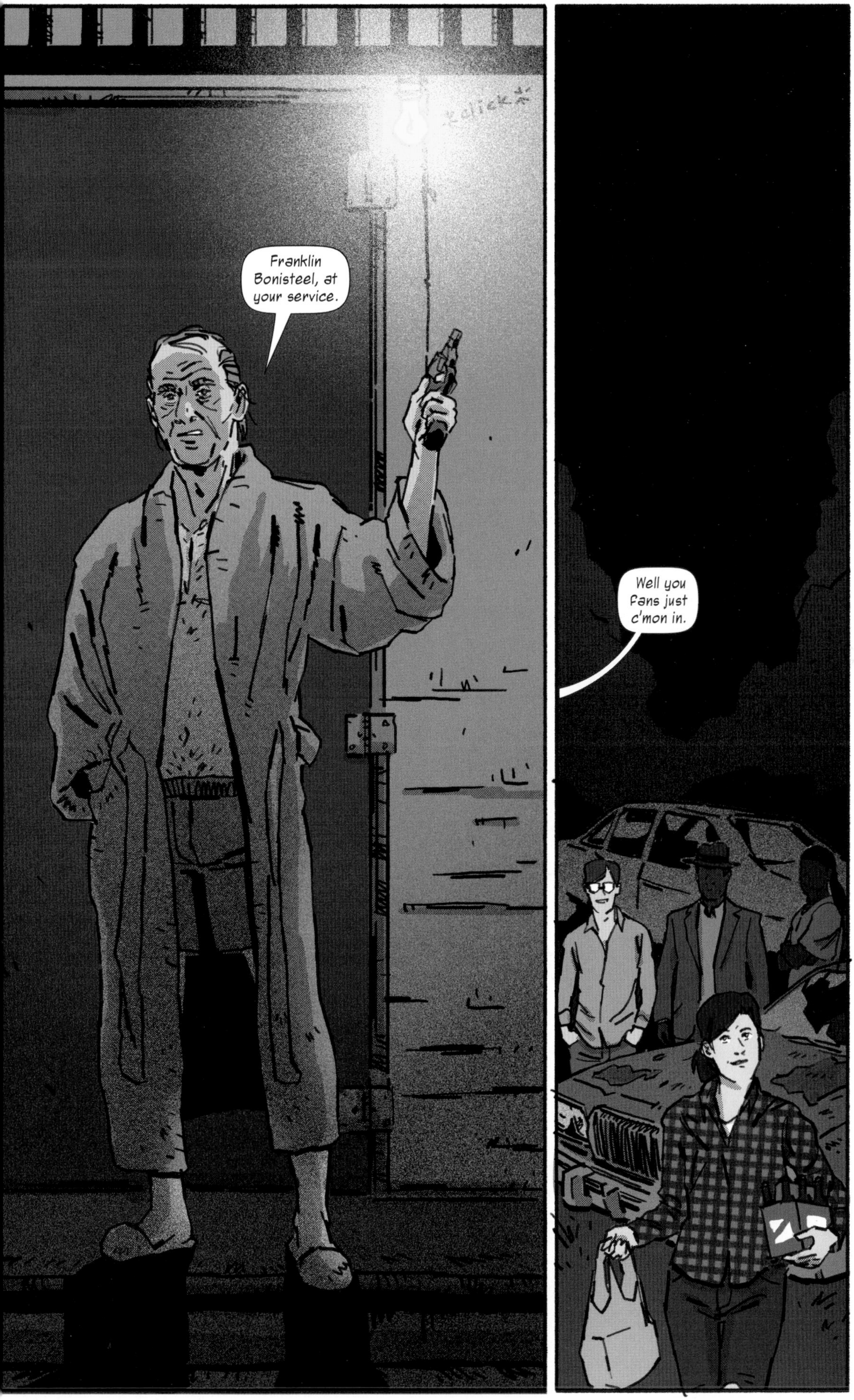
klick
Franklin Bonisteel, at your service.
Well you fans just c'mon in.

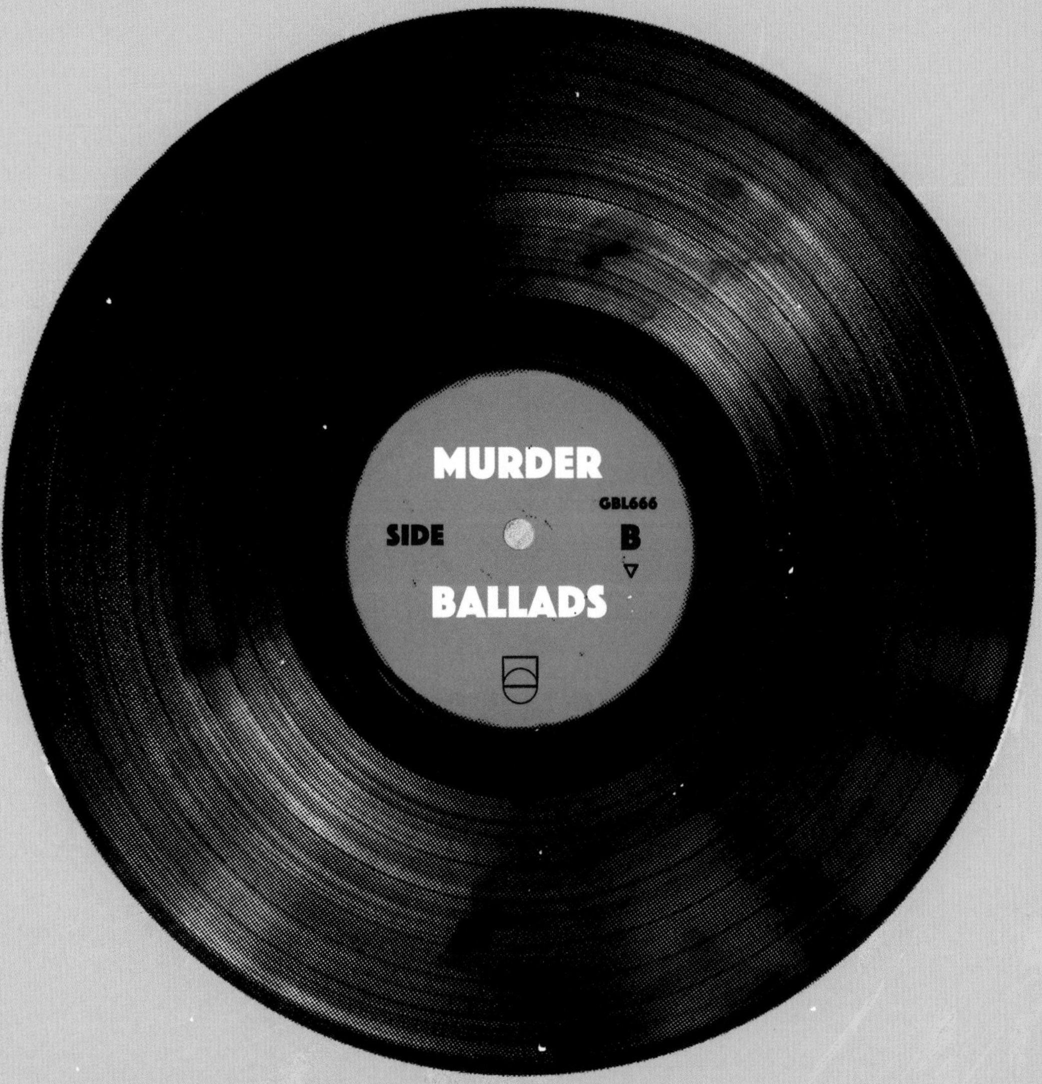
MURDER
GBL666
SIDE
B
BALLADS

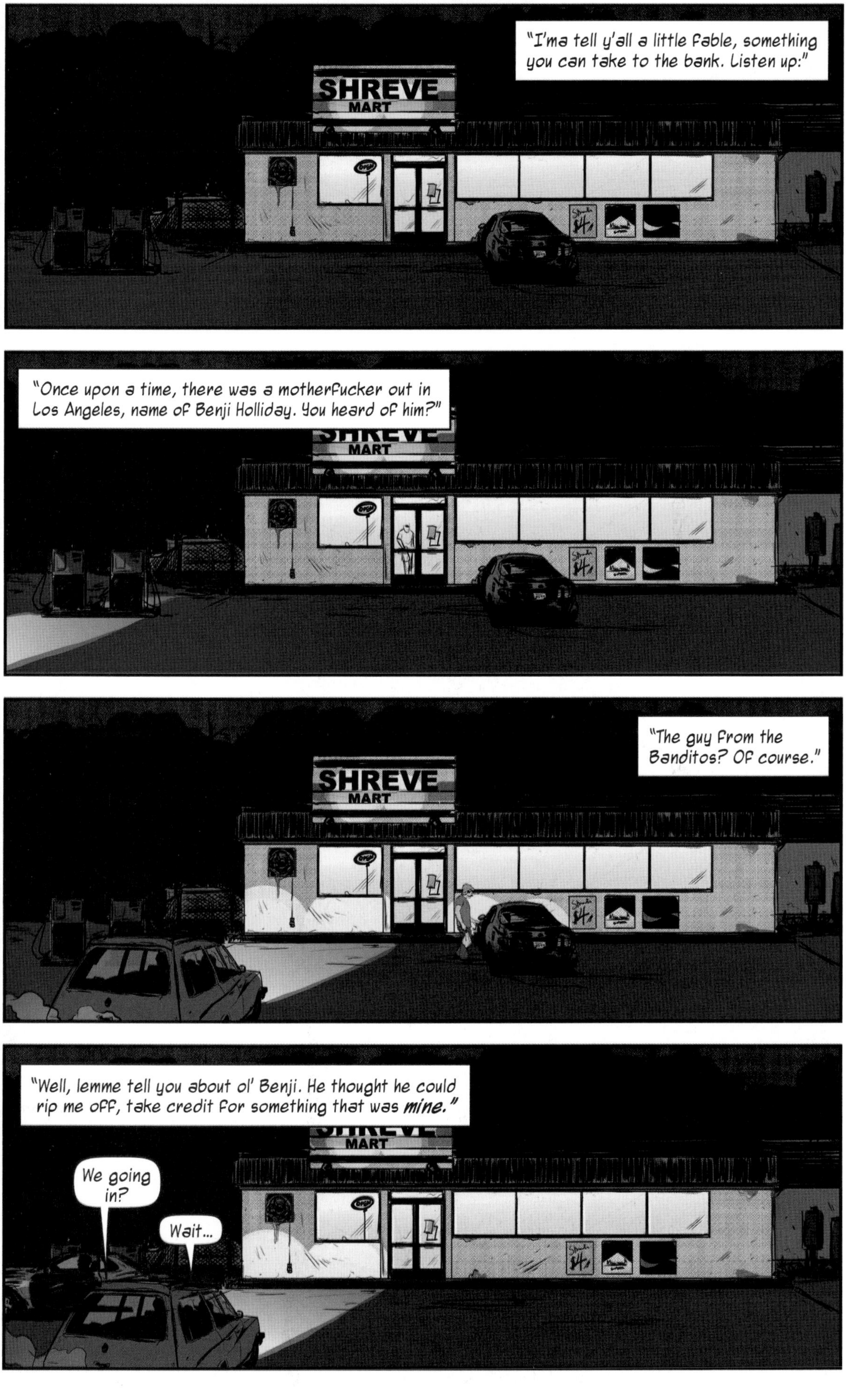
"I'ma tell y'all a little fable, something you can take to the bank. Listen up:"
SHREVE MART
"Once upon a time, there was a motherfucker out in Los Angeles, name of Benji Holliday. You heard of him?"
"The guy from the Banditos? Of course."
"Well, lemme tell you about ol' Benji. He thought he could rip me off, take credit for something that was *mine.*"
We going in?
Wait...

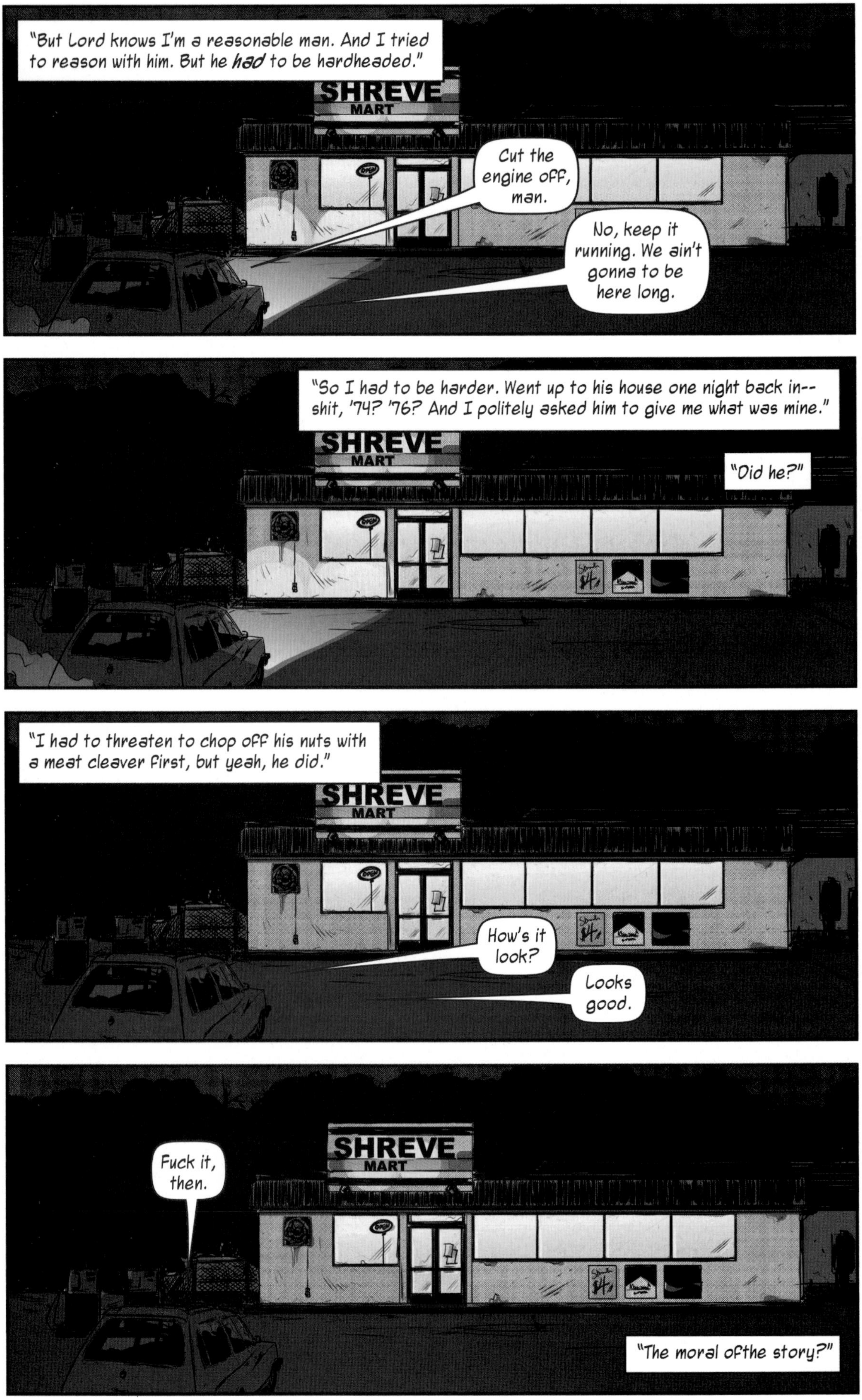
"But Lord knows I'm a reasonable man. And I tried to reason with him. But he *had* to be hardheaded."
SHREVE MART
Cut the engine off, man.
No, keep it running. We ain't gonna to be here long.
"So I had to be harder. Went up to his house one night back in--shit, '74? '76? And I politely asked him to give me what was mine."
SHREVE MART
"Did he?"
"I had to threaten to chop off his nuts with a meat cleaver first, but yeah, he did."
SHREVE MART
How's it look?
Looks good.
SHREVE MART
Fuck it, then.
"The moral ofthe story?"

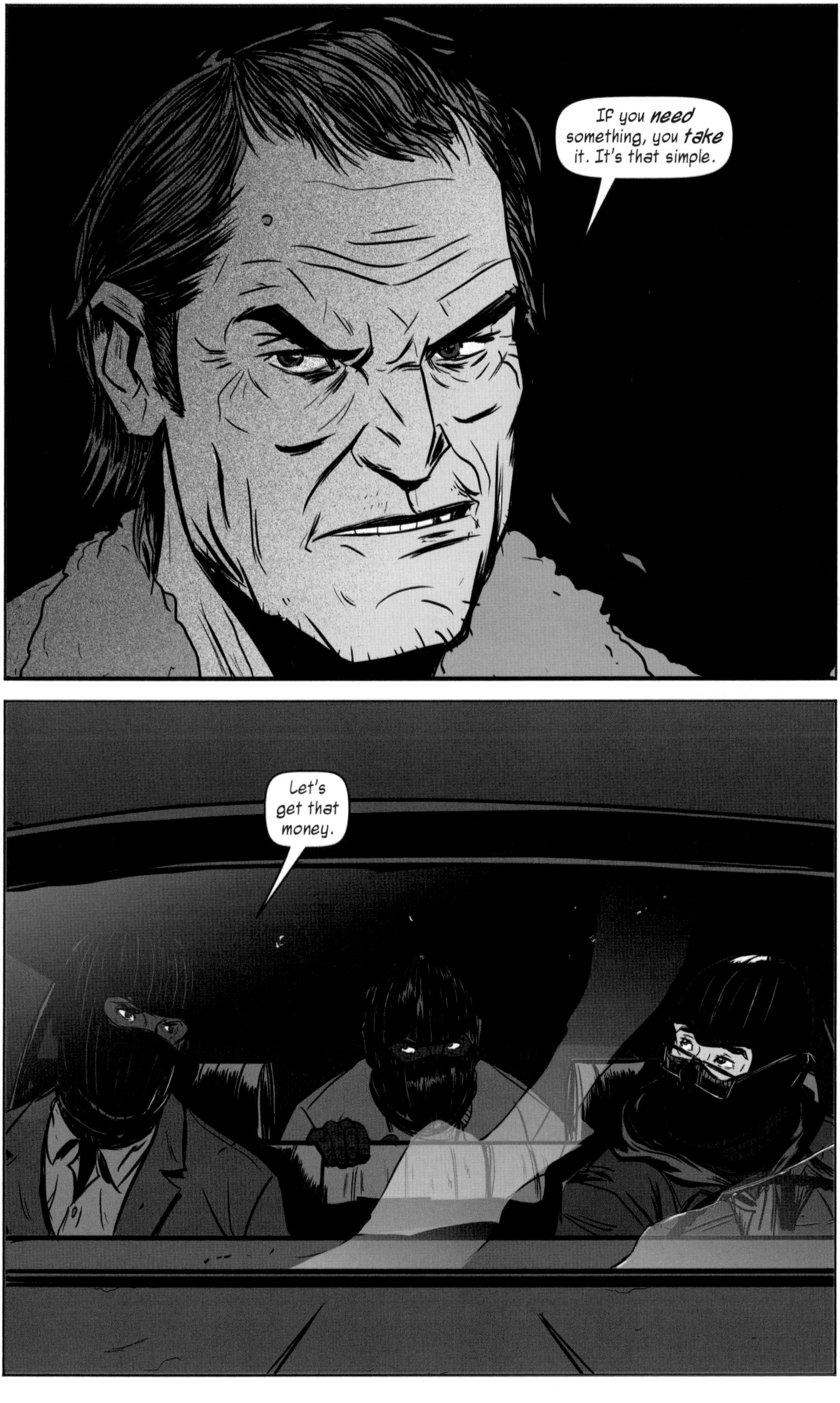
If you *need* something, you *take* it. It's that simple.
Let's get that money.

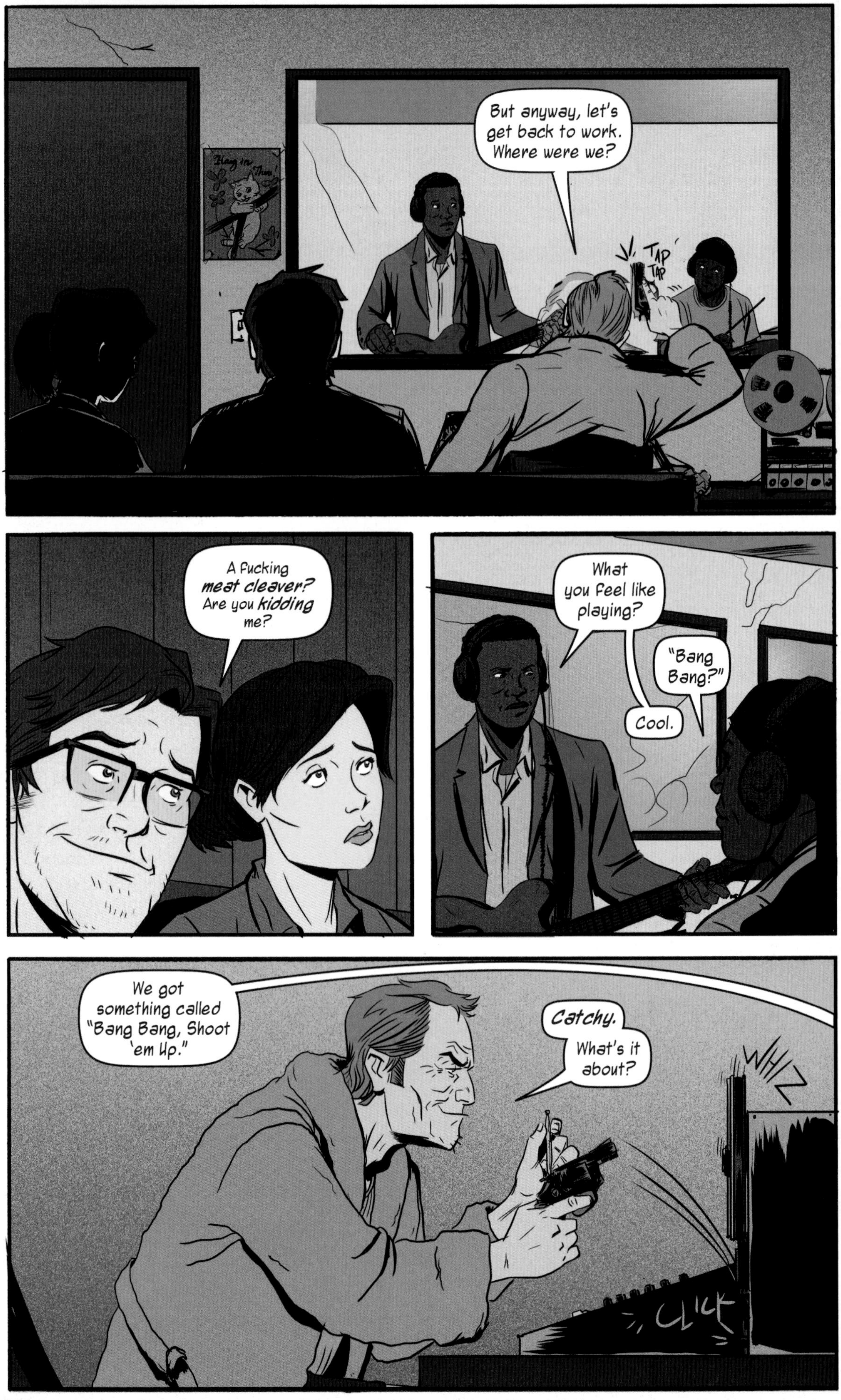

But anyway, let's get back to work. Where were we?
TAP TAP
A fucking *meat cleaver?* Are you *kidding* me?
What you feel like playing?
"Bang Bang?"
Cool.
We got something called "Bang Bang, Shoot 'em Up."
Catchy. What's it about?
WHIZ
CLICK

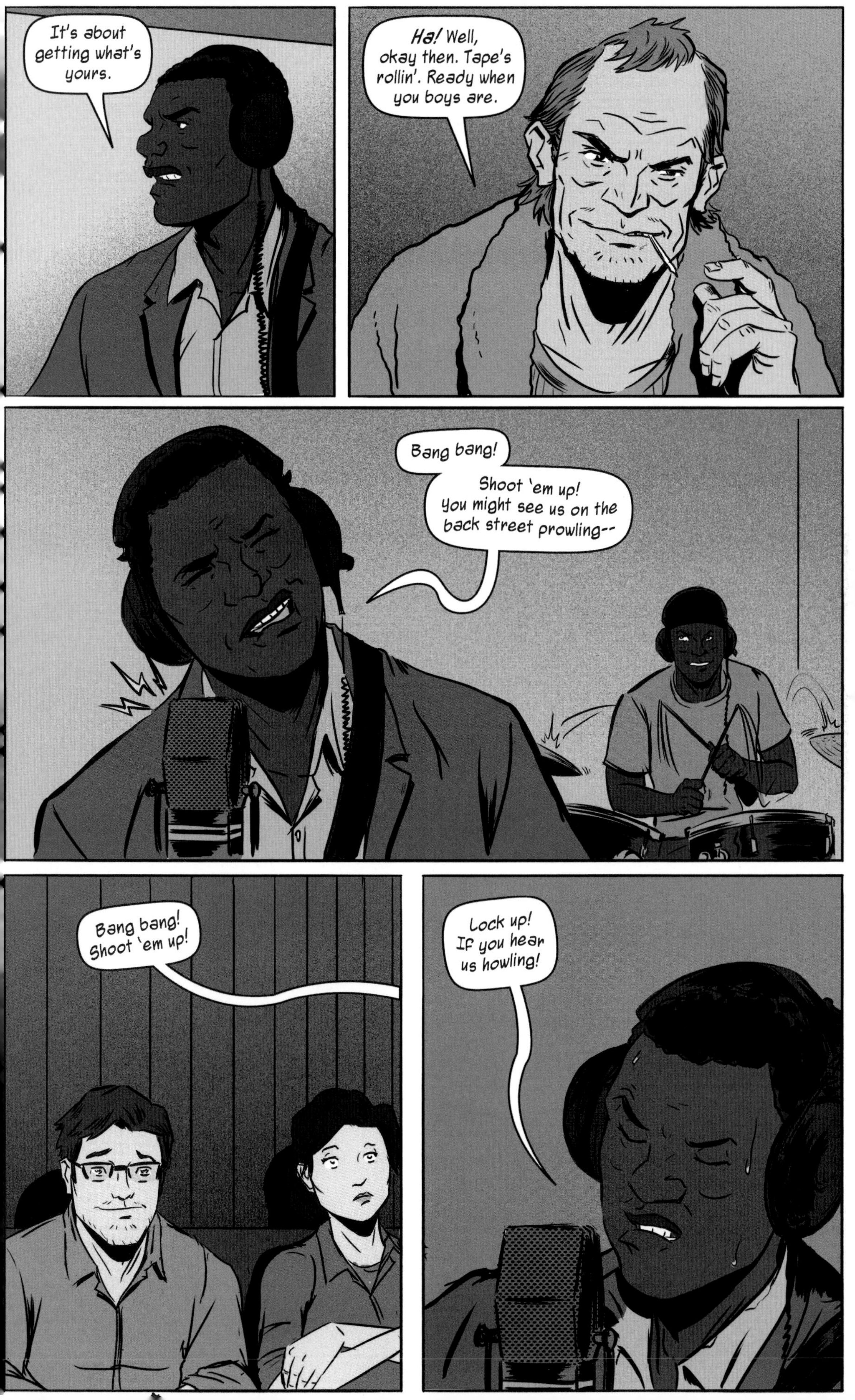
It's about getting what's yours.
Ha! Well, okay then. Tape's rollin'. Ready when you boys are.
Bang bang!
Shoot 'em up! You might see us on the back street prowling--
Bang bang! Shoot 'em up!
Lock up! If you hear us howling!

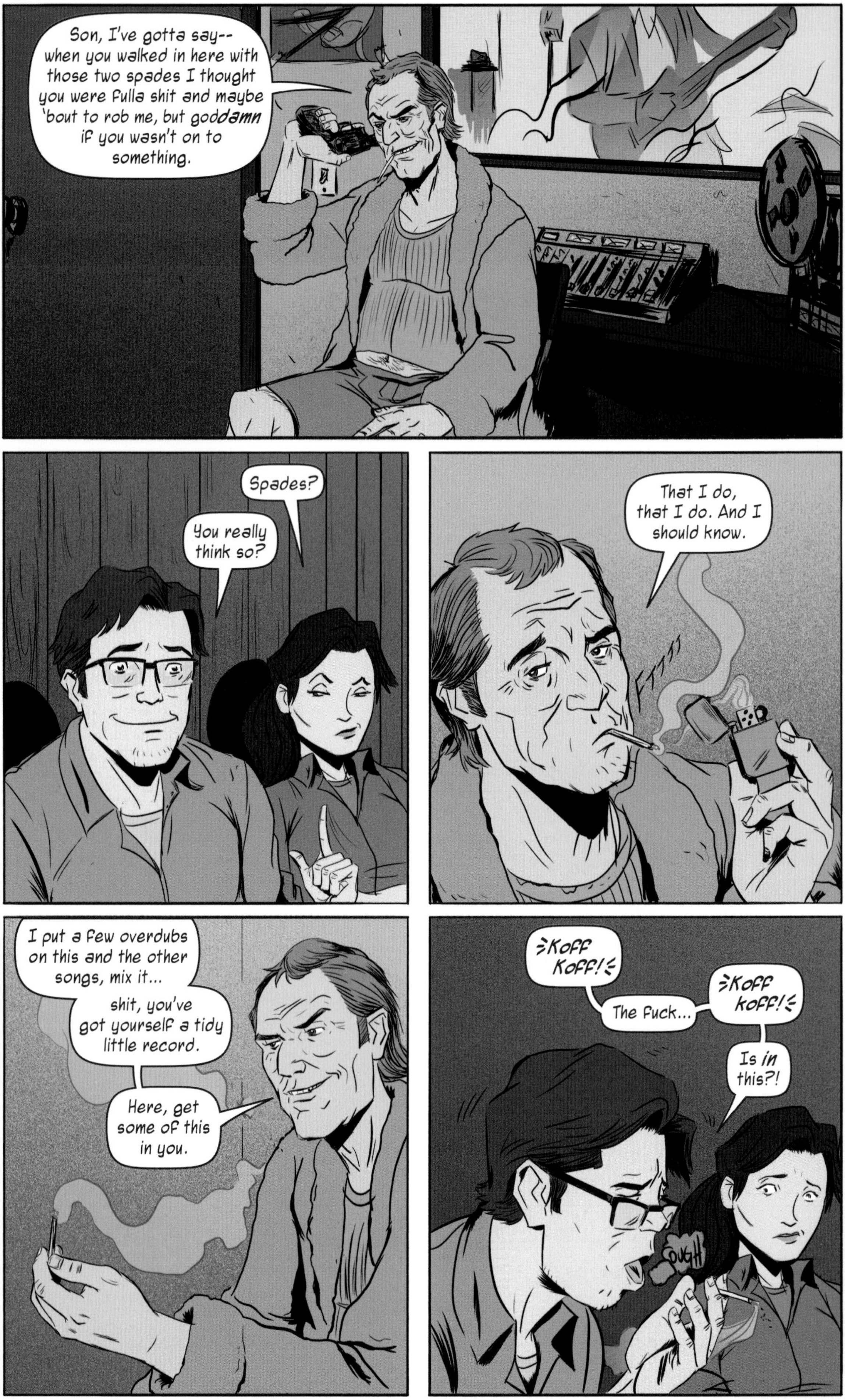
Son, I've gotta say-- when you walked in here with those two spades I thought you were fulla shit and maybe 'bout to rob me, but god*damn* if you wasn't on to something.
Spades?
You really think so?
That I do, that I do. And I should know.
FTTTT
I put a few overdubs on this and the other songs, mix it...
shit, you've got yourself a tidy little record.
Here, get some of this in you.
KOFF KOFF!
The fuck...
KOFF KOFF!
Is *in* this?!
COUGH

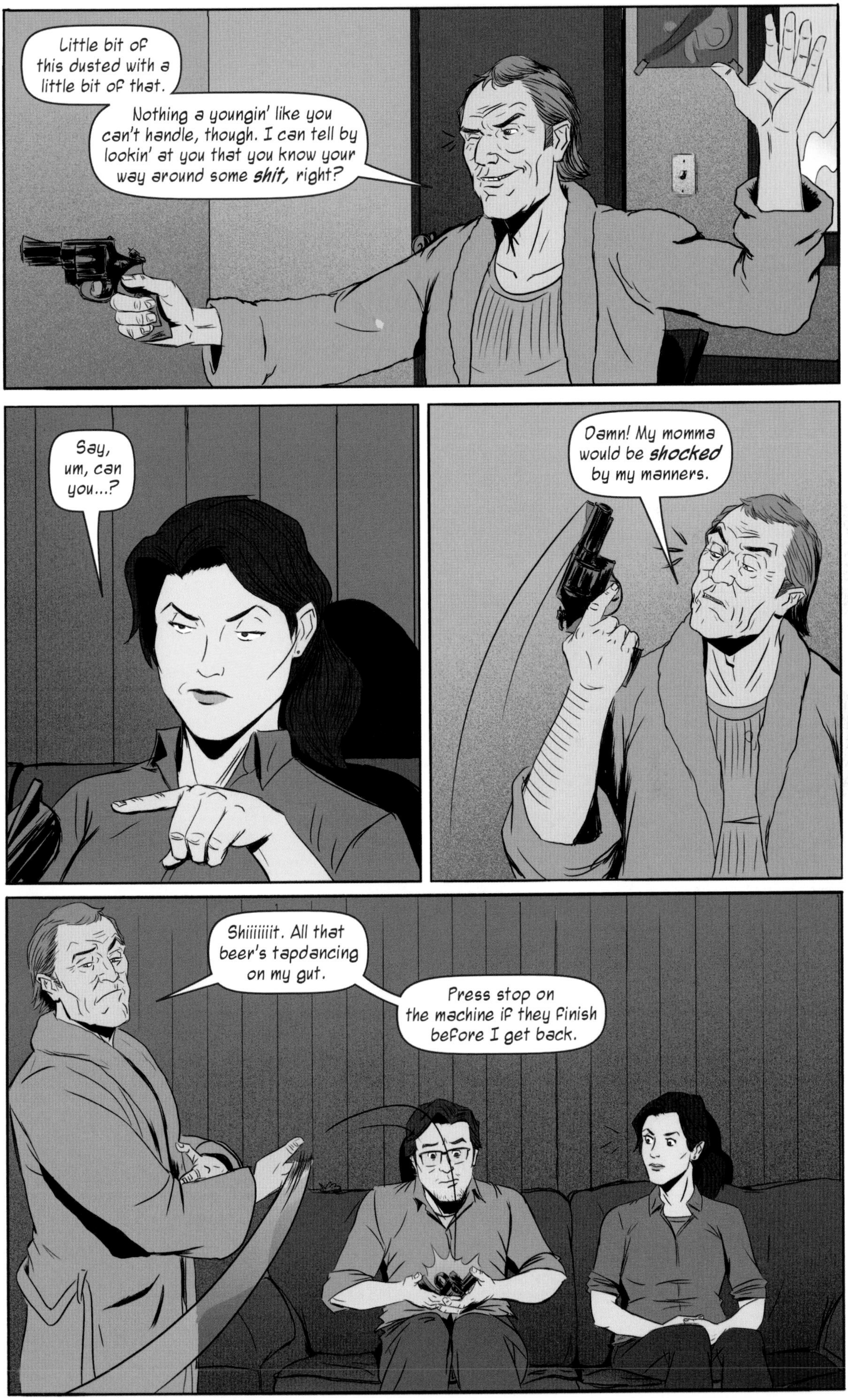

Little bit of this dusted with a little bit of that.
Nothing a youngin' like you can't handle, though. I can tell by lookin' at you that you know your way around some shit, right?
Say, um, can you...?
Damn! My momma would be shocked by my manners.
Shiiiiiiit. All that beer's tapdancing on my gut.
Press stop on the machine if they finish before I get back.

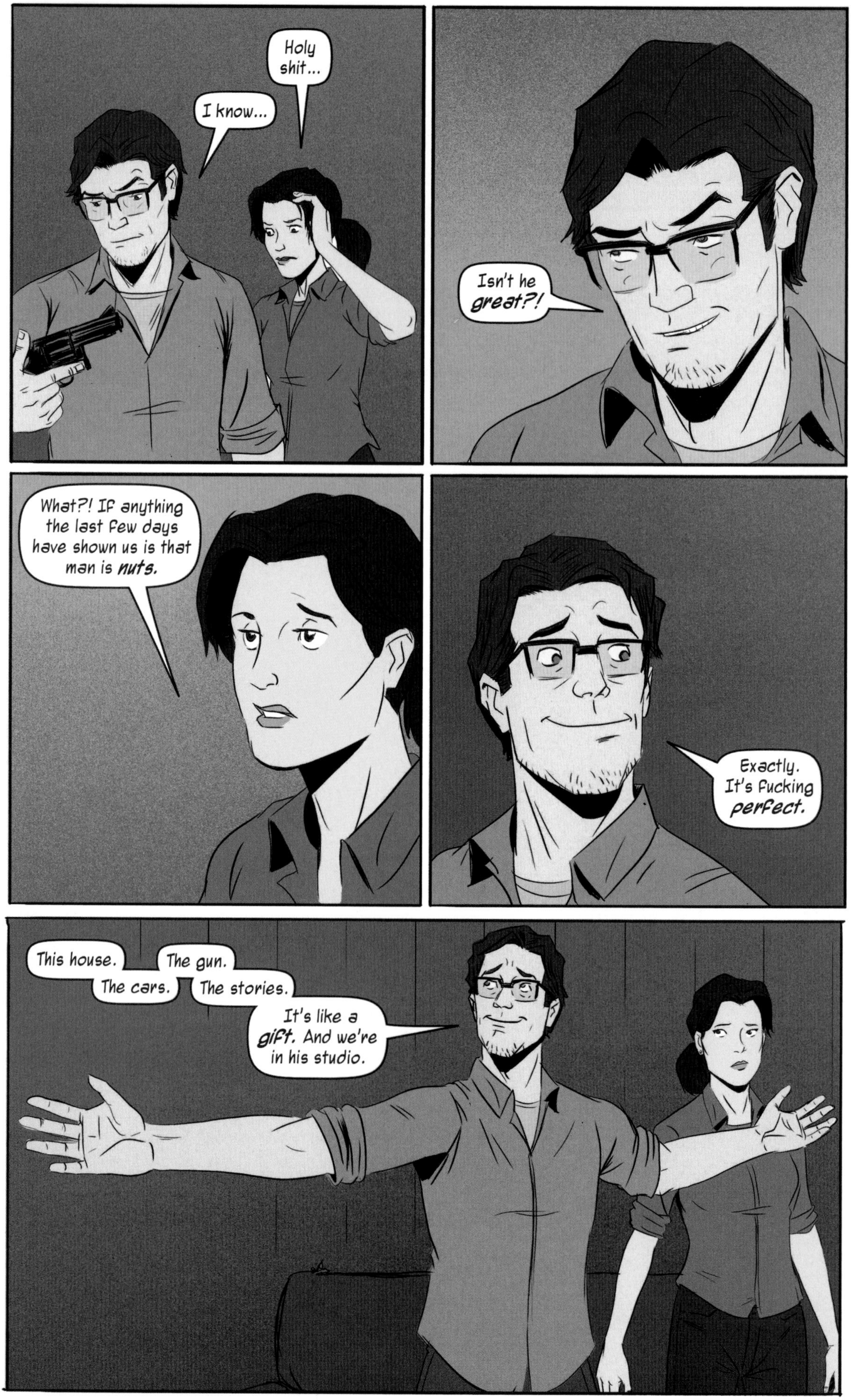
Holy shit...
I know...
Isn't he *great?!*
What?! If anything the last few days have shown us is that man is *nuts.*
Exactly. It's fucking *perfect.*
This house.
The gun.
The cars.
The stories.
It's like a *gift.* And we're in his studio.

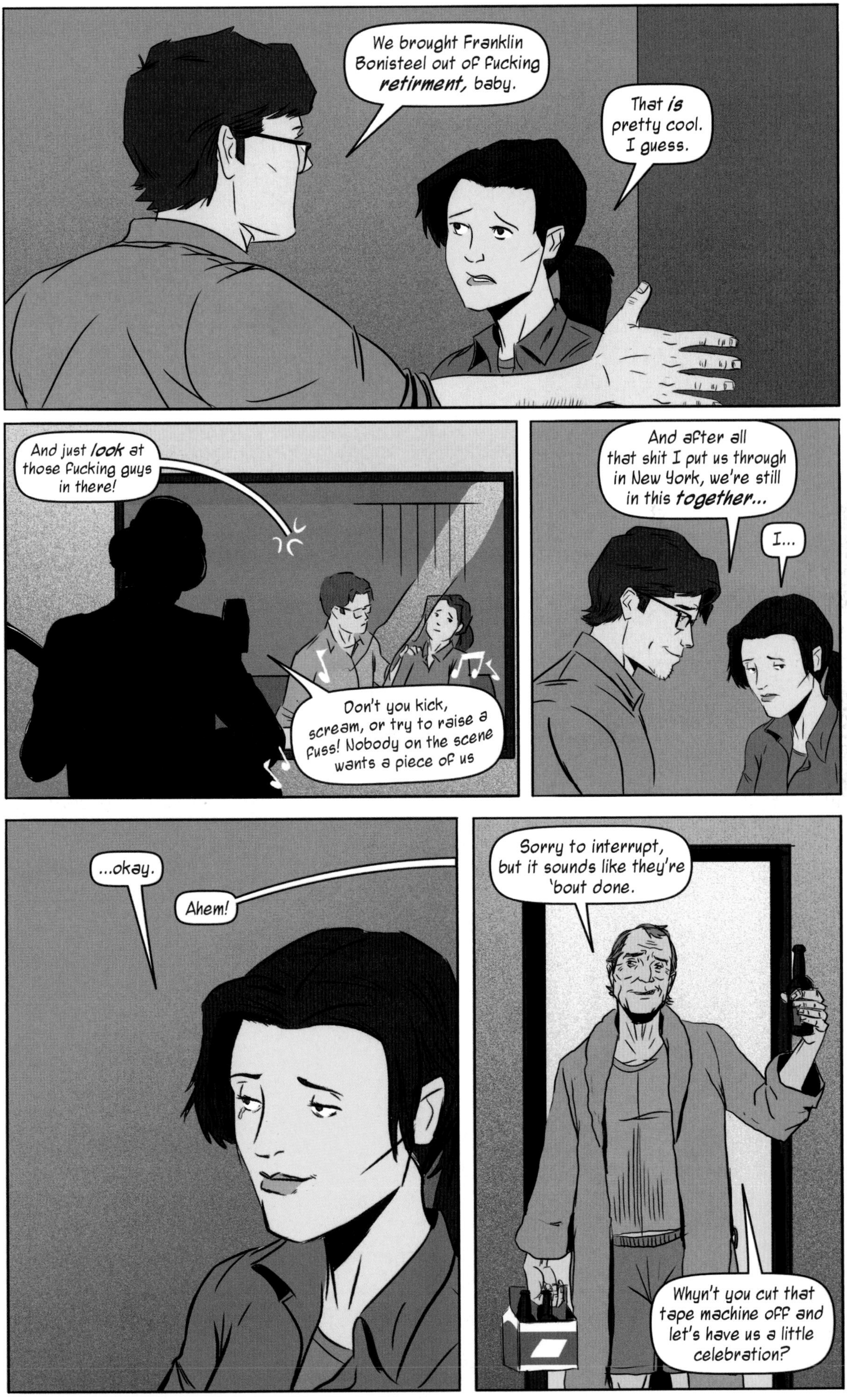
We brought Franklin Bonisteel out of fucking *retirment,* baby.
That *is* pretty cool. I guess.
And just *look* at those fucking guys in there!
Don't you kick, scream, or try to raise a fuss! Nobody on the scene wants a piece of us
And after all that shit I put us through in New York, we're still in this *together...*
I...
...okay.
Ahem!
Sorry to interrupt, but it sounds like they're 'bout done.
Whyn't you cut that tape machine off and let's have us a little celebration?

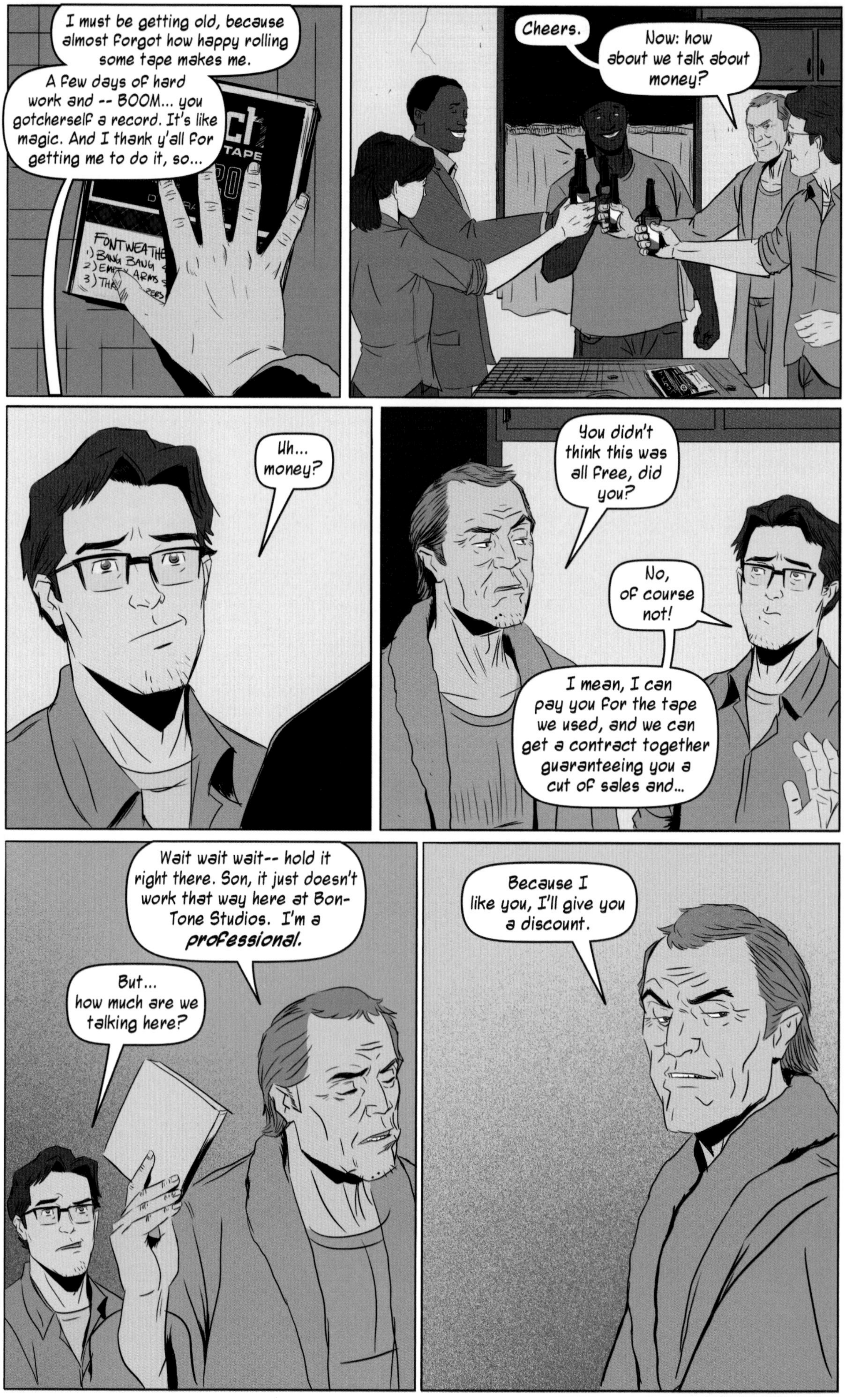
I must be getting old, because almost forgot how happy rolling some tape makes me.
A few days of hard work and -- BOOM... you gotcherself a record. It's like magic. And I thank y'all for getting me to do it, so...
Cheers.
Now: how about we talk about money?
Uh... money?
You didn't think this was all free, did you?
No, of course not!
I mean, I can pay you for the tape we used, and we can get a contract together guaranteeing you a cut of sales and...
Wait wait wait-- hold it right there. Son, it just doesn't work that way here at Bon-Tone Studios. I'm a *professional.*
But... how much are we talking here?
Because I like you, I'll give you a discount.

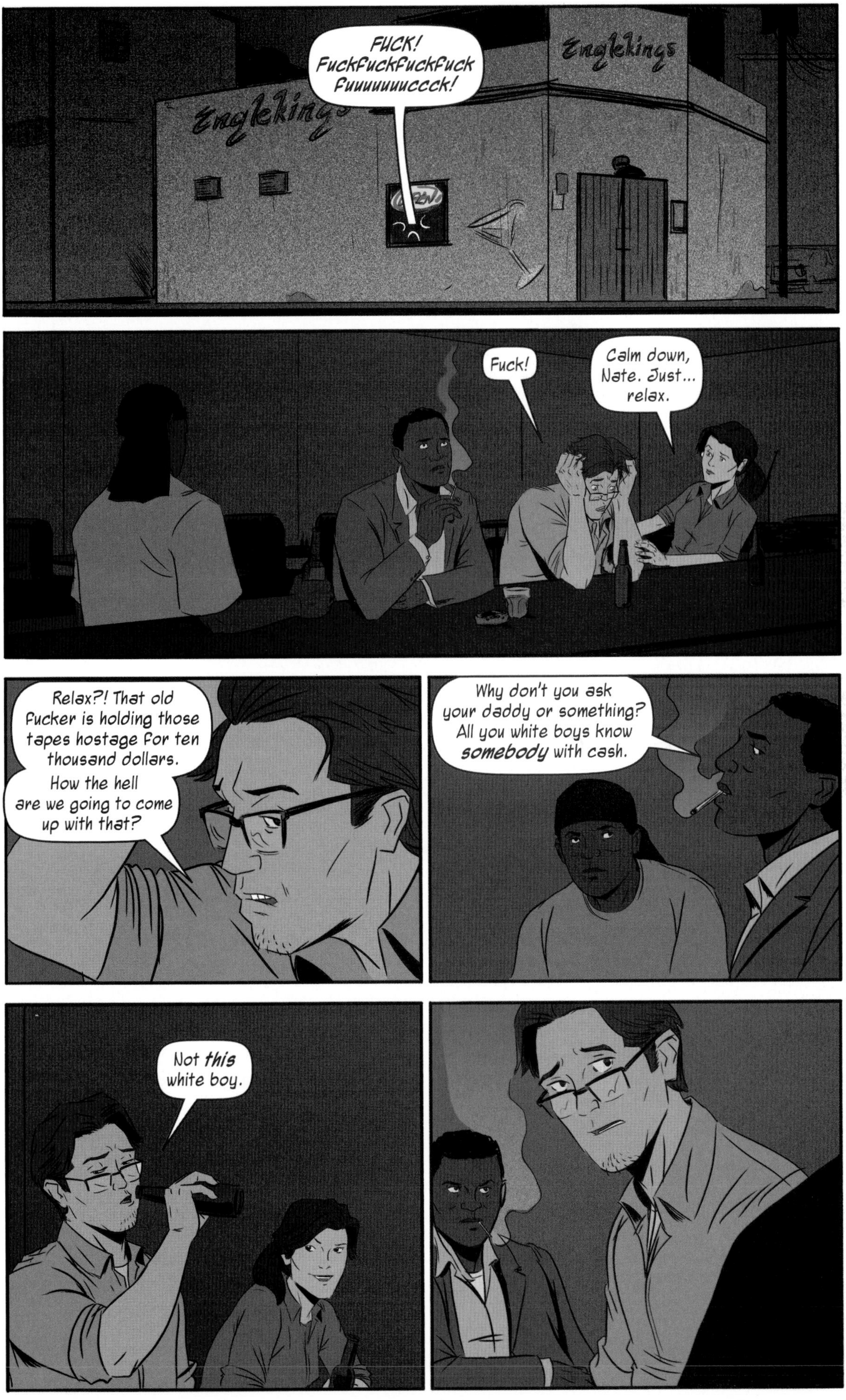
FUCK! Fuckfuckfuckfuck Fuuuuuuccck!
Englekings
Fuck!
Calm down, Nate. Just... relax.
Relax?! That old fucker is holding those tapes hostage for ten thousand dollars.
How the hell are we going to come up with that?
Why don't you ask your daddy or something? All you white boys know *somebody* with cash.
Not *this* white boy.

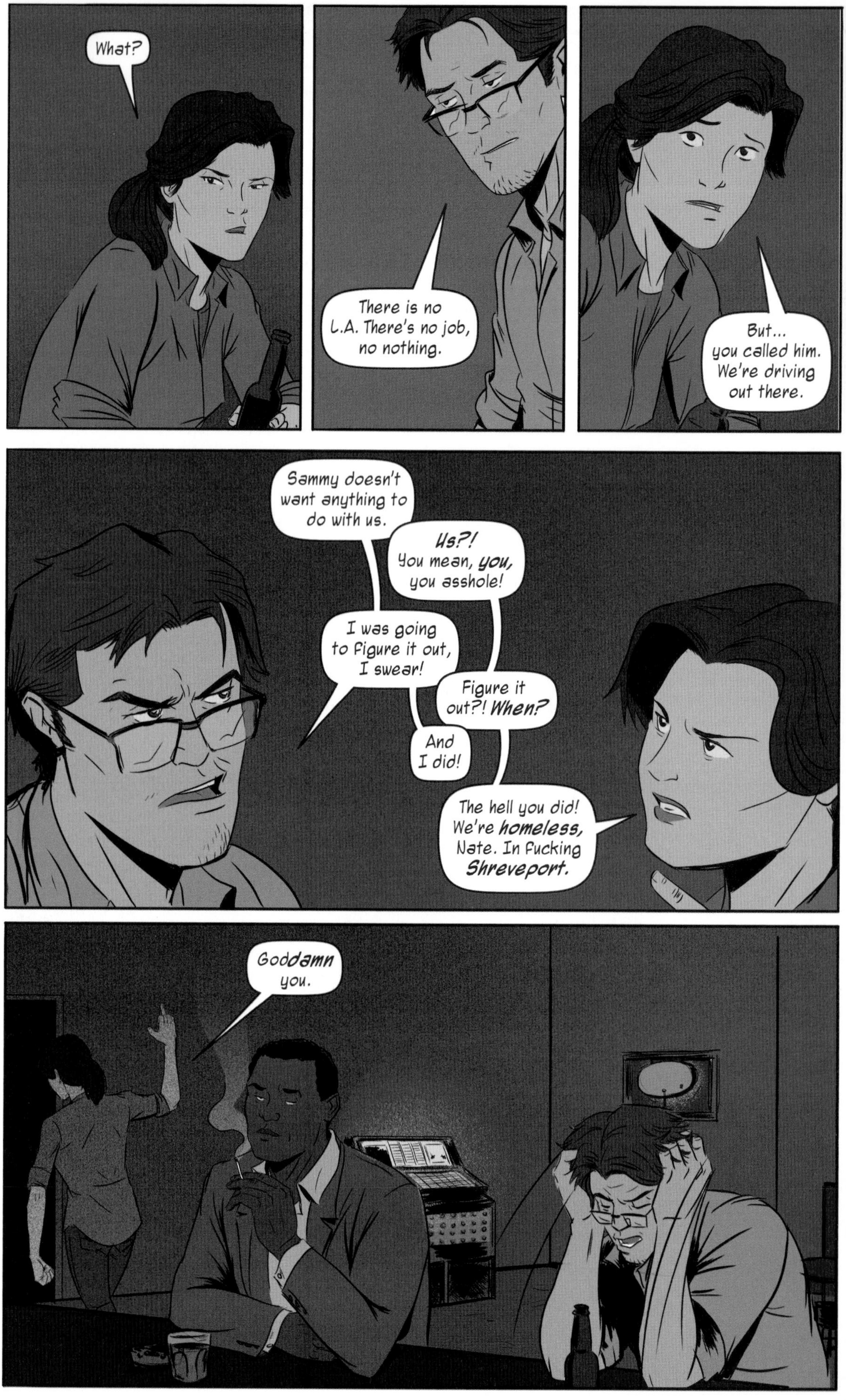
What?
There is no L.A. There's no job, no nothing.
But... you called him. We're driving out there.
Sammy doesn't want anything to do with us.
Us?! You mean, you, you asshole!
I was going to figure it out, I swear!
Figure it out?! When?
And I did!
The hell you did! We're homeless, Nate. In fucking Shreveport.
Goddamn you.

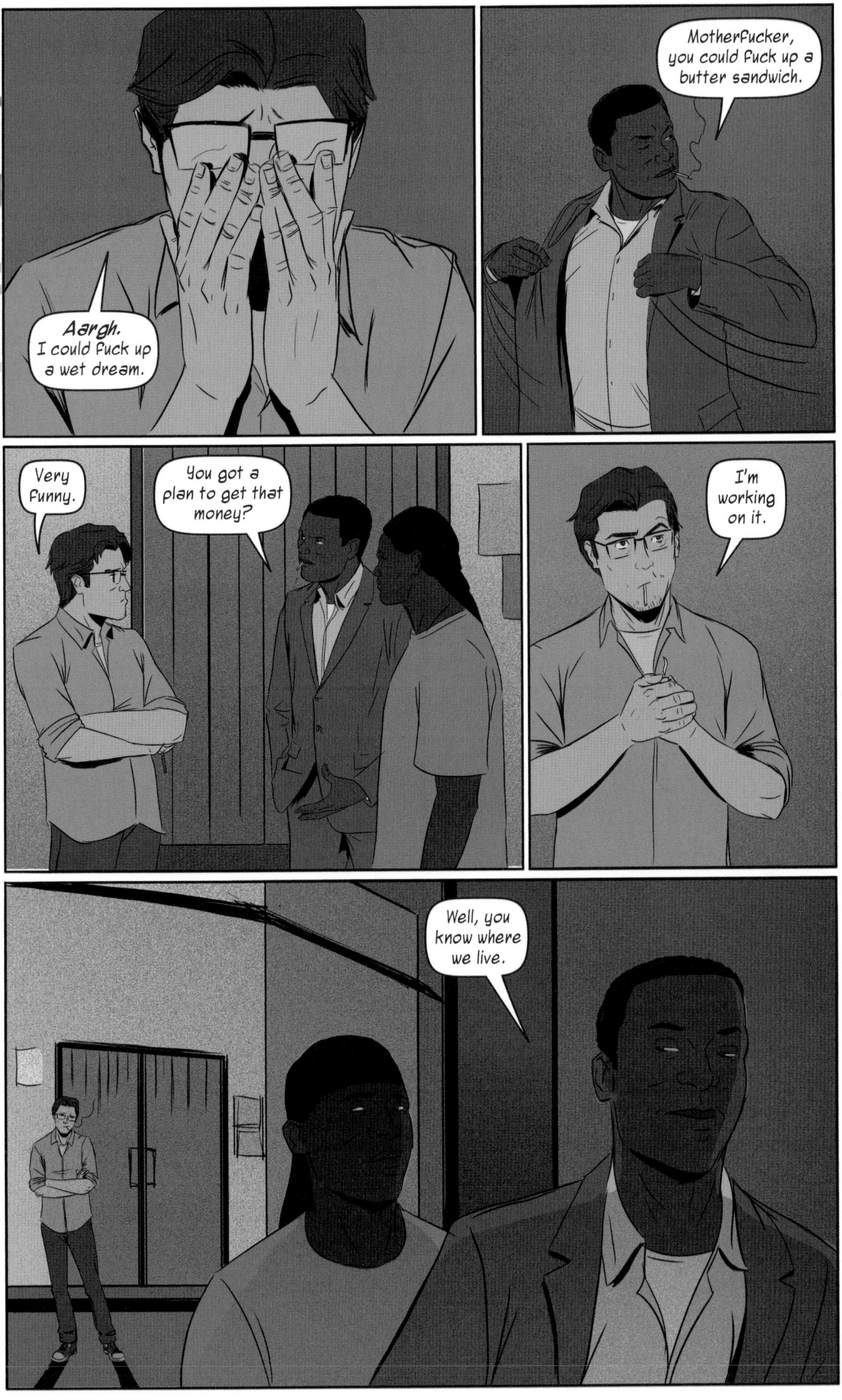
Aargh. I could fuck up a wet dream.
Motherfucker, you could fuck up a butter sandwich.
Very funny.
You got a plan to get that money?
I'm working on it.
Well, you know where we live.

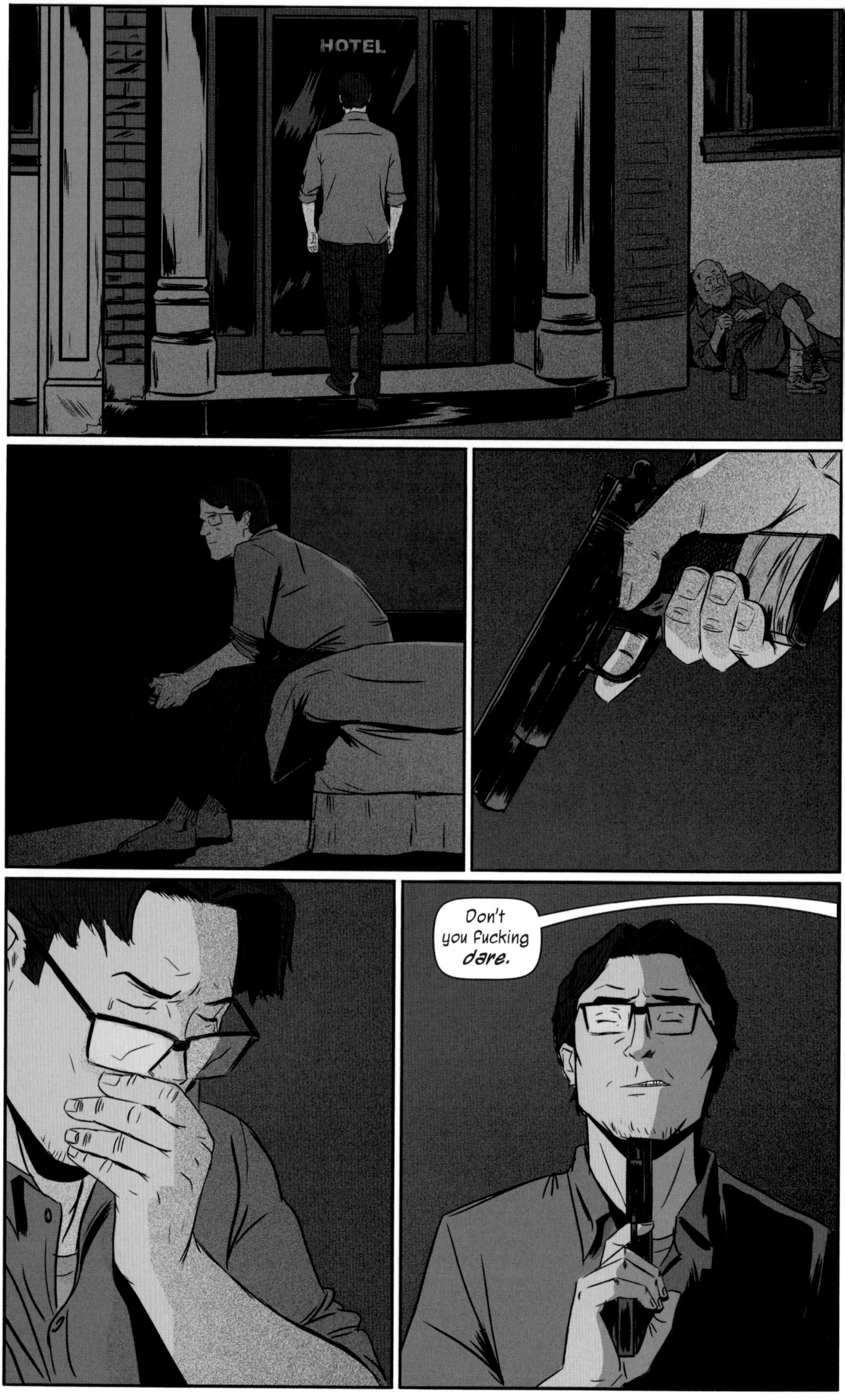
HOTEL
Don't you fucking dare.

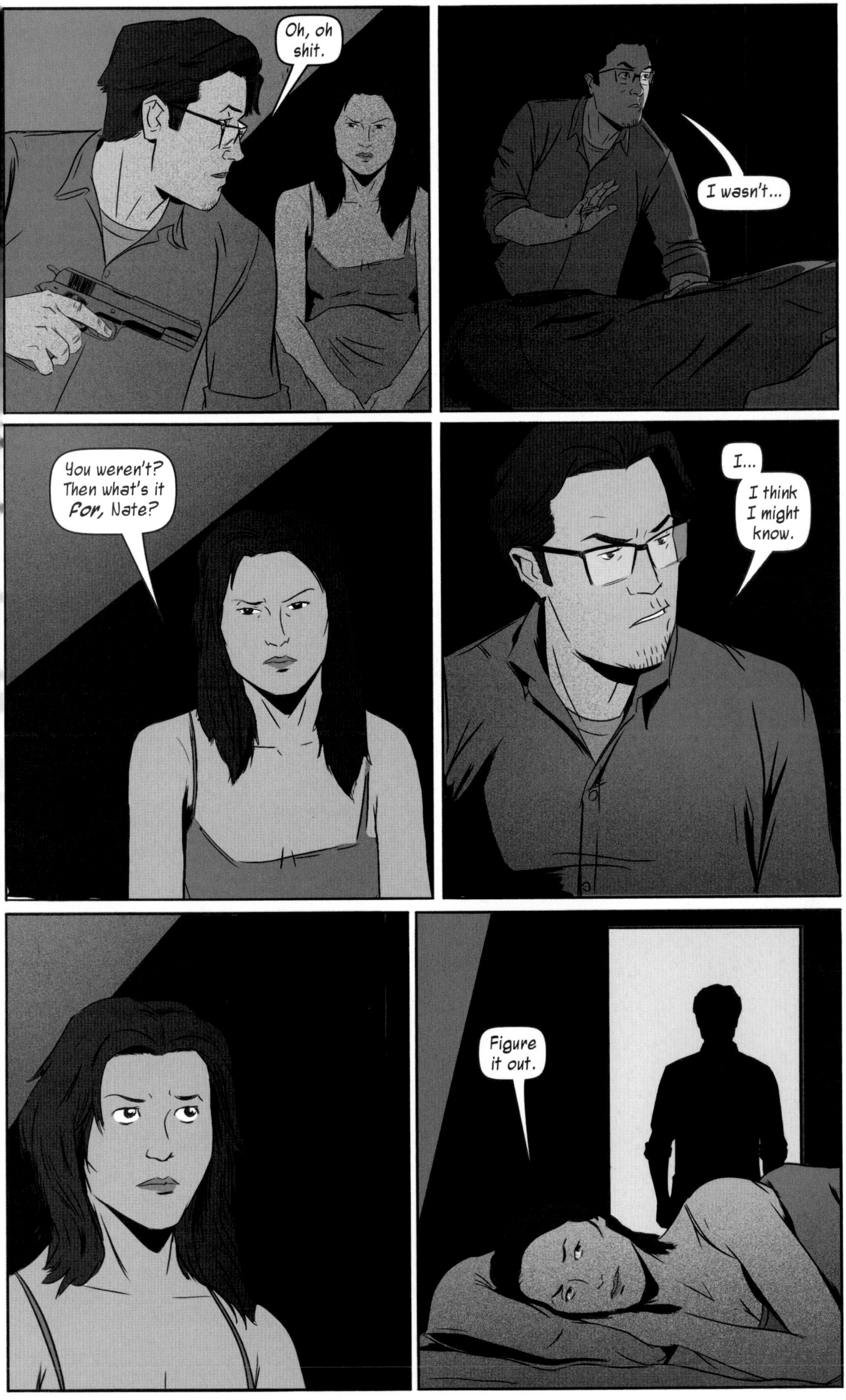
Oh, oh shit.
I wasn't...
You weren't? Then what's it *for*, Nate?
I...
I think I might know.
Figure it out.

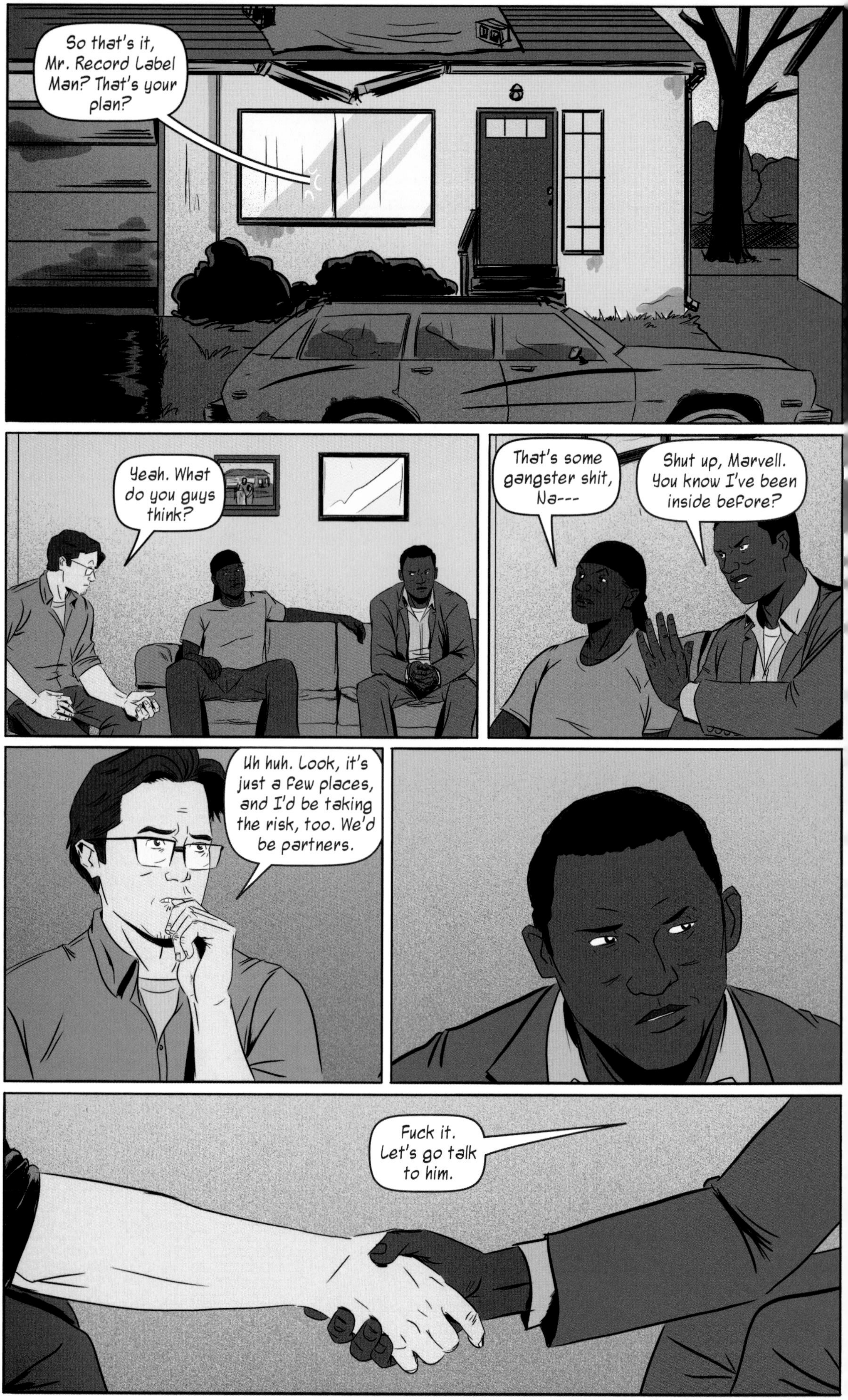

So that's it, Mr. Record Label Man? That's your plan?
Yeah. What do you guys think?
That's some gangster shit, Na---
Shut up, Marvell. You know I've been inside before?
Uh huh. Look, it's just a few places, and I'd be taking the risk, too. We'd be partners.
Fuck it. Let's go talk to him.

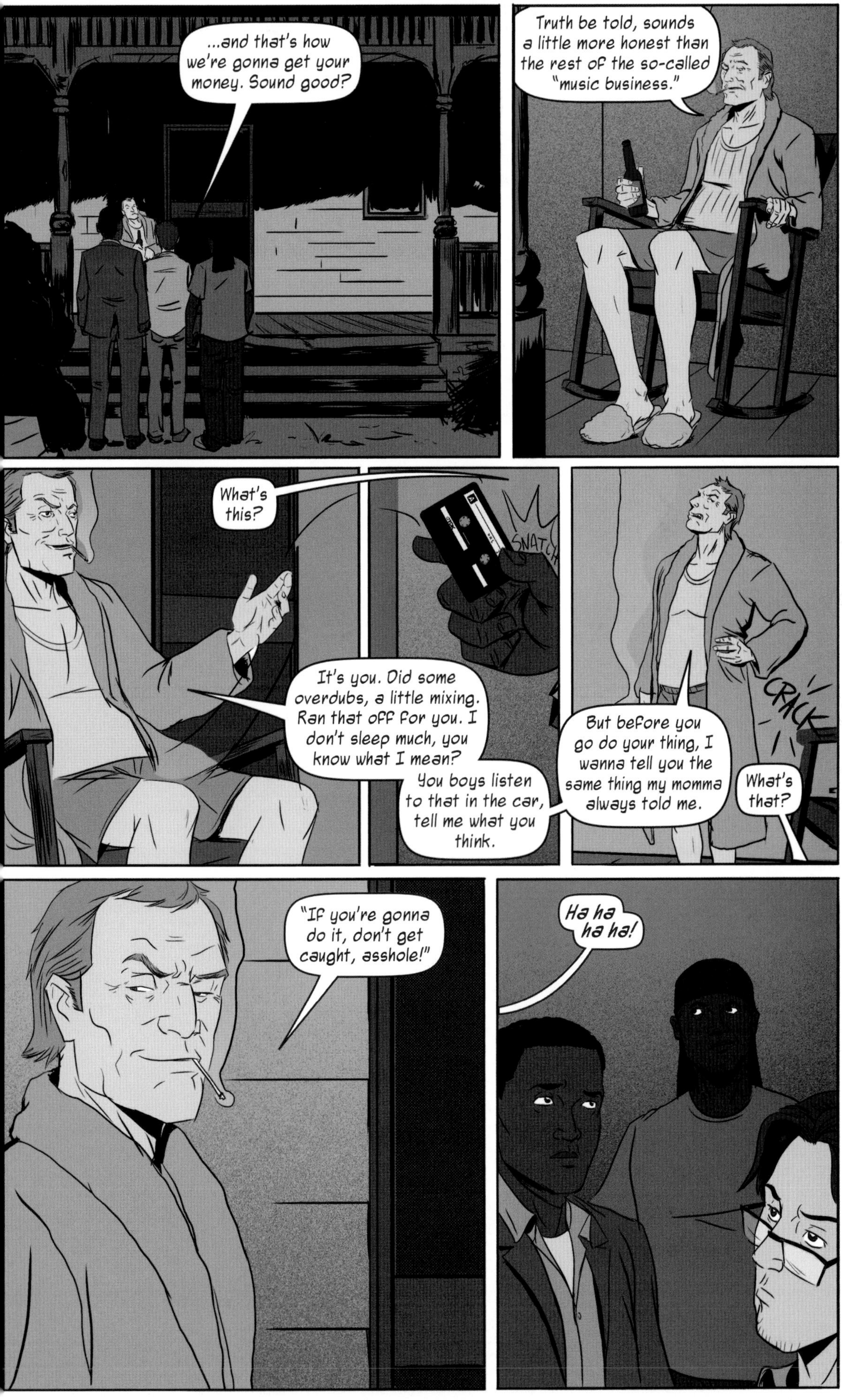
...and that's how we're gonna get your money. Sound good?
Truth be told, sounds a little more honest than the rest of the so-called "music business."
What's this?
SNATCH
It's you. Did some overdubs, a little mixing. Ran that off for you. I don't sleep much, you know what I mean?
You boys listen to that in the car, tell me what you think.
CRACK
But before you go do your thing, I wanna tell you the same thing my momma always told me.
What's that?
"If you're gonna do it, don't get caught, asshole!"
Ha ha ha ha!

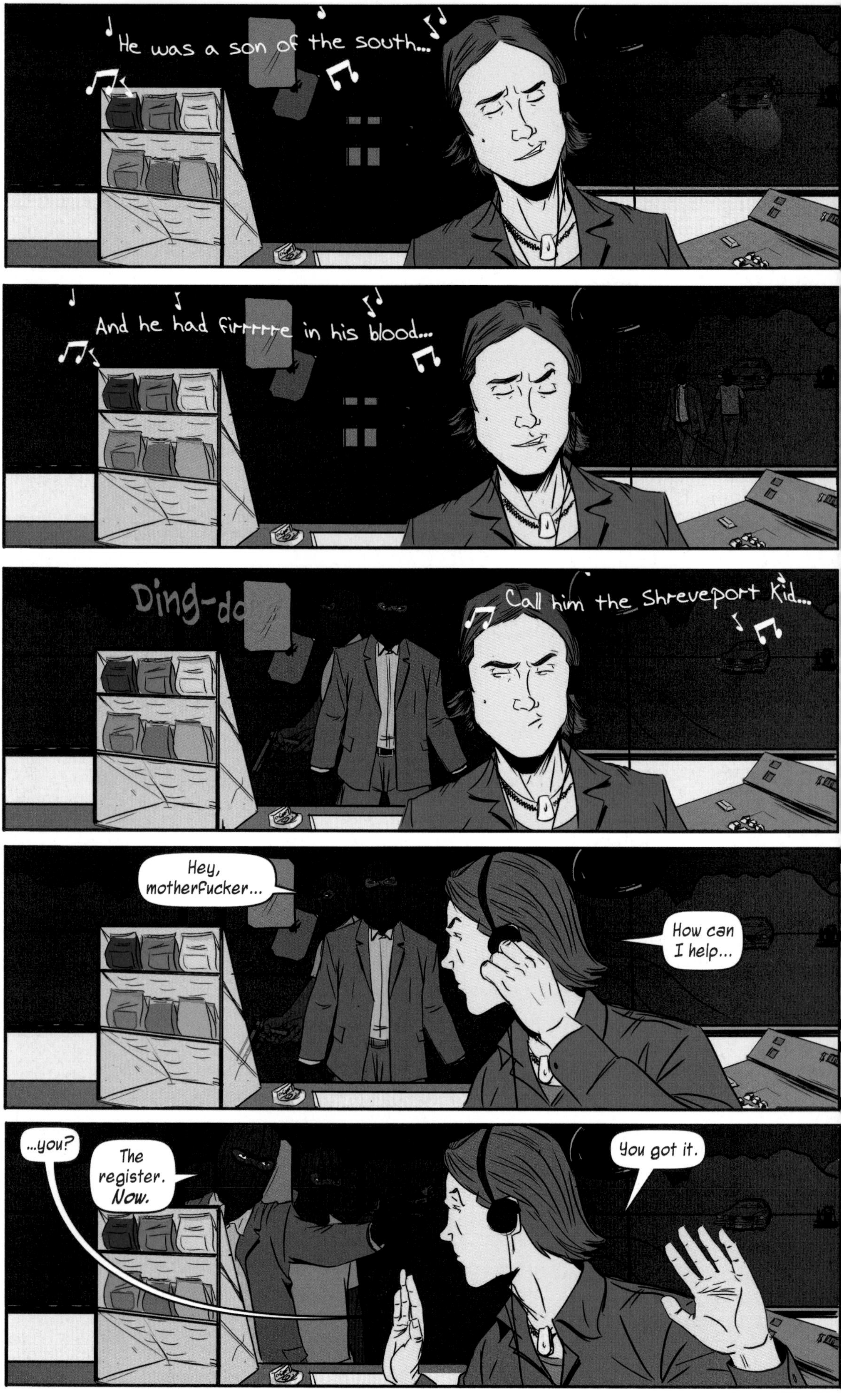
He was a son of the south...
And he had firrrrre in his blood...
Ding-do
Call him the Shreveport Kid...
Hey, motherfucker...
How can I help...
...you?
The register. Now.
You got it.

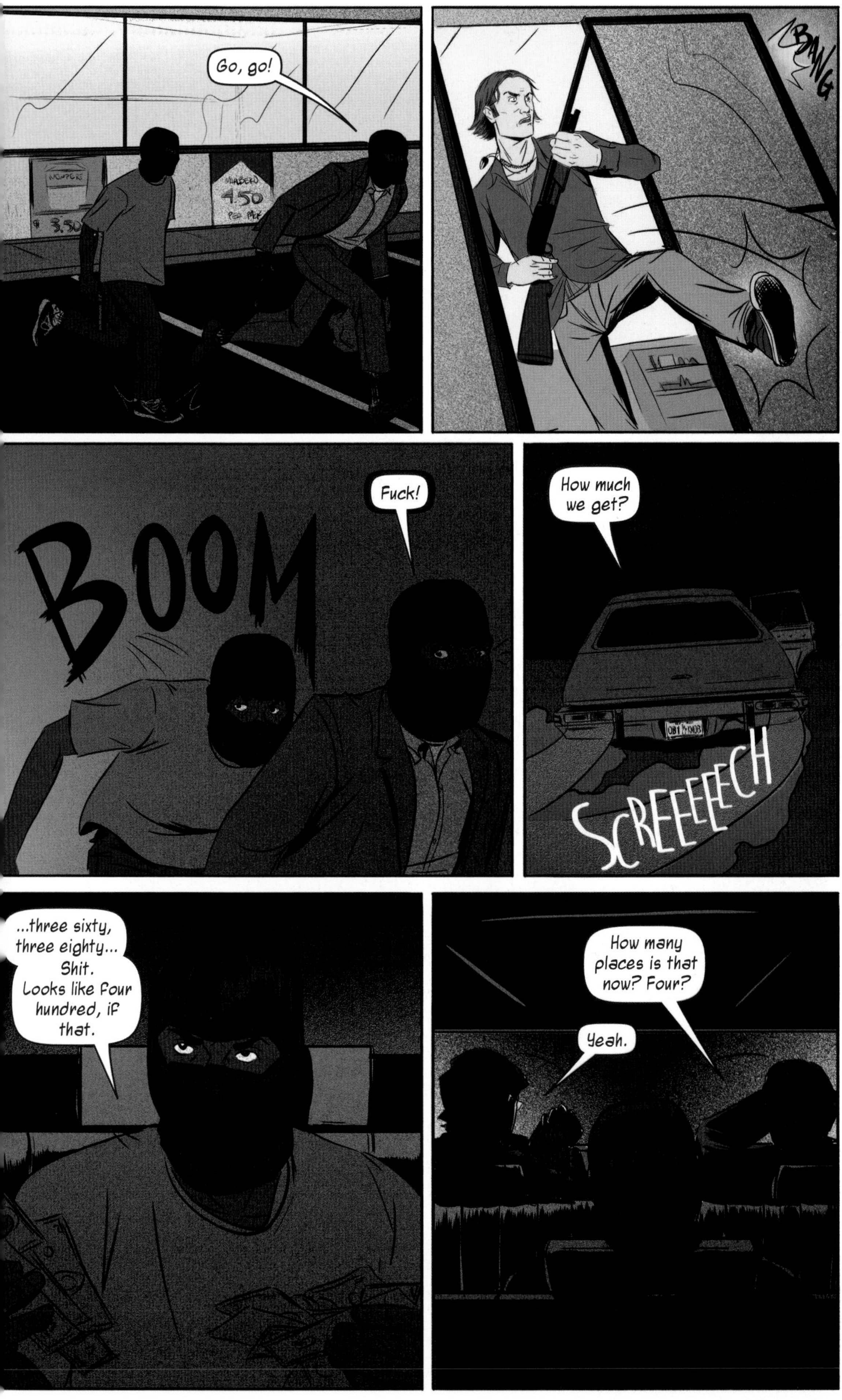
Go, go!
BANG
BOOM
Fuck!
How much we get?
SCREEEEECH
...three sixty, three eighty... Shit. Looks like four hundred, if that.
How many places is that now? Four?
Yeah.

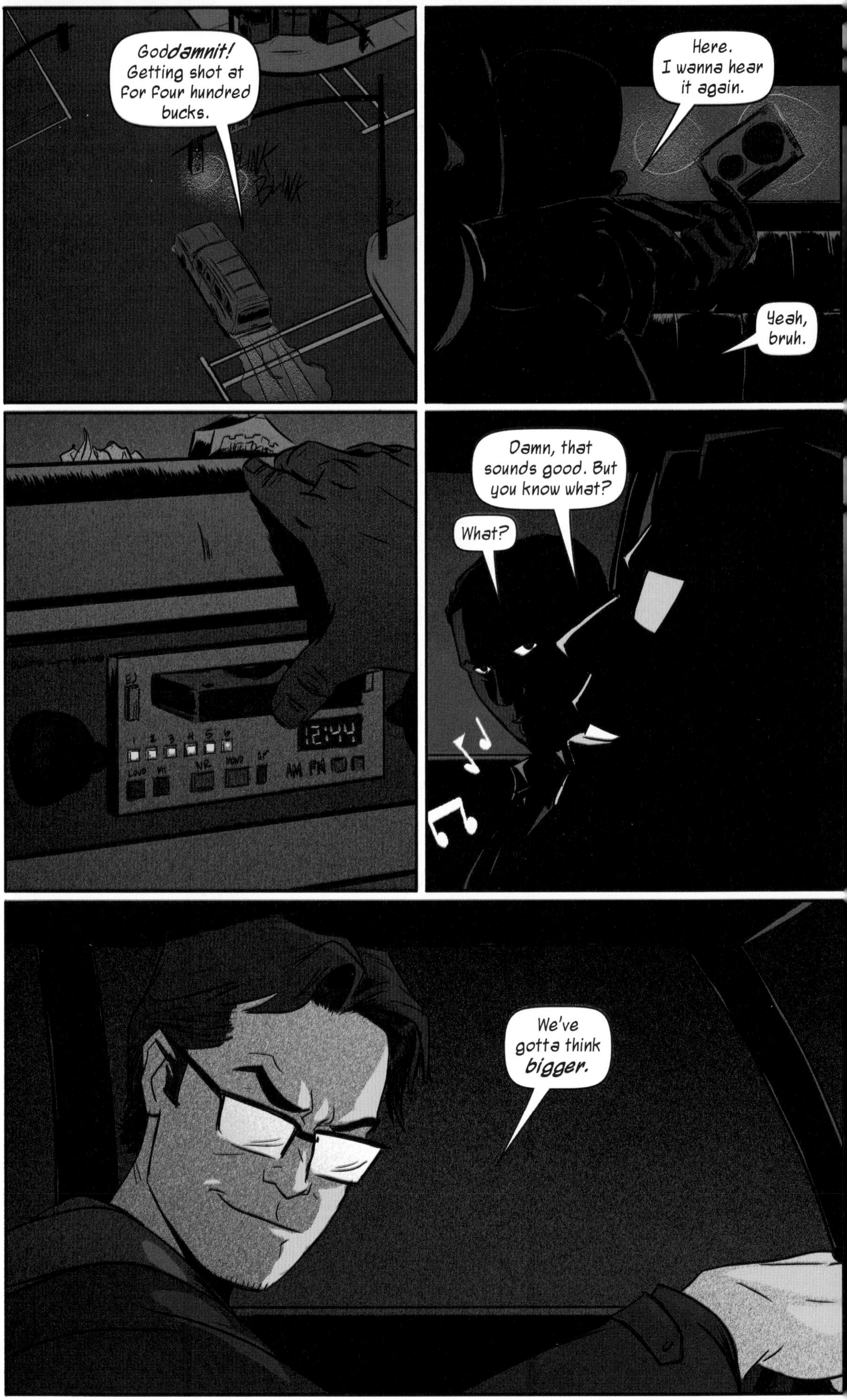
Goddamnit! Getting shot at for four hundred bucks.
BLINK
BLINK
Here. I wanna hear it again.
Yeah, bruh.
12:44
Damn, that sounds good. But you know what?
What?
We've gotta think bigger.

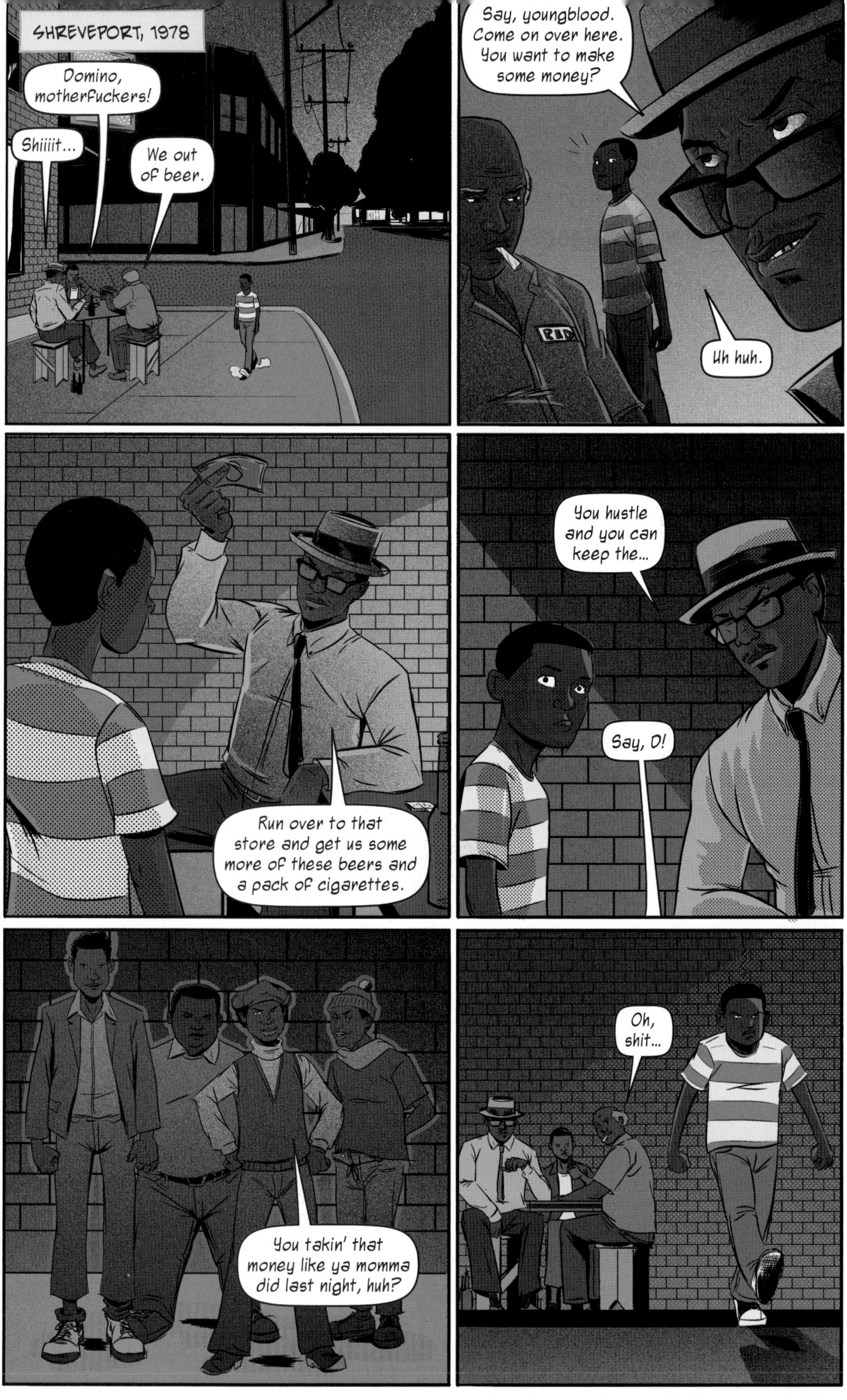
SHREVEPORT, 1978
Domino, motherfuckers!
Shiiiit...
We out of beer.
Say, youngblood. Come on over here. You want to make some money?
Uh huh.
Run over to that store and get us some more of these beers and a pack of cigarettes.
You hustle and you can keep the...
Say, D!
You takin' that money like ya momma did last night, huh?
Oh, shit...

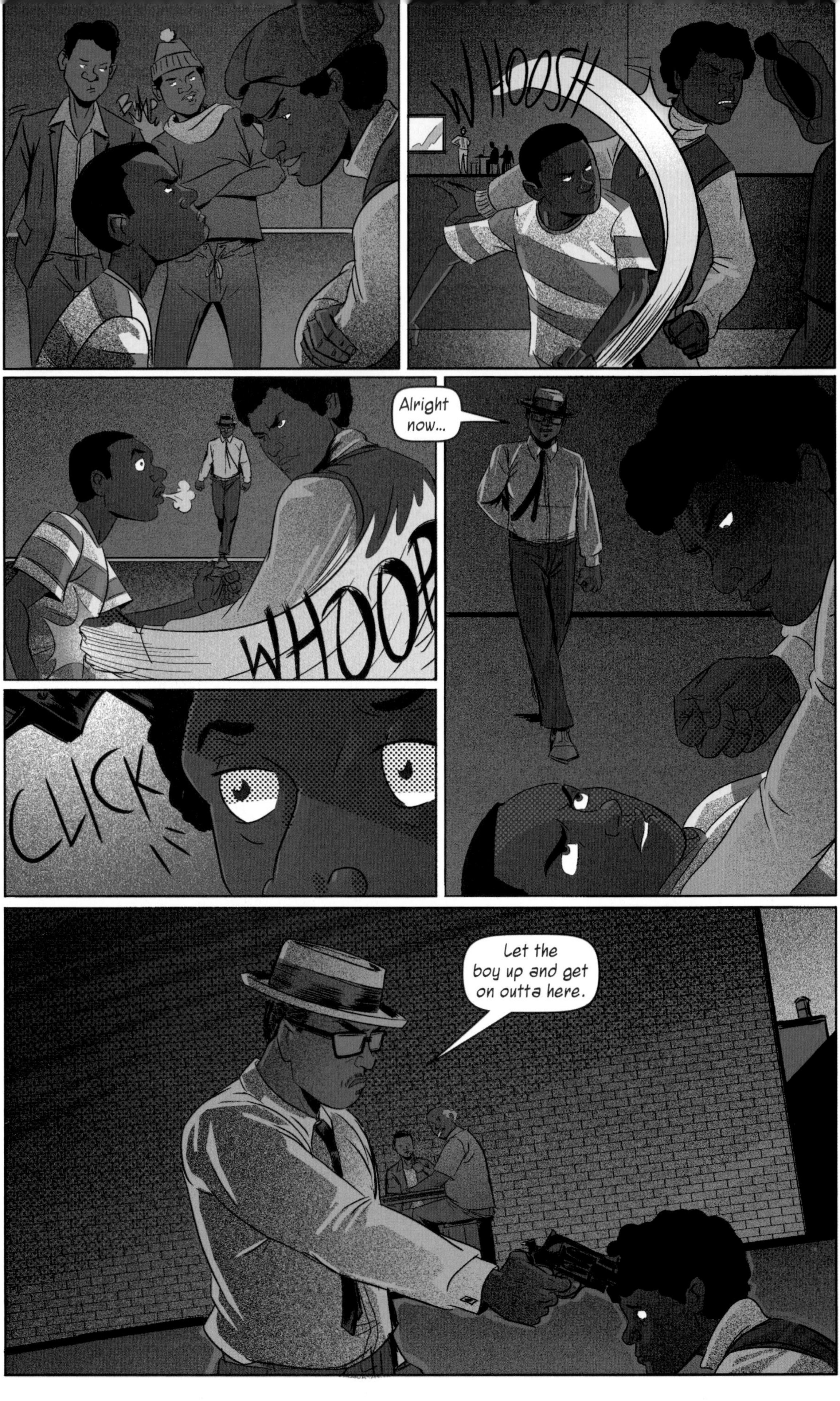
BUMP
WHOOSH
Alright now...
WHOOP
CLICK
Let the boy up and get on outta here.

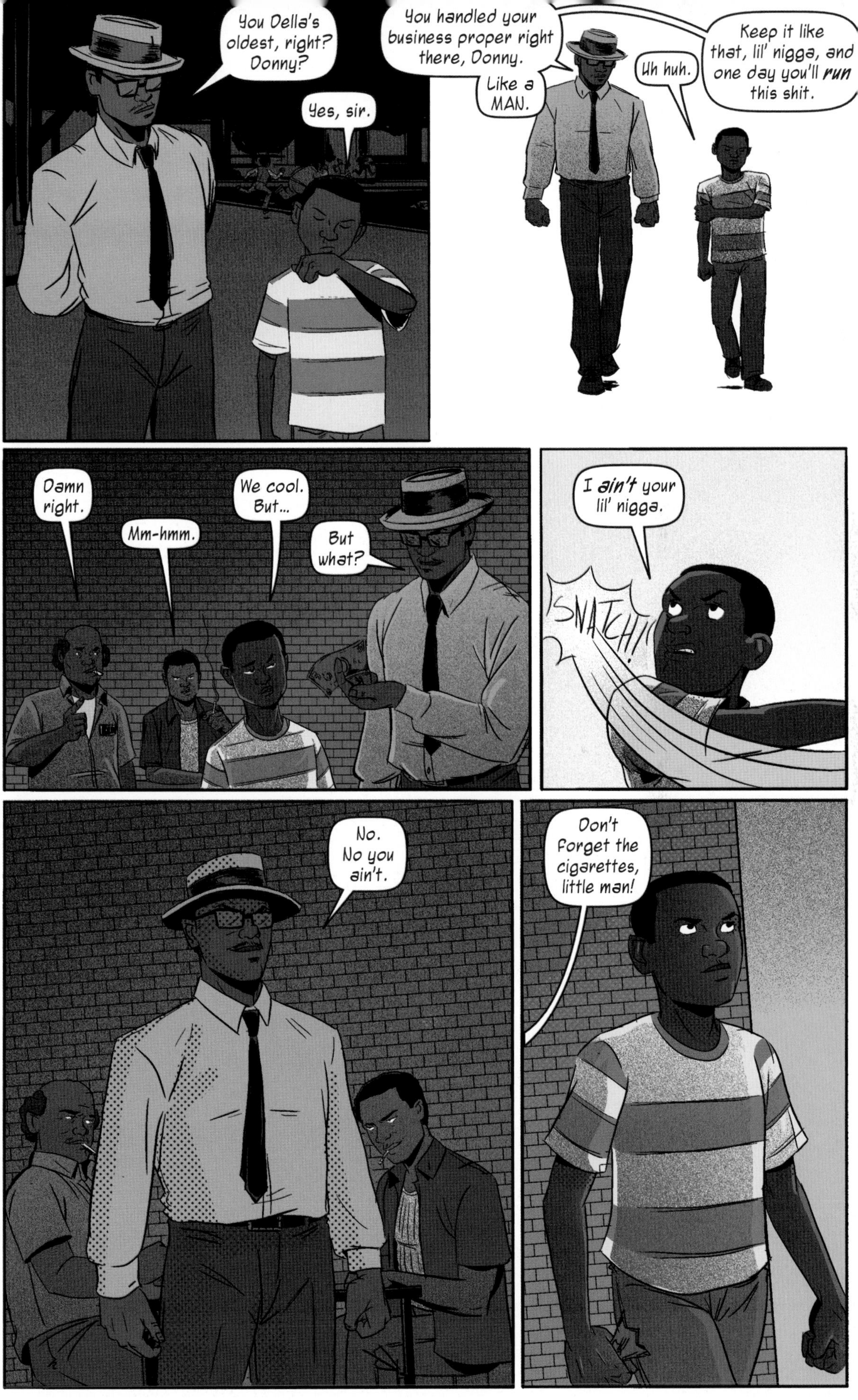
You Della's oldest, right? Donny?
Yes, sir.
You handled your business proper right there, Donny.
Like a MAN.
Uh huh.
Keep it like that, lil' nigga, and one day you'll *run* this shit.
Damn right.
Mm-hmm.
We cool. But...
But what?
I *ain't* your lil' nigga.
SNATCH!!
No. No you ain't.
Don't forget the cigarettes, little man!

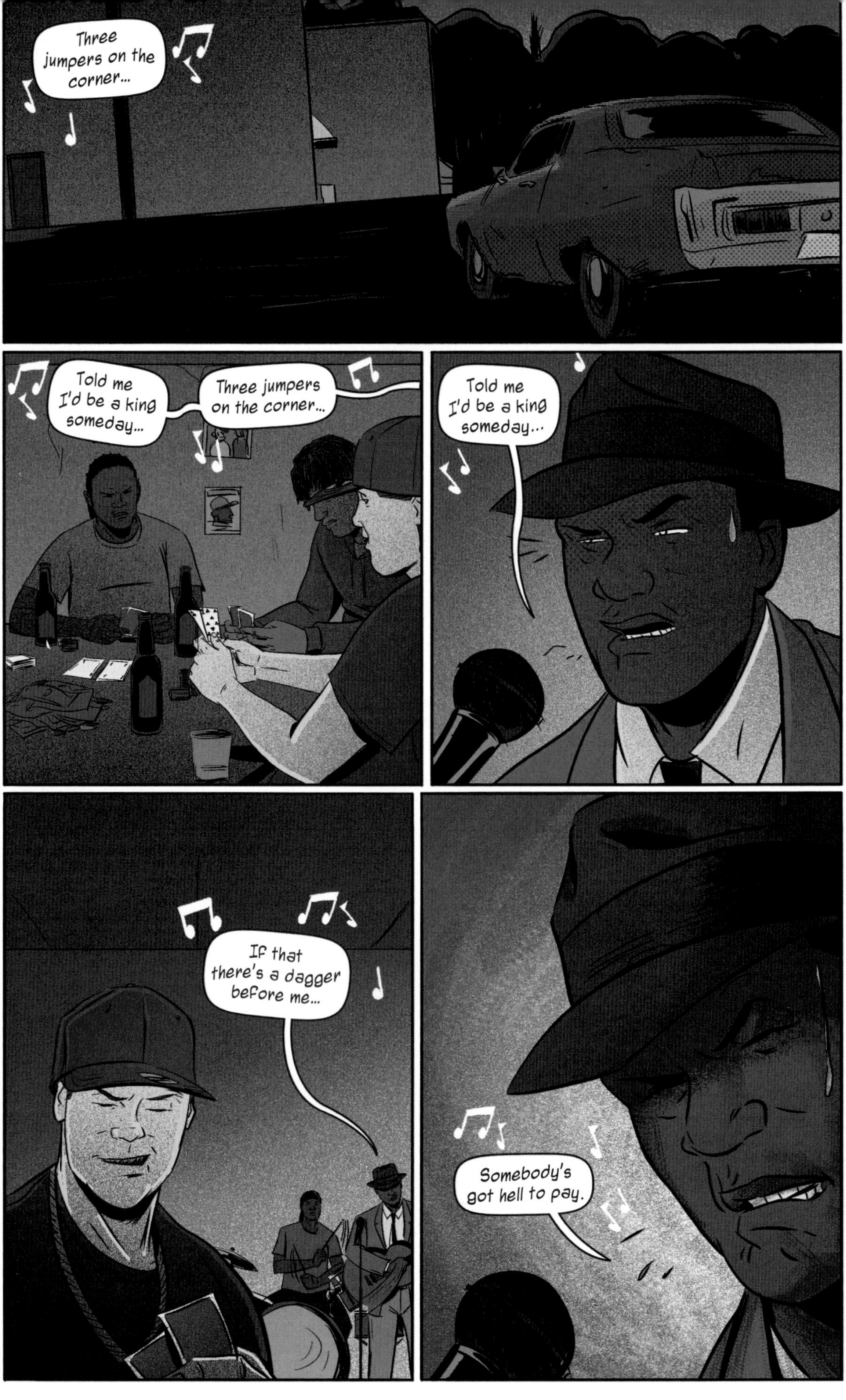
Three jumpers on the corner...
Told me I'd be a king someday...
Three jumpers on the corner...
Told me I'd be a king someday...
If that there's a dagger before me...
Somebody's got hell to pay.

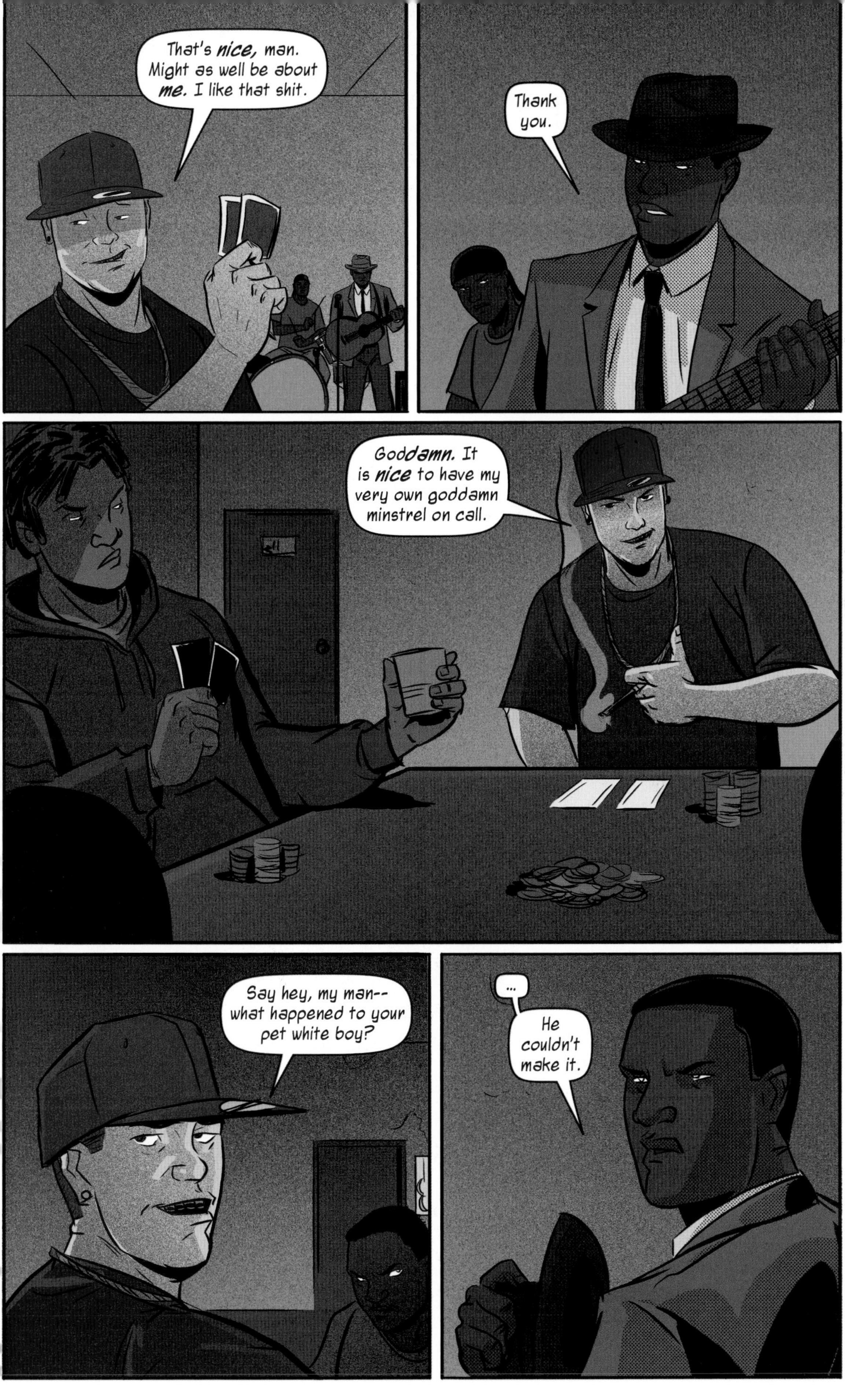
That's *nice,* man. Might as well be about *me.* I like that shit.
Thank you.
God*damn.* It is *nice* to have my very own goddamn minstrel on call.
Say hey, my man-- what happened to your pet white boy?
...
He couldn't make it.

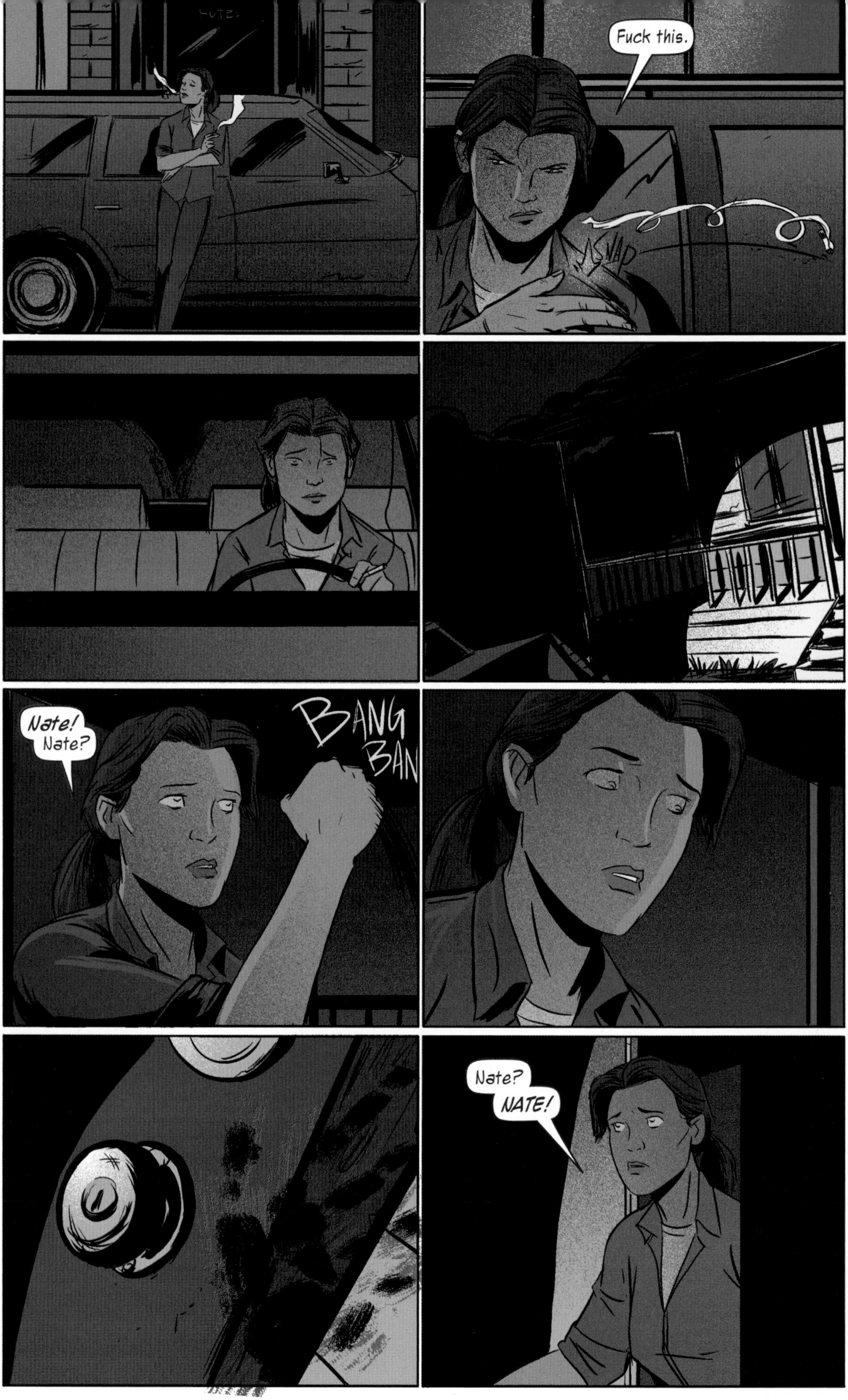
Fuck this.
SNAP
Nate!
Nate?
BANG
BAN
Nate?
NATE!

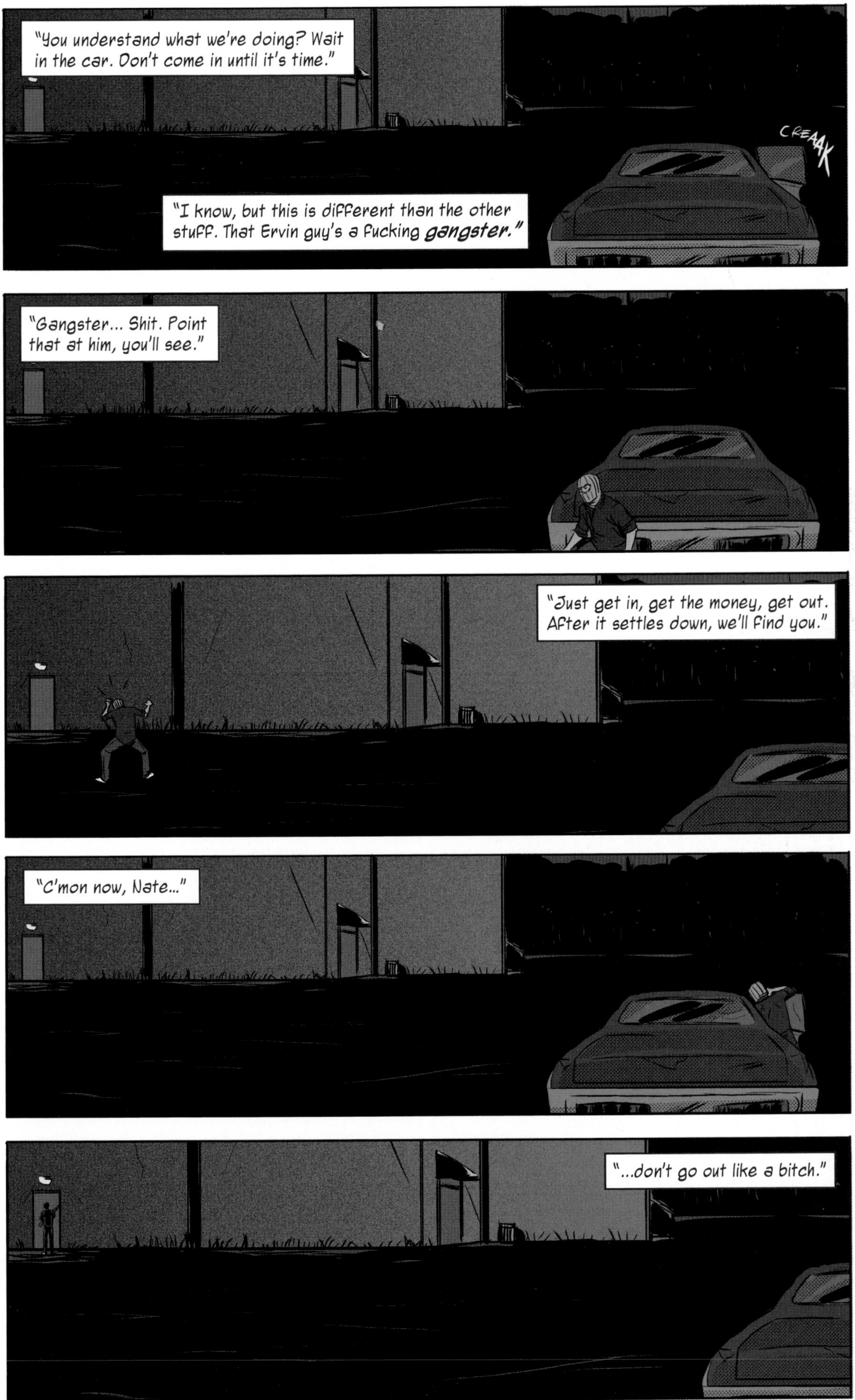
"You understand what we're doing? Wait in the car. Don't come in until it's time."
CREAAAK
"I know, but this is different than the other stuff. That Ervin guy's a fucking *gangster.*"
"Gangster... Shit. Point that at him, you'll see."
"Just get in, get the money, get out. After it settles down, we'll find you."
"C'mon now, Nate..."
"...don't go out like a bitch."

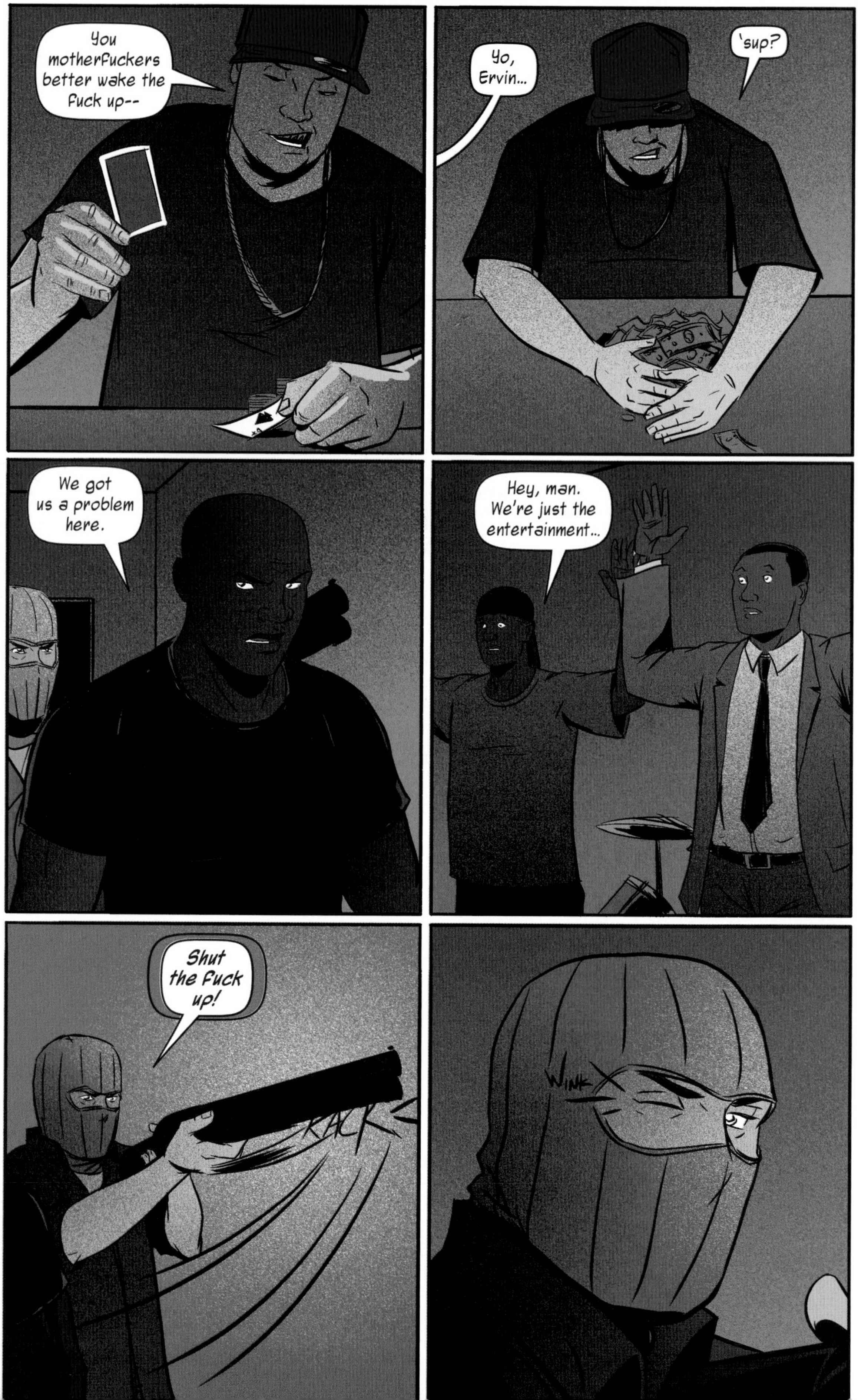
You motherfuckers better wake the fuck up--
Yo, Ervin...
'sup?
We got us a problem here.
Hey, man. We're just the entertainment...
Shut the fuck up!
RACK
WINK

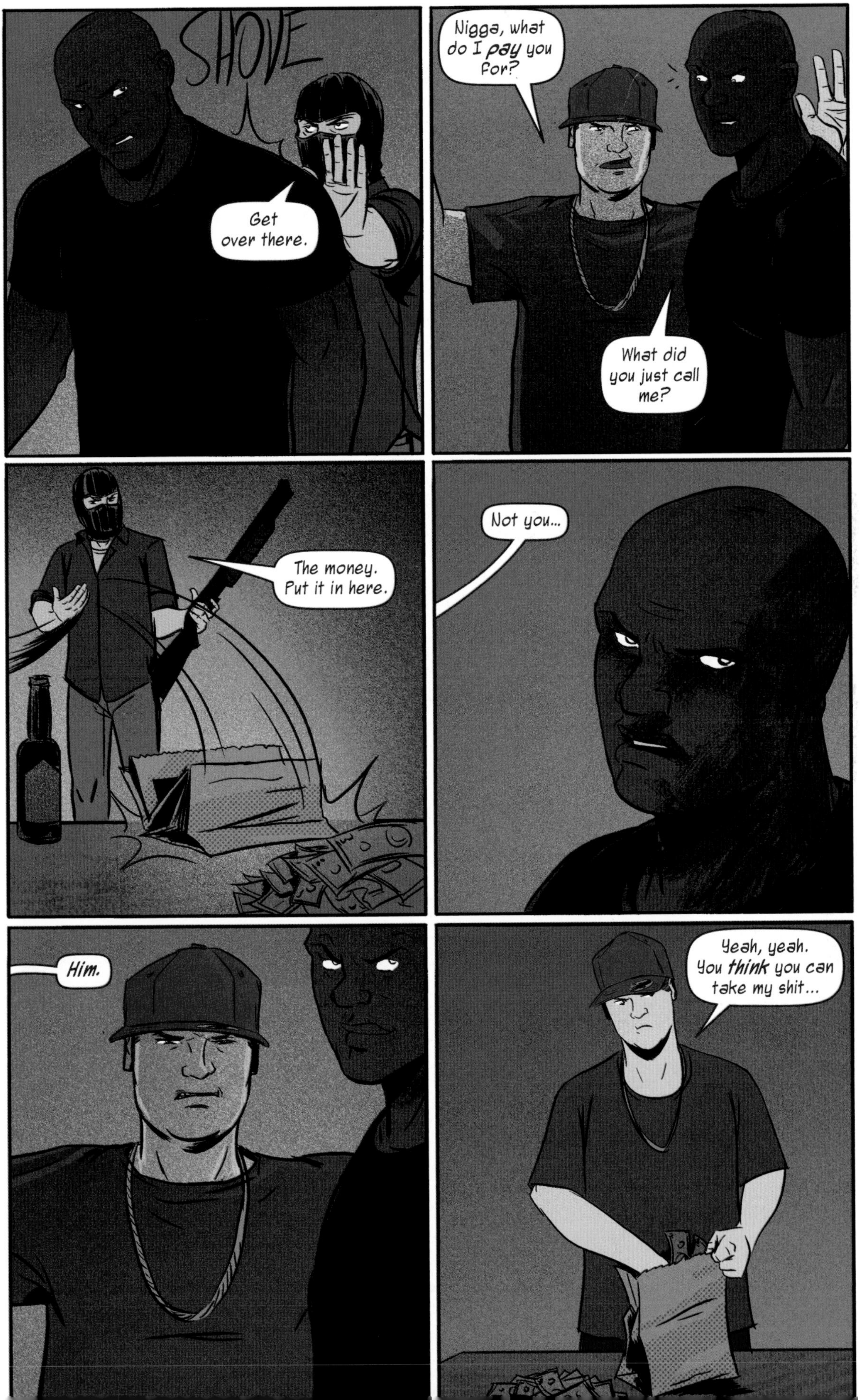
SHOVE
Get over there.
Nigga, what do I *pay* you for?
What did you just call me?
The money. Put it in here.
Not you...
Him.
Yeah, yeah. You *think* you can take my shit...

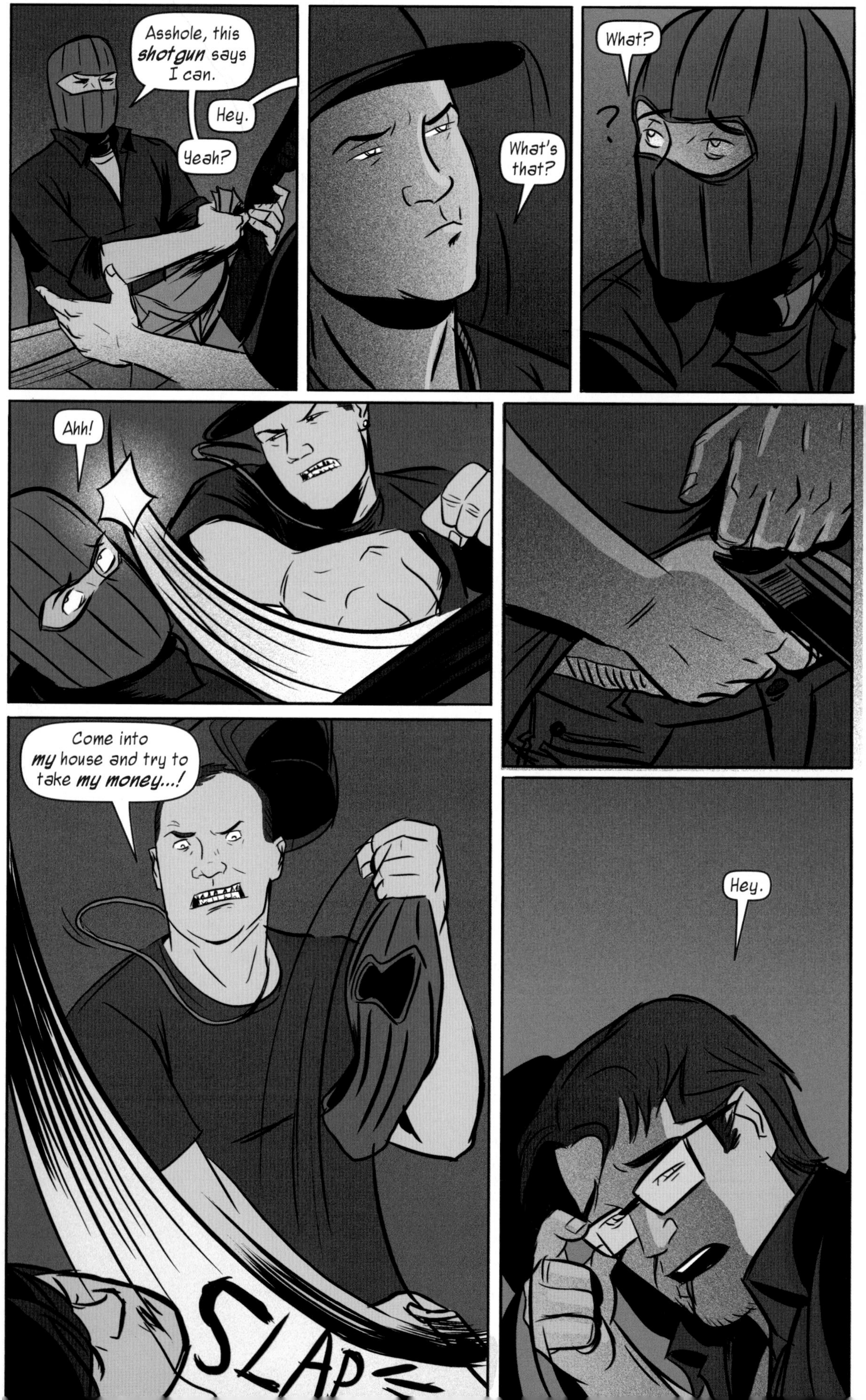
Asshole, this **shotgun** says I can.
Hey.
Yeah?
What's that?
What?
?
Ahh!
Come into **my** house and try to take **my money...!**
SLAP
Hey.

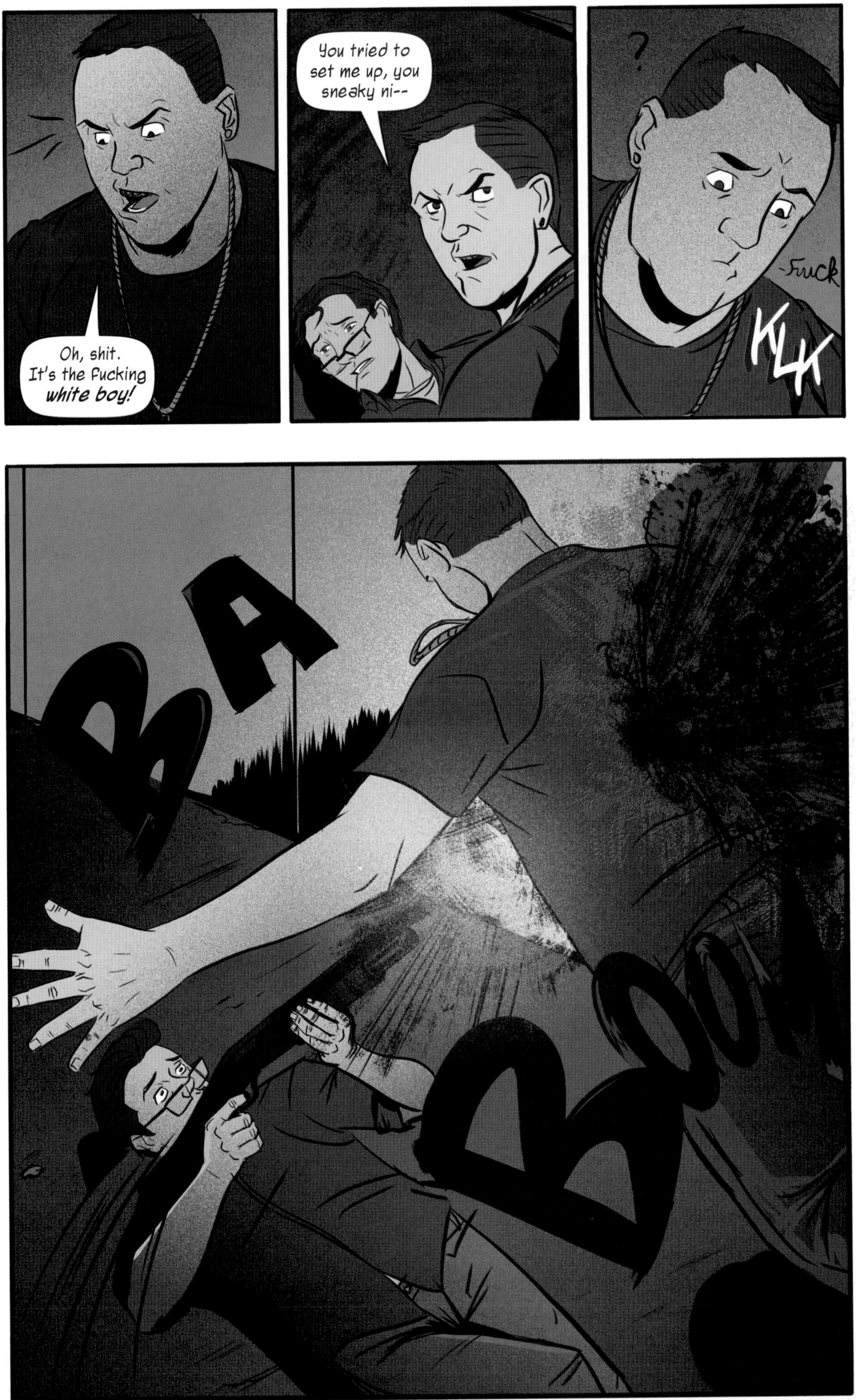

Oh, shit. It's the fucking *white boy!*
You tried to set me up, you sneaky ni--
?
-Fuck
KLIK
BA
BOOM

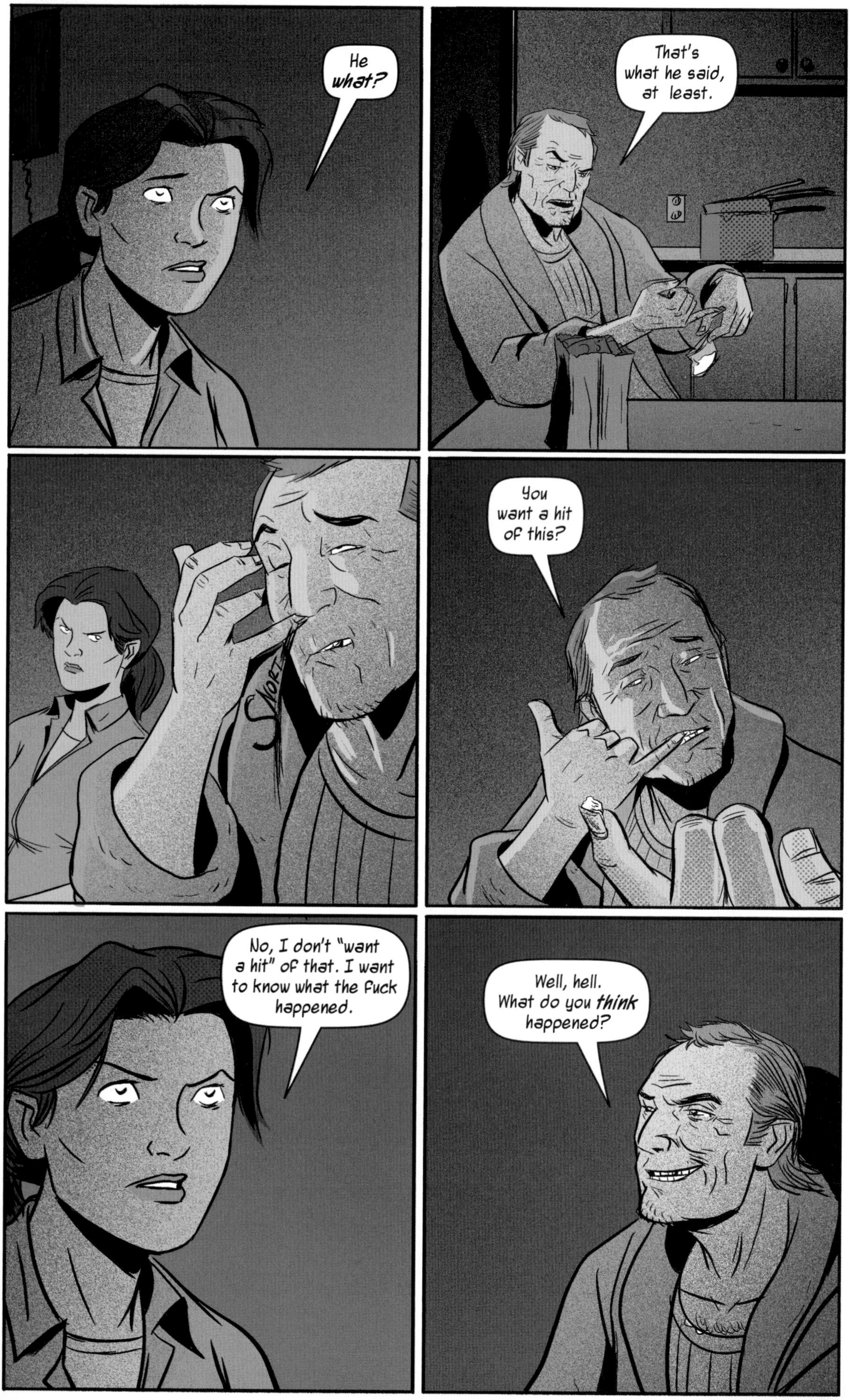
He what?
That's what he said, at least.
You want a hit of this?
No, I don't "want a hit" of that. I want to know what the fuck happened.
Well, hell. What do you think happened?

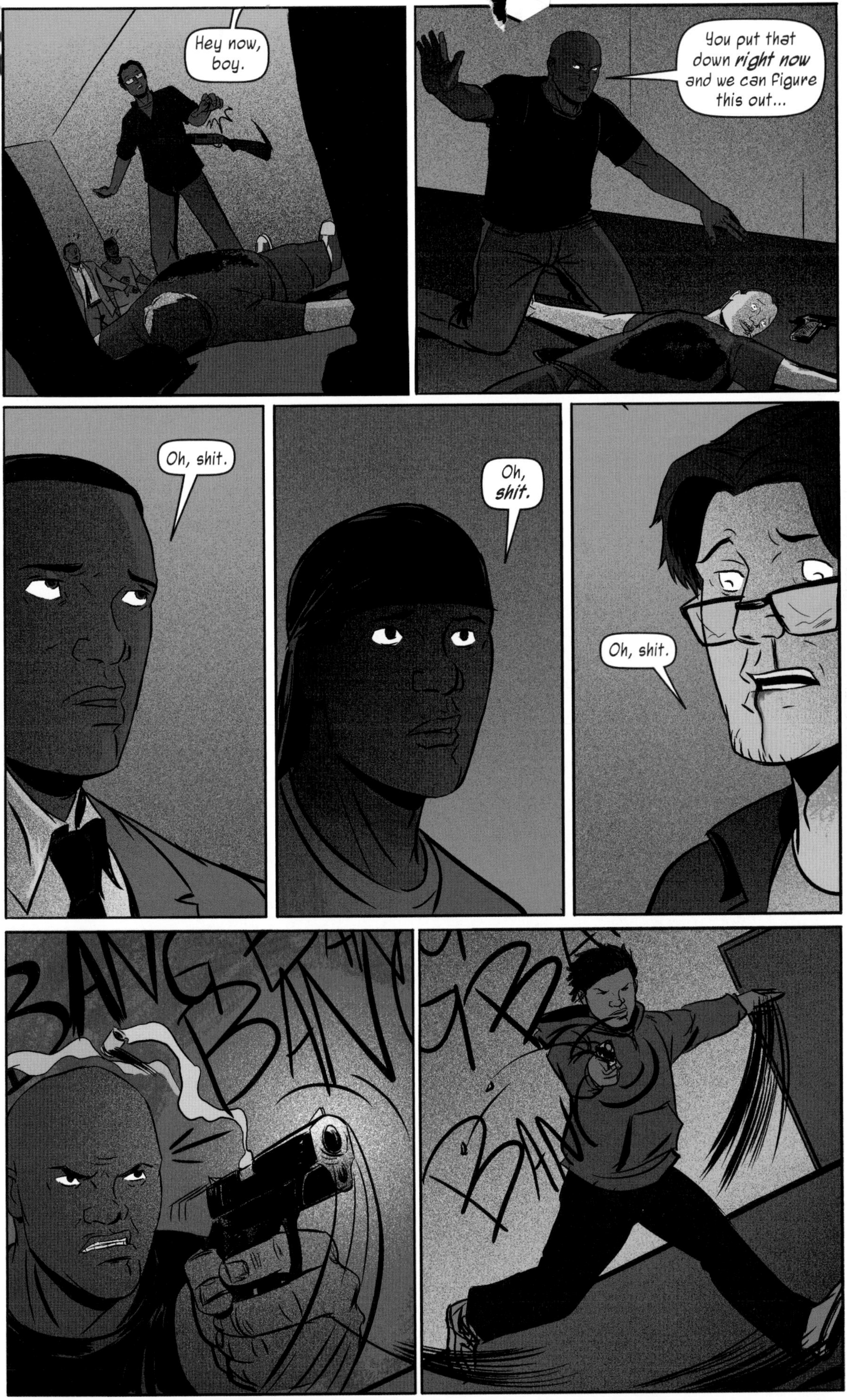
Hey now, boy.
You put that down right now and we can figure this out...
Oh, shit.
Oh, shit.
Oh, shit.
BANG
BANG

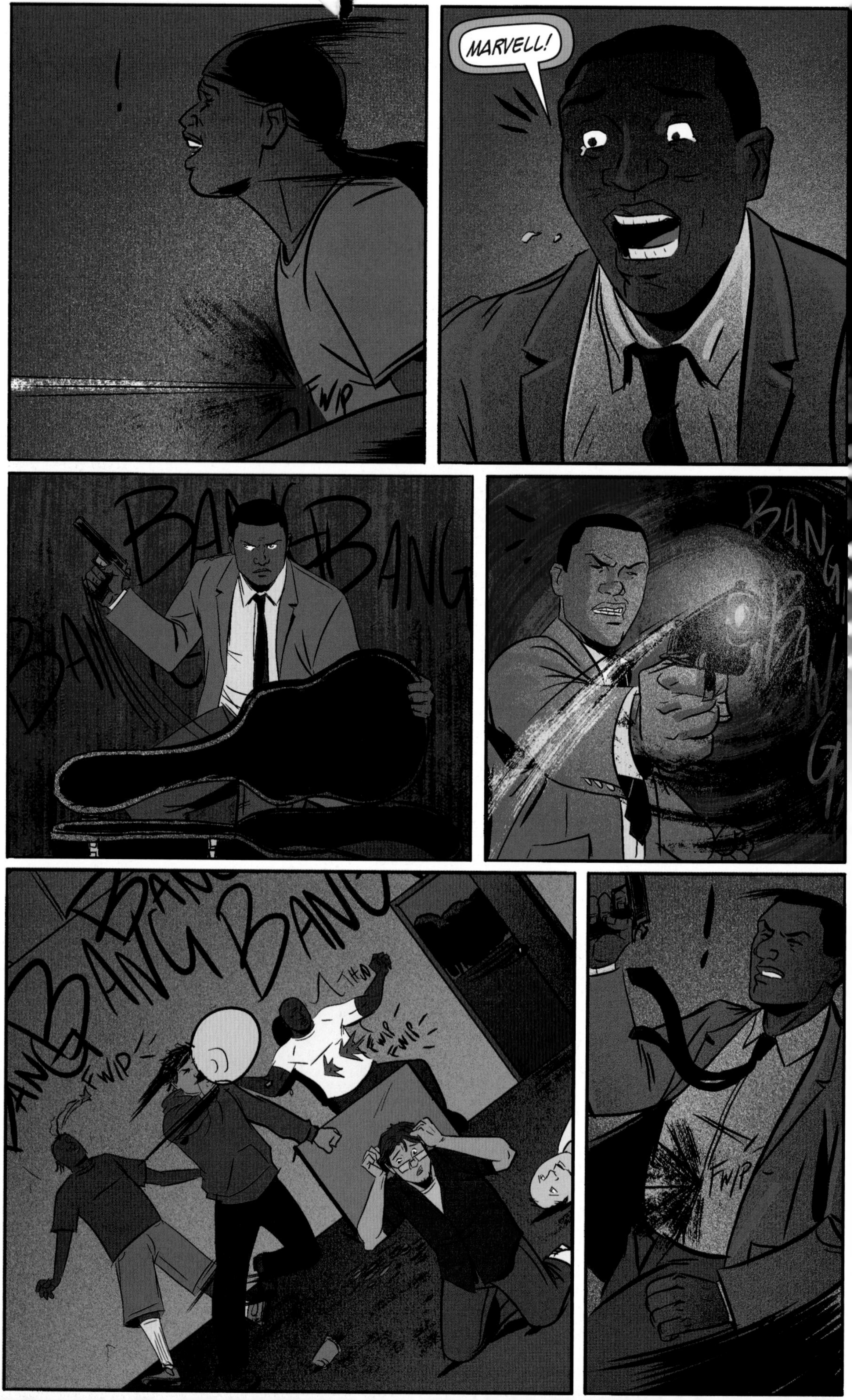
!
FWIP
MARVELL!
BANG BANG BANG
BANG
BANG
BANG BANG BANG
BANG
FWIP
FWIP
THO
FWIP FWIP
!
FWIP

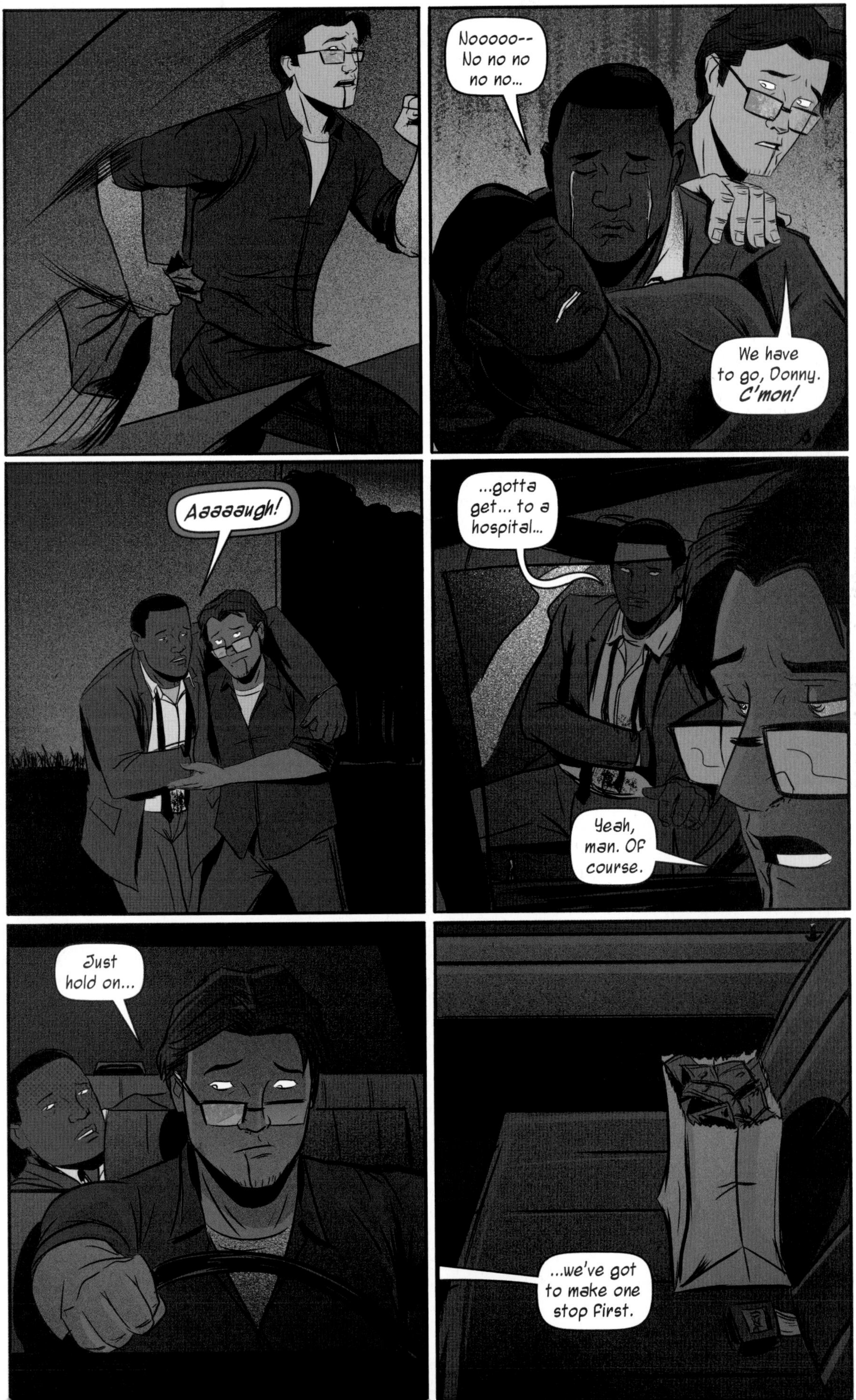
Nooooo-- No no no no no...
We have to go, Donny. C'mon!
Aaaaaugh!
...gotta get... to a hospital...
Yeah, man. Of course.
Just hold on...
...we've got to make one stop first.

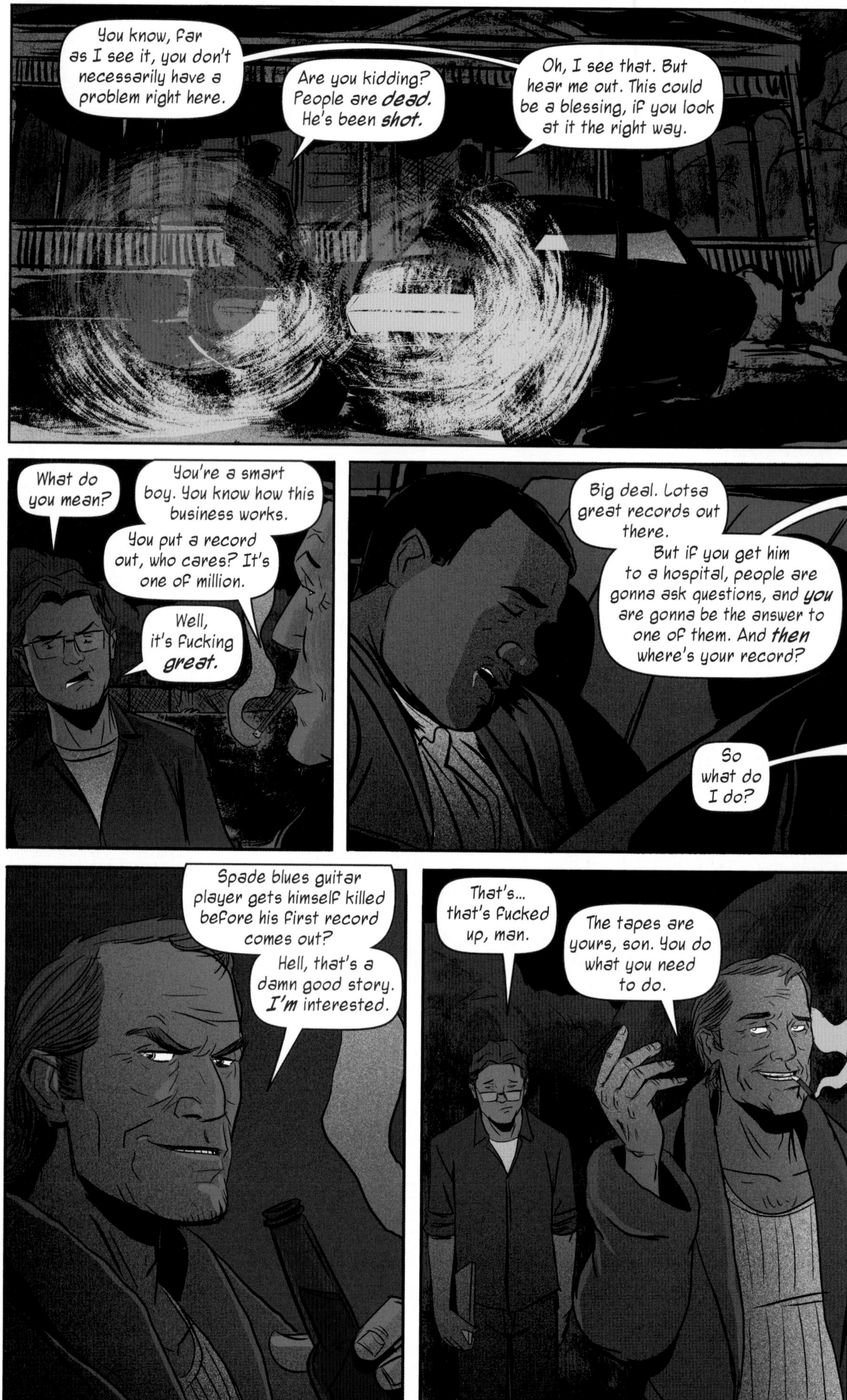
You know, far as I see it, you don't necessarily have a problem right here.
Are you kidding? People are *dead.* He's been *shot.*
Oh, I see that. But hear me out. This could be a blessing, if you look at it the right way.
What do you mean?
You're a smart boy. You know how this business works.
You put a record out, who cares? It's one of million.
Well, it's fucking *great.*
Big deal. Lotsa great records out there.
But if you get him to a hospital, people are gonna ask questions, and *you* are gonna be the answer to one of them. And *then* where's your record?
So what do I do?
Spade blues guitar player gets himself killed before his first record comes out?
Hell, that's a damn good story. *I'm* interested.
That's... that's fucked up, man.
The tapes are yours, son. You do what you need to do.

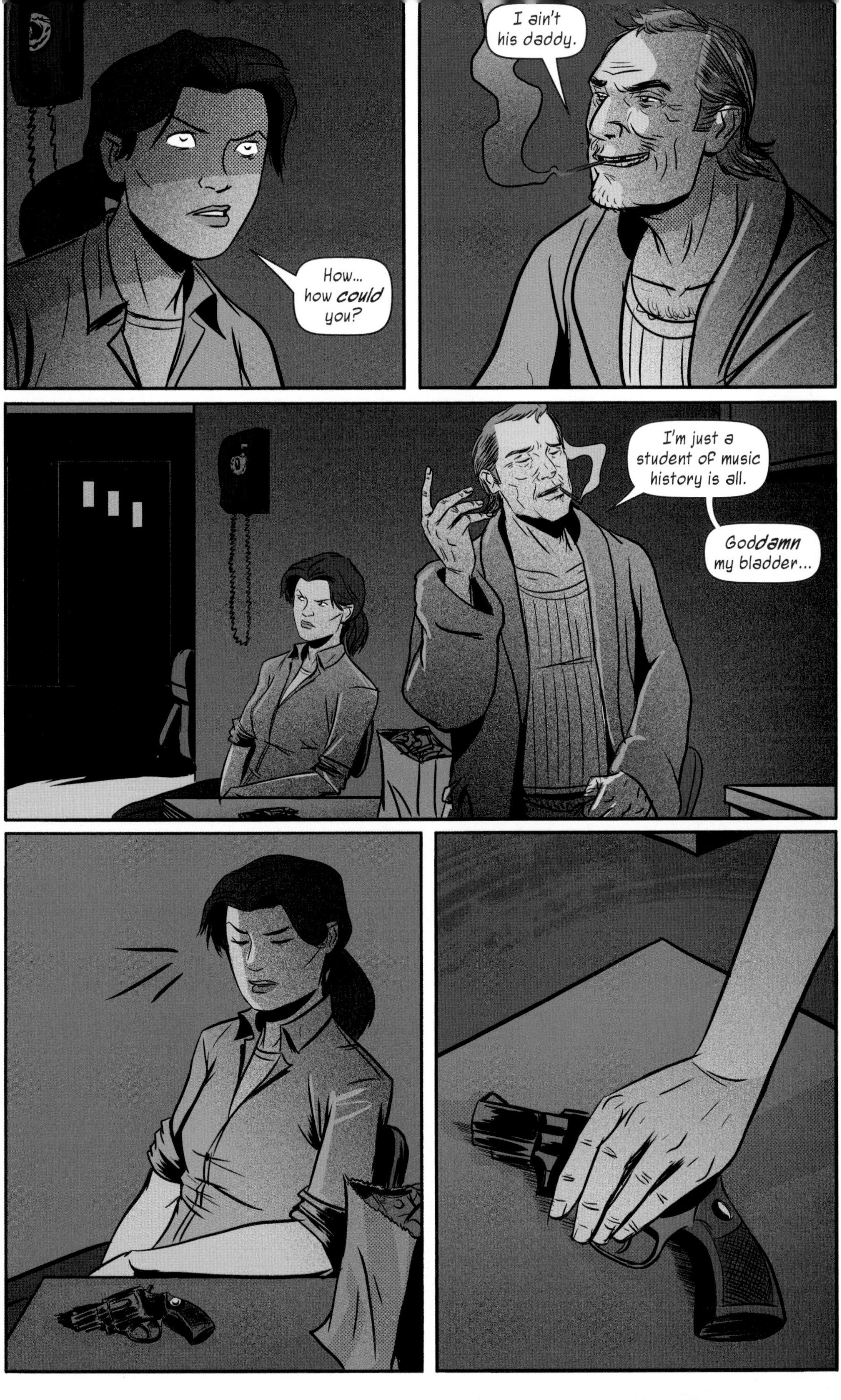
How... how could you?
I ain't his daddy.
I'm just a student of music history is all.
Goddamn my bladder...

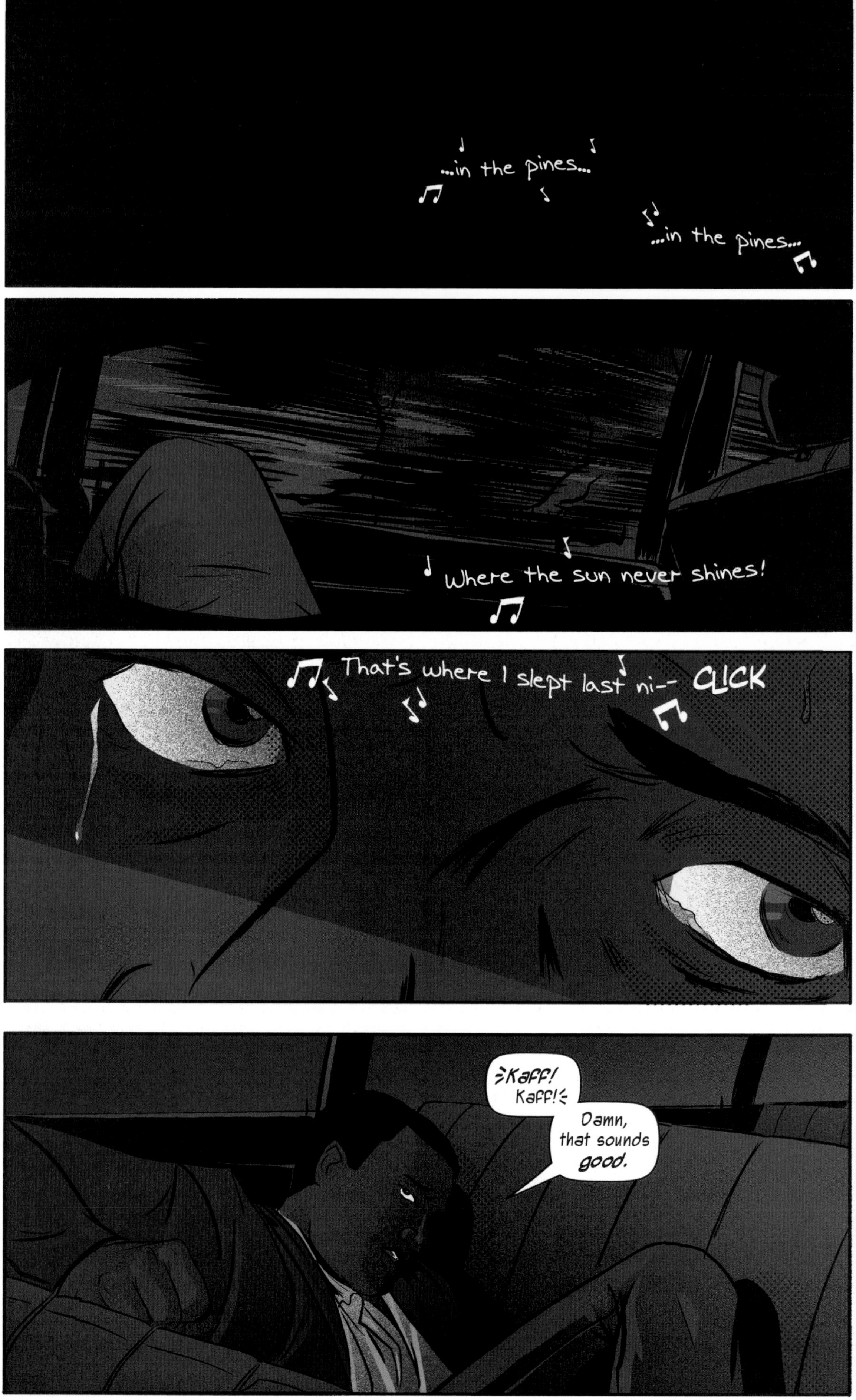
...in the pines...
...in the pines...
Where the sun never shines!
That's where I slept last ni--
CLICK
Kaff! Kaff!
Damn, that sounds good.

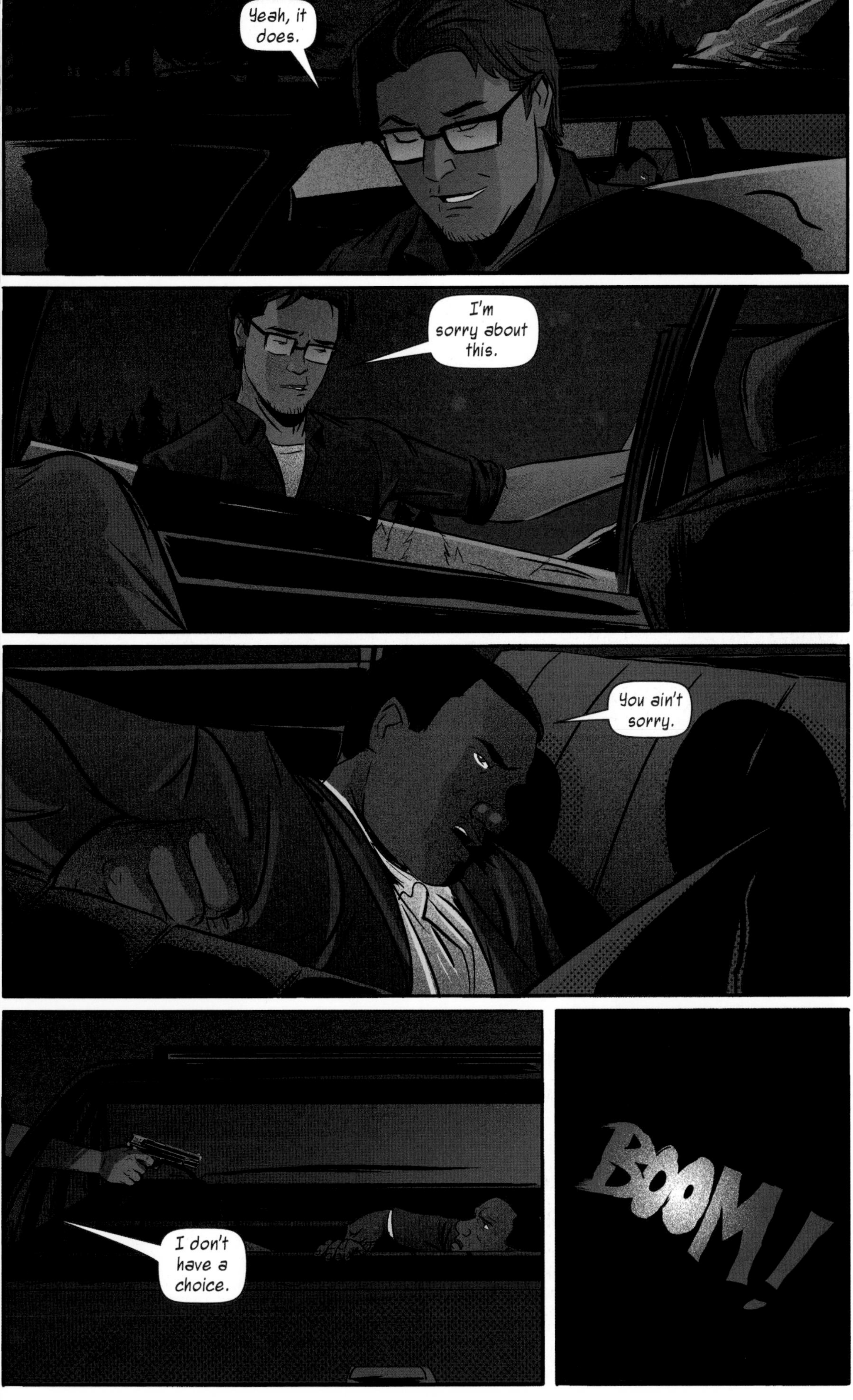
Yeah, it does.
I'm sorry about this.
You ain't sorry.
I don't have a choice.
BOOM!

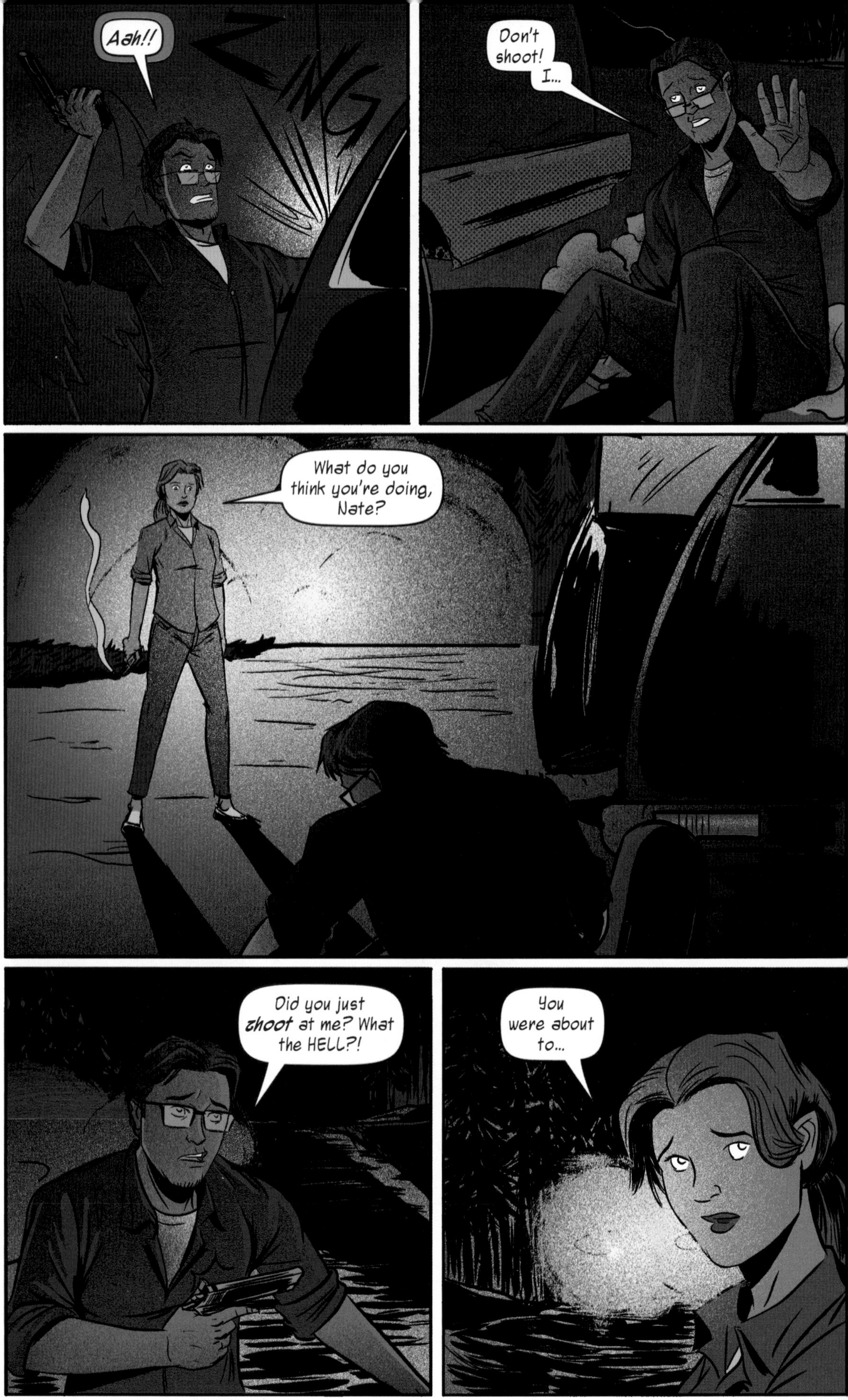
Aah!!
ZING
Don't shoot! I...
What do you think you're doing, Nate?
Did you just *shoot* at me? What the HELL?!
You were about to...

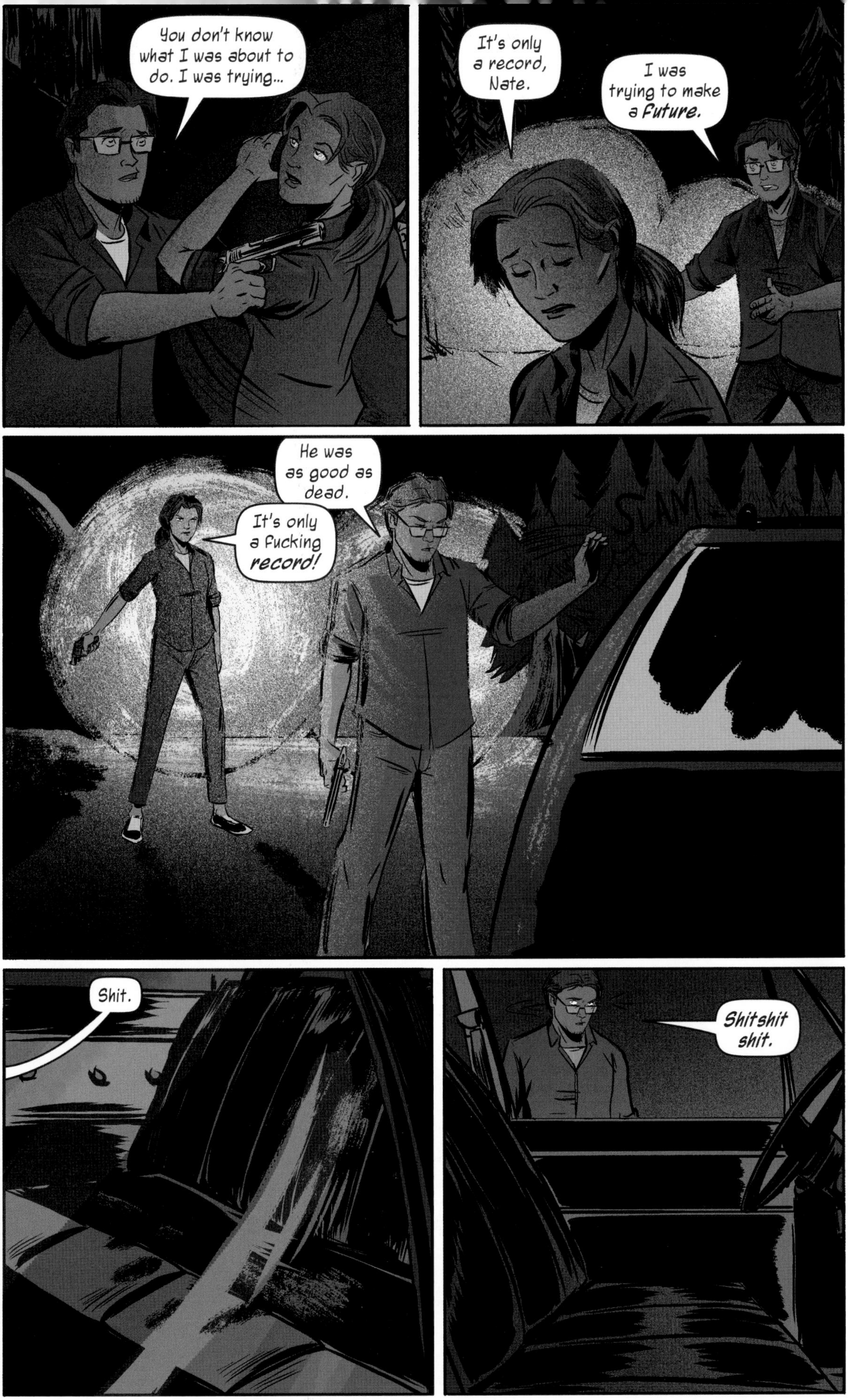
You don't know what I was about to do. I was trying...
It's only a record, Nate.
I was trying to make a *future.*
It's only a fucking *record!*
He was as good as dead.
SLAM
Shit.
Shitshit shit.

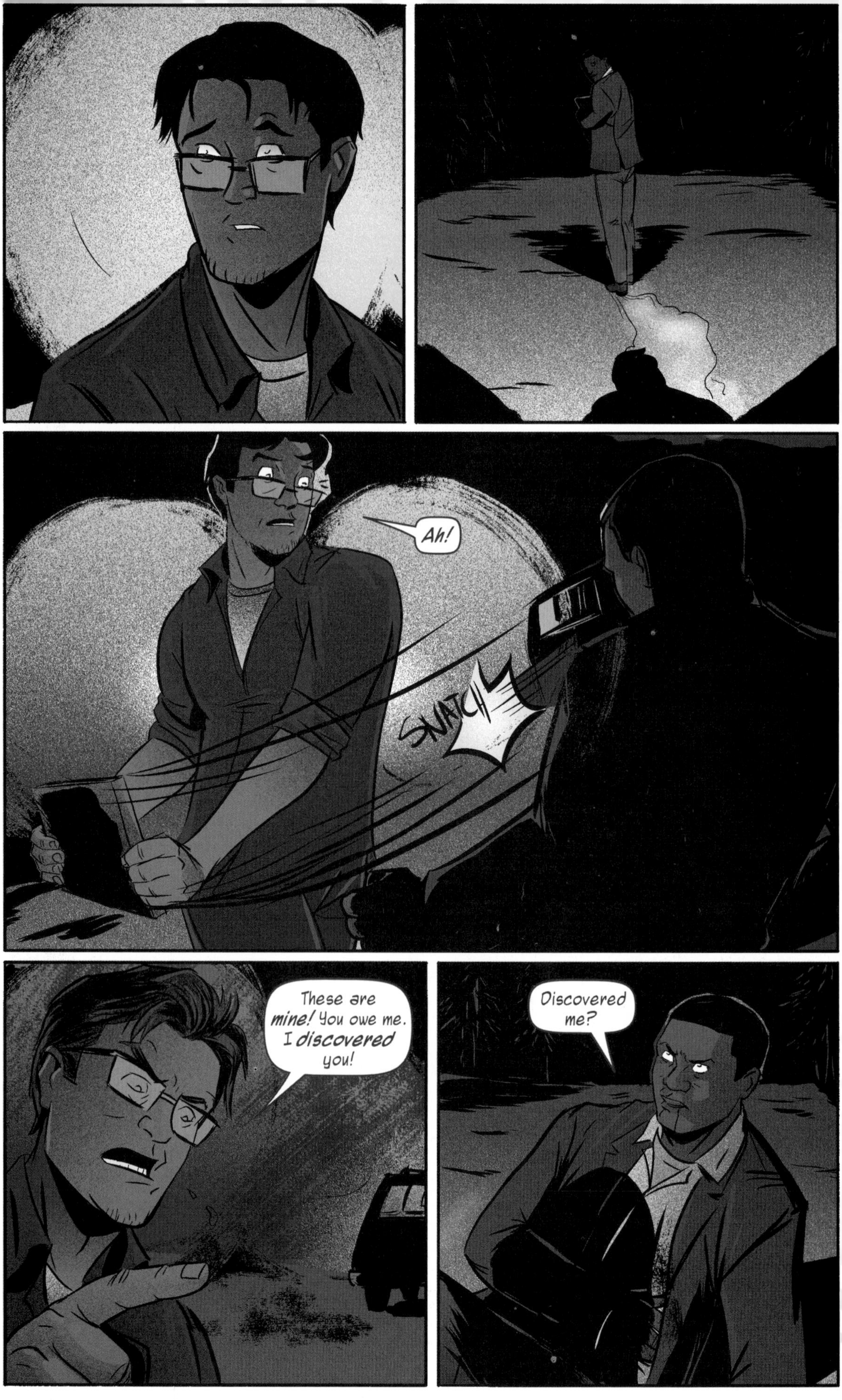
Ah!
SNATCH
These are mine! You owe me. I discovered you!
Discovered me?

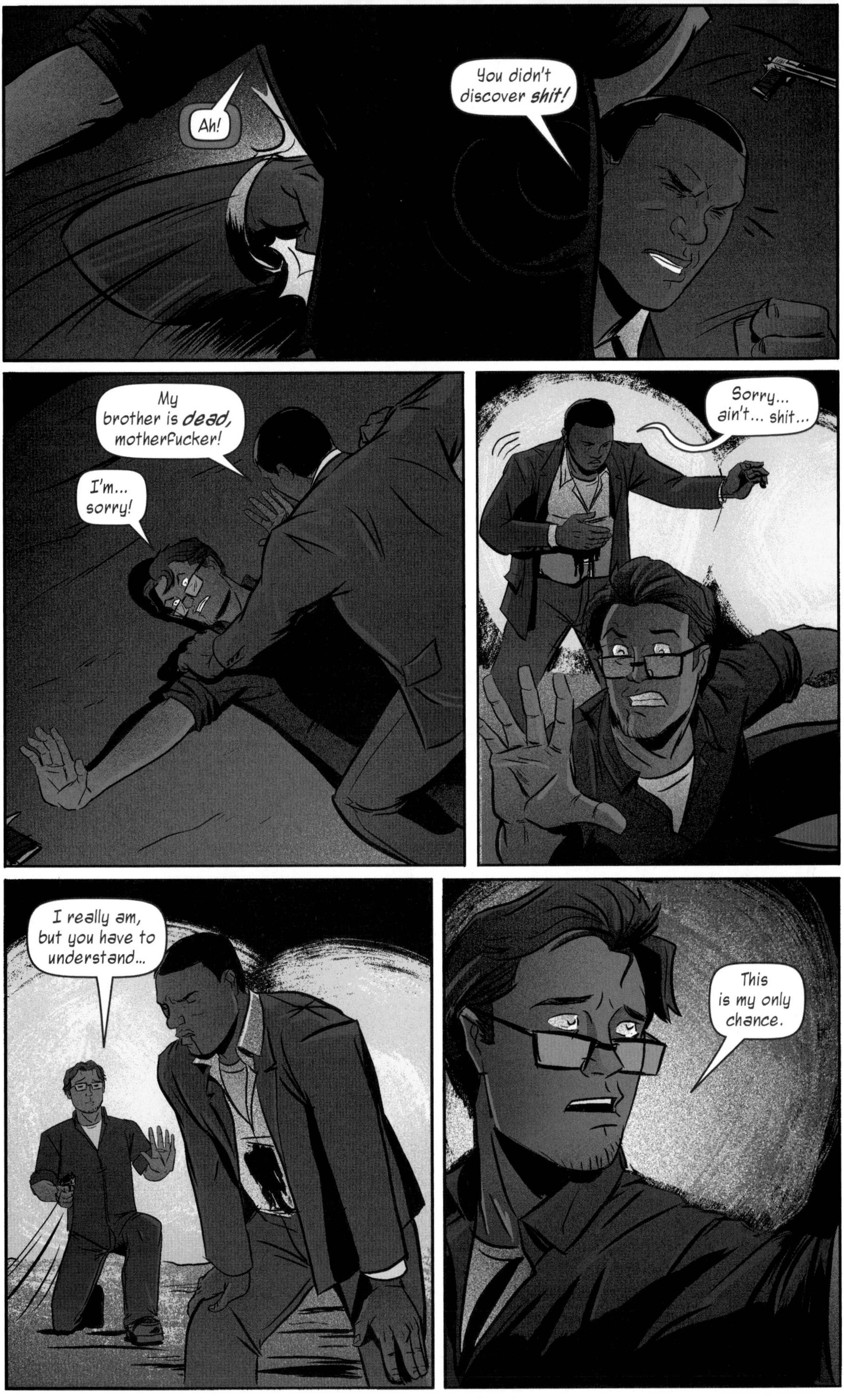
Ah!
You didn't discover shit!
My brother is dead, motherfucker!
I'm... sorry!
Sorry... ain't... shit...
I really am, but you have to understand...
This is my only chance.

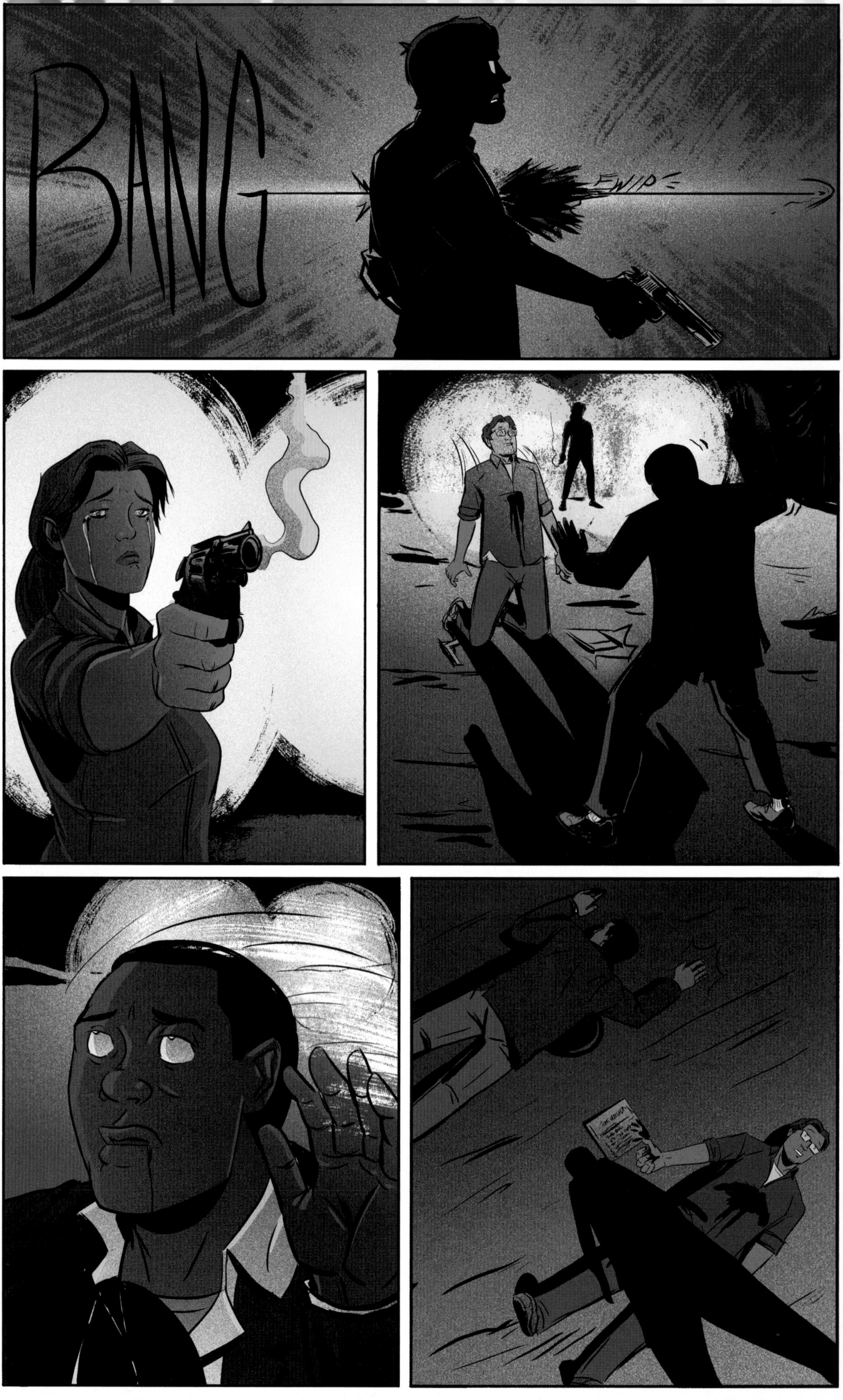
BANG
FWIP

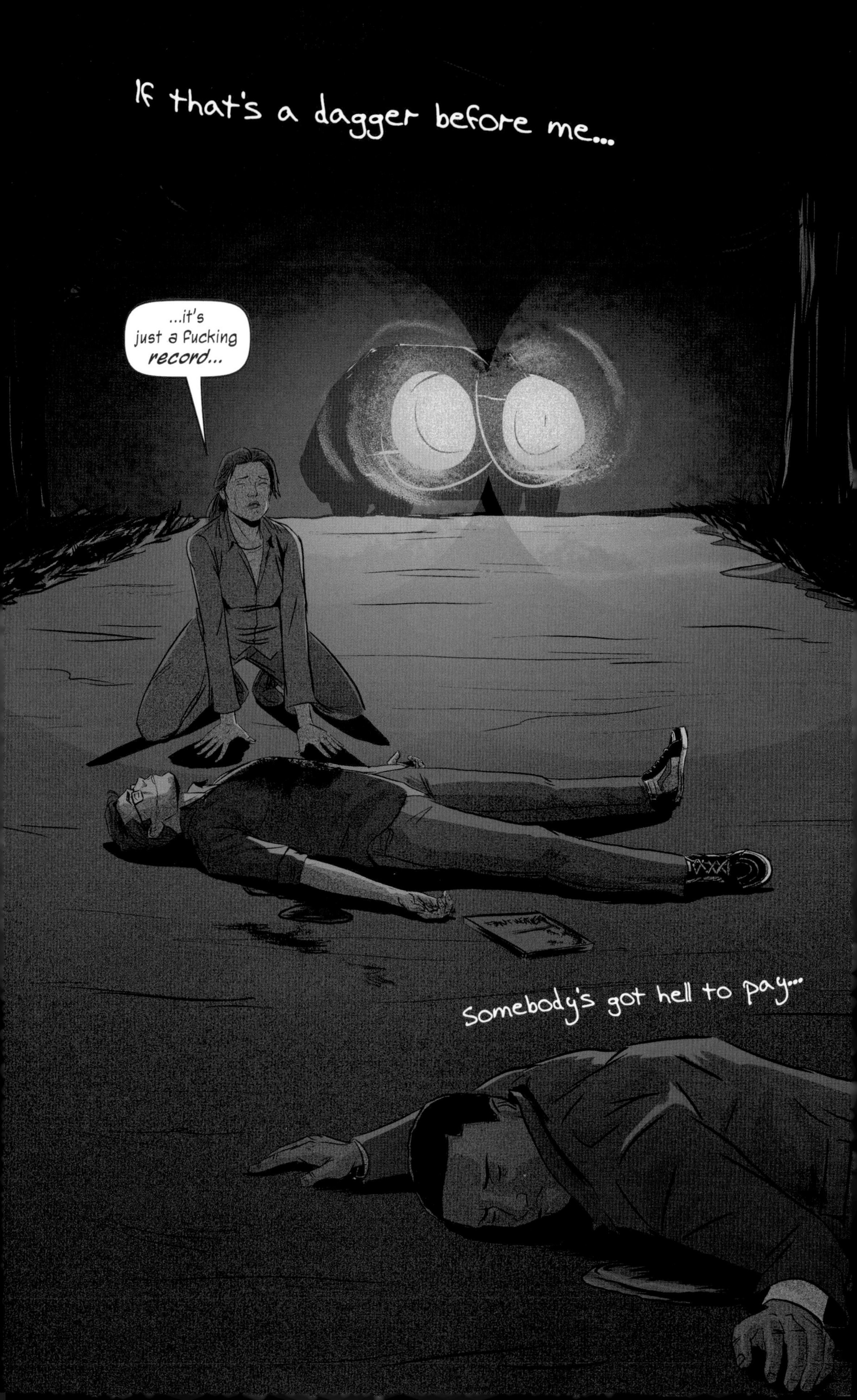
If that's a dagger before me...
...it's just a fucking record...
Somebody's got hell to pay...

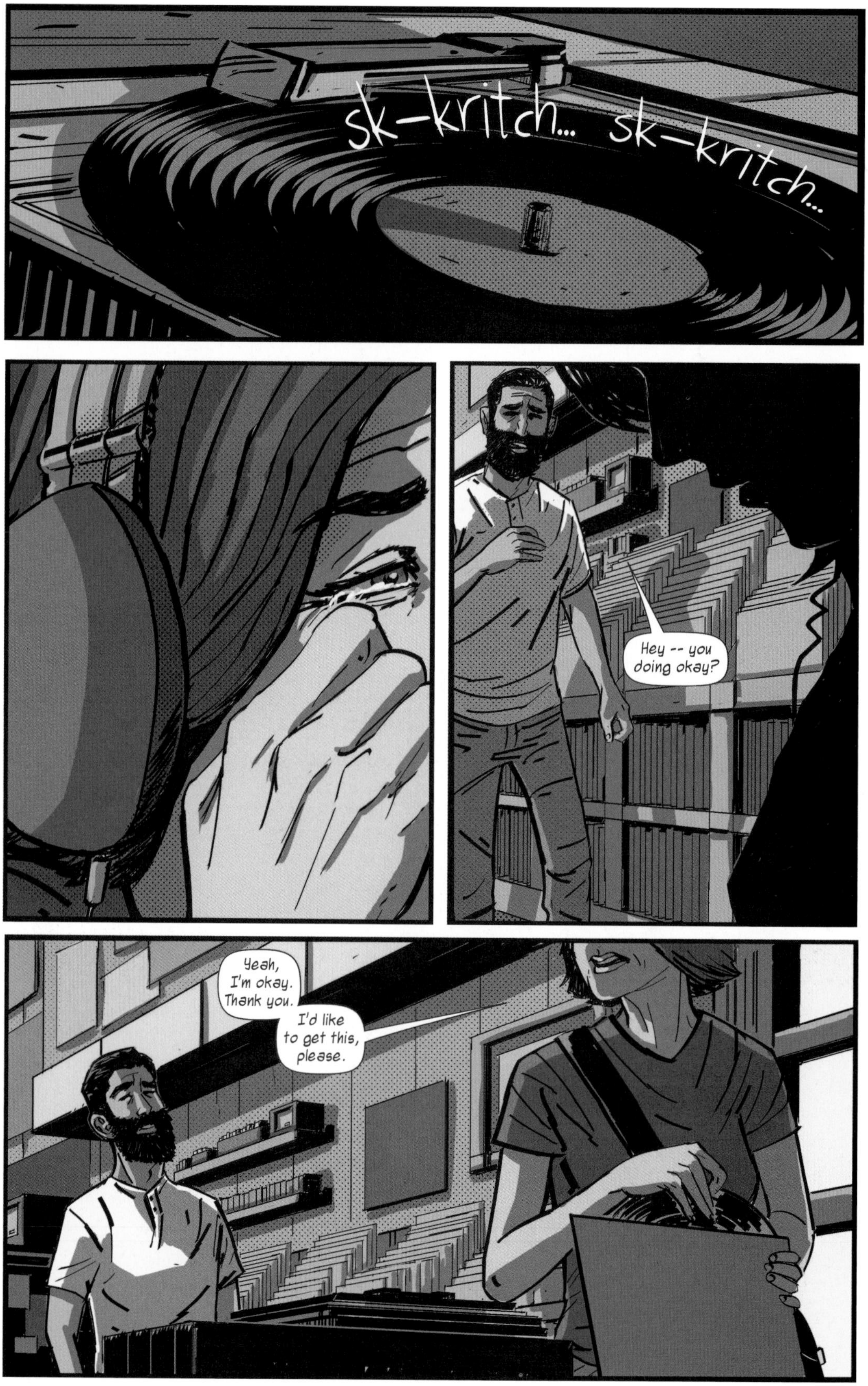
sk-kritch... sk-kritch...
Hey -- you doing okay?
Yeah, I'm okay. Thank you.
I'd like to get this, please.

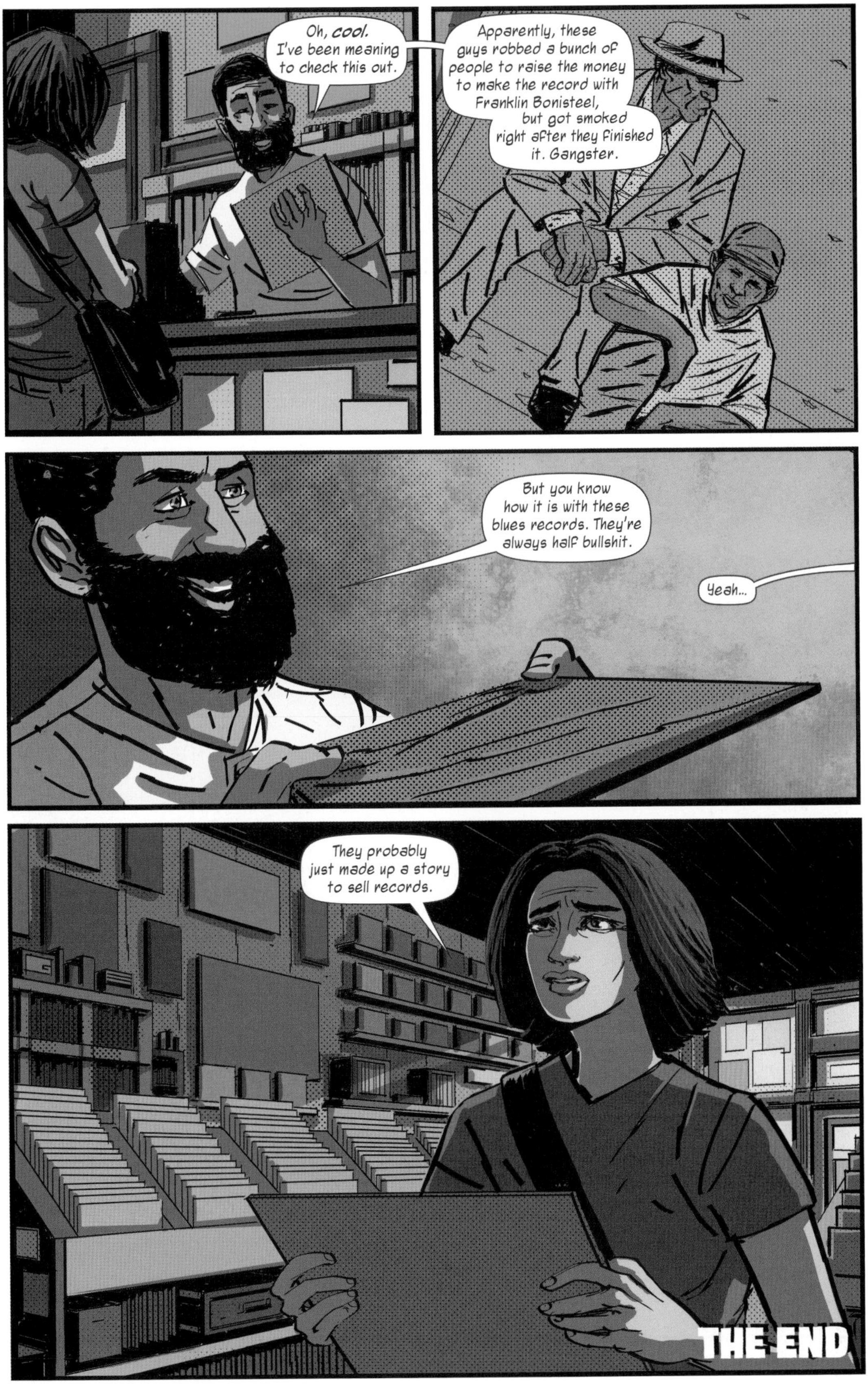
Oh, cool. I've been meaning to check this out.
Apparently, these guys robbed a bunch of people to raise the money to make the record with Franklin Bonisteel,
but got smoked right after they finished it. Gangster.
But you know how it is with these blues records. They're always half bullshit.
Yeah...
They probably just made up a story to sell records.
THE END

Now for your enjoyment comes
THE BALLAD OF FRANKLIN BONISTEEL
AKA "THE SHREVEPORT KID"
BY GABE SORIA AND WARREN PLEECE

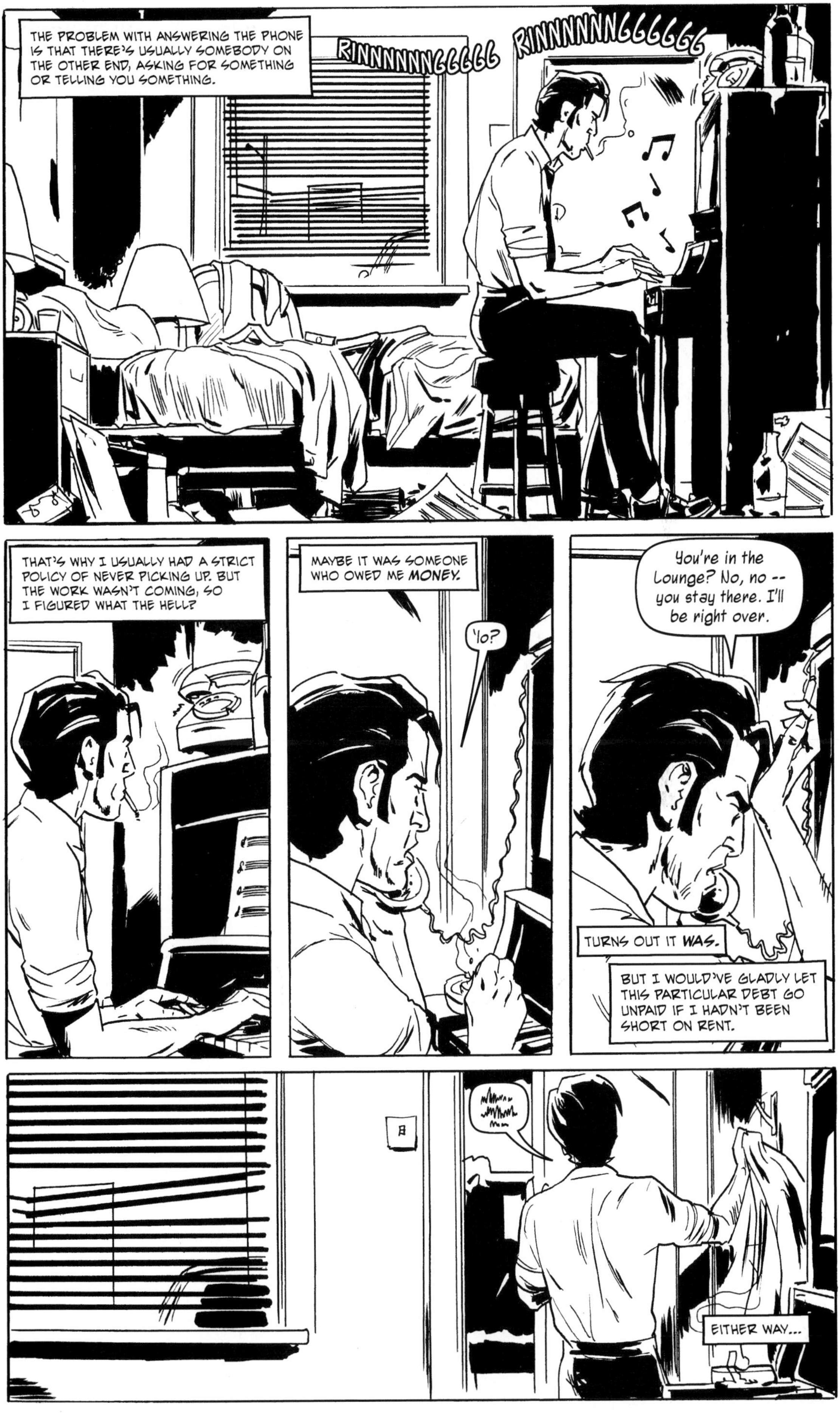
THE PROBLEM WITH ANSWERING THE PHONE IS THAT THERE'S USUALLY SOMEBODY ON THE OTHER END, ASKING FOR SOMETHING OR TELLING YOU SOMETHING.
RINNNNNNGGGGG RINNNNNNGGGGGG
THAT'S WHY I USUALLY HAD A STRICT POLICY OF NEVER PICKING UP. BUT THE WORK WASN'T COMING, SO I FIGURED WHAT THE HELL?
MAYBE IT WAS SOMEONE WHO OWED ME MONEY.
'lo?
You're in the Lounge? No, no -- you stay there. I'll be right over.
TURNS OUT IT WAS.
BUT I WOULD'VE GLADLY LET THIS PARTICULAR DEBT GO UNPAID IF I HADN'T BEEN SHORT ON RENT.
EITHER WAY...

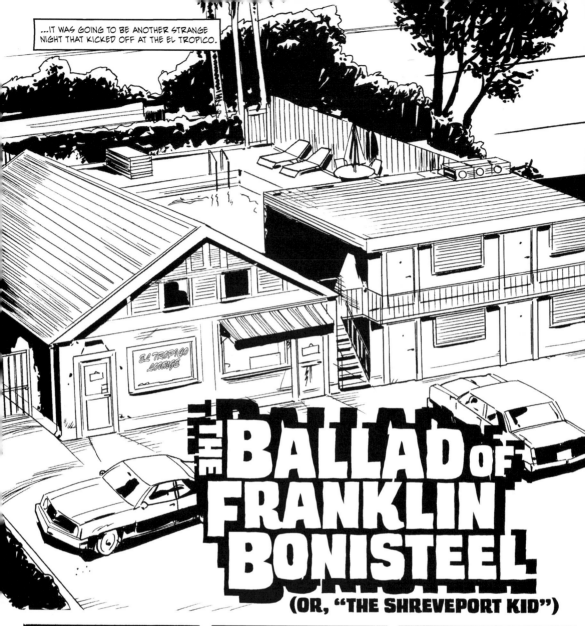

...IT WAS GOING TO BE ANOTHER STRANGE NIGHT THAT KICKED OFF AT THE EL TROPICO.

THE BALLAD OF FRANKLIN BONISTEEL

(OR, "THE SHREVEPORT KID")

Pete Reyes

Piano player, accidental detective. El Tropico, Room 104.

Marguerite Dumas

Former late-night TV horror host, current woman of leisure. El Tropico, Room 108.

Franklin Bonisteel

Producer. Bon-Tone Studios, Burbank.

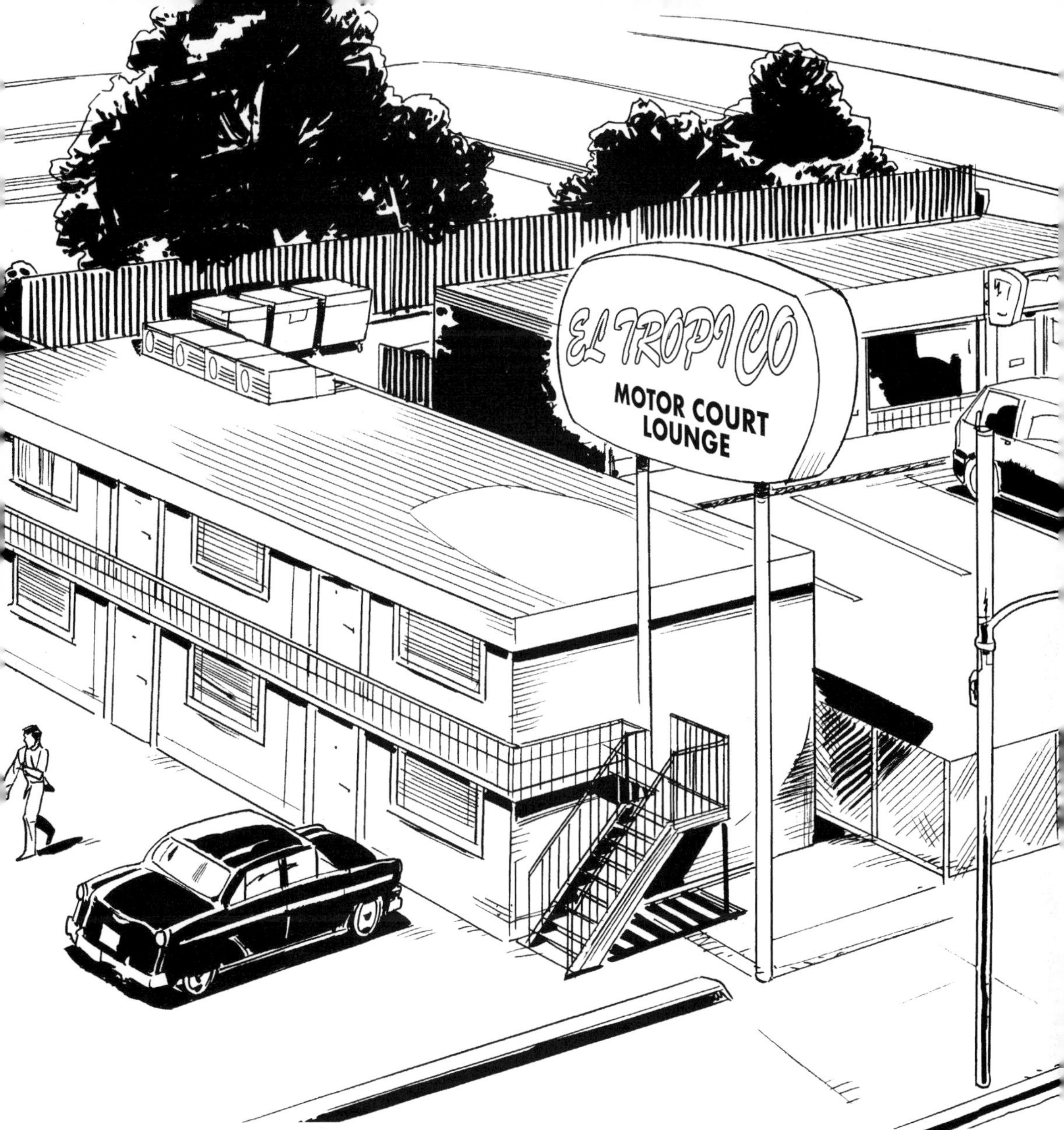
EL TROPICO
MOTOR COURT
LOUNGE

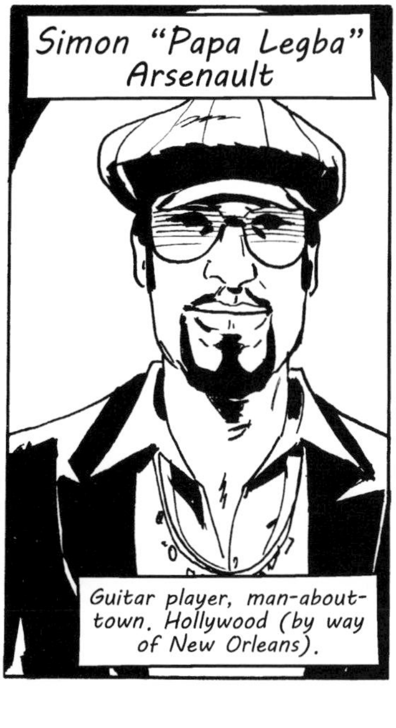
Simon "Papa Legba" Arsenault
Guitar player, man-about-town. Hollywood (by way of New Orleans).

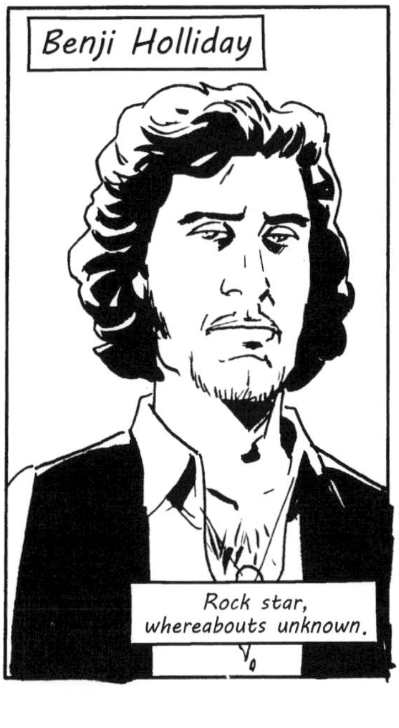
Benji Holliday
Rock star, whereabouts unknown.

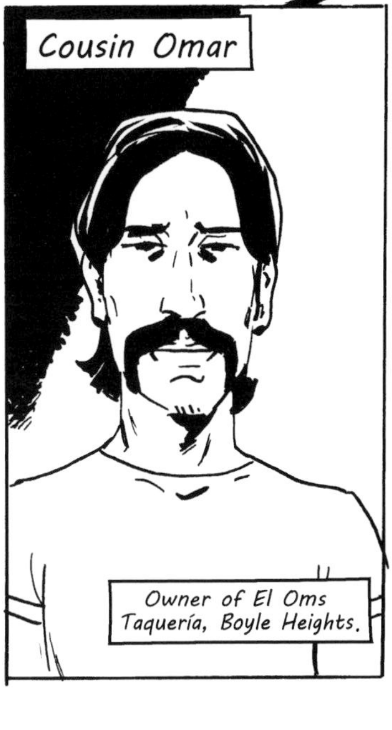
Cousin Omar
Owner of El Oms Taquería, Boyle Heights.

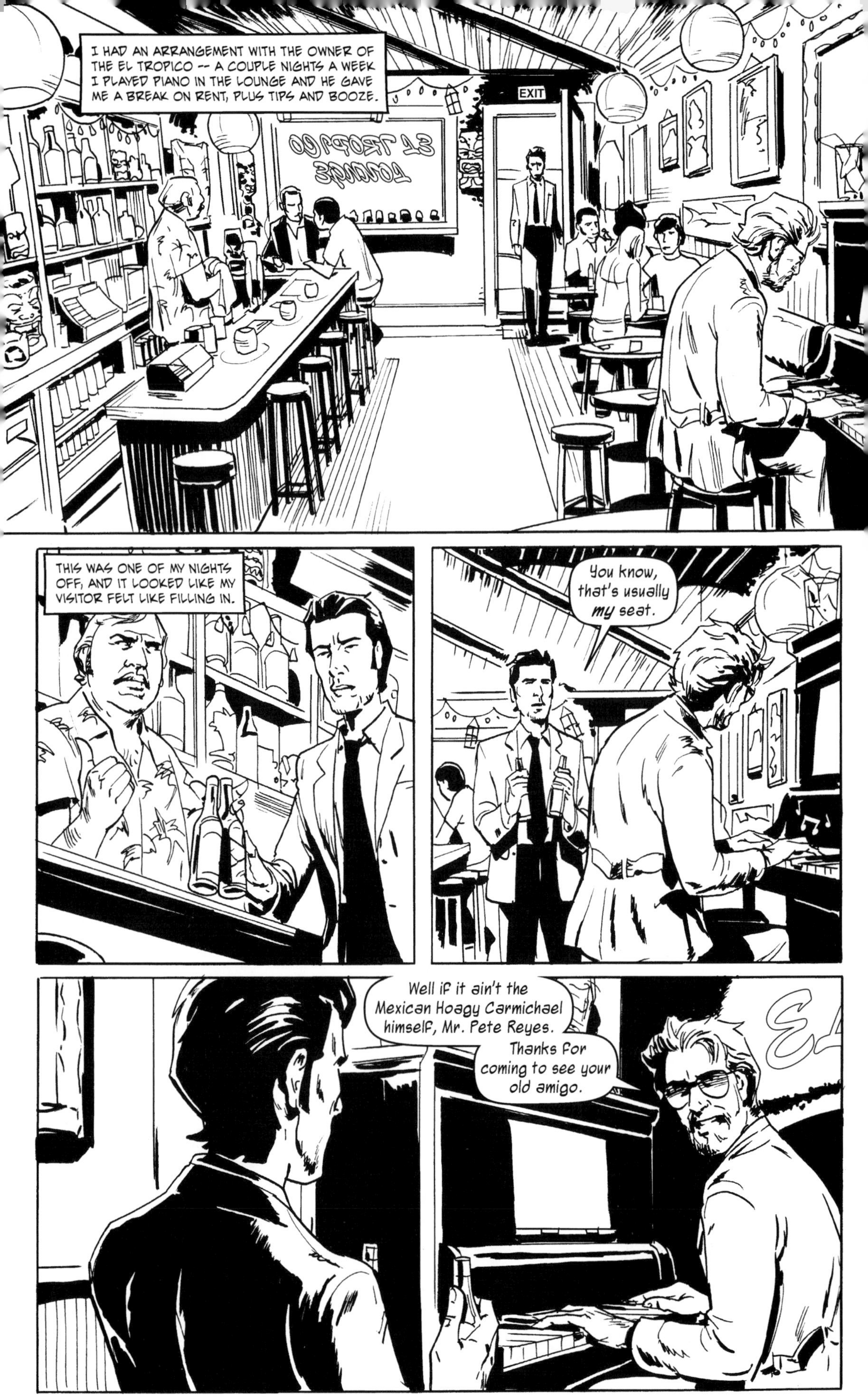
I HAD AN ARRANGEMENT WITH THE OWNER OF THE EL TROPICO -- A COUPLE NIGHTS A WEEK I PLAYED PIANO IN THE LOUNGE AND HE GAVE ME A BREAK ON RENT, PLUS TIPS AND BOOZE.
EXIT
THIS WAS ONE OF MY NIGHTS OFF, AND IT LOOKED LIKE MY VISITOR FELT LIKE FILLING IN.
You know, that's usually *my* seat.
Well if it ain't the Mexican Hoagy Carmichael himself, Mr. Pete Reyes.
Thanks for coming to see your old amigo.

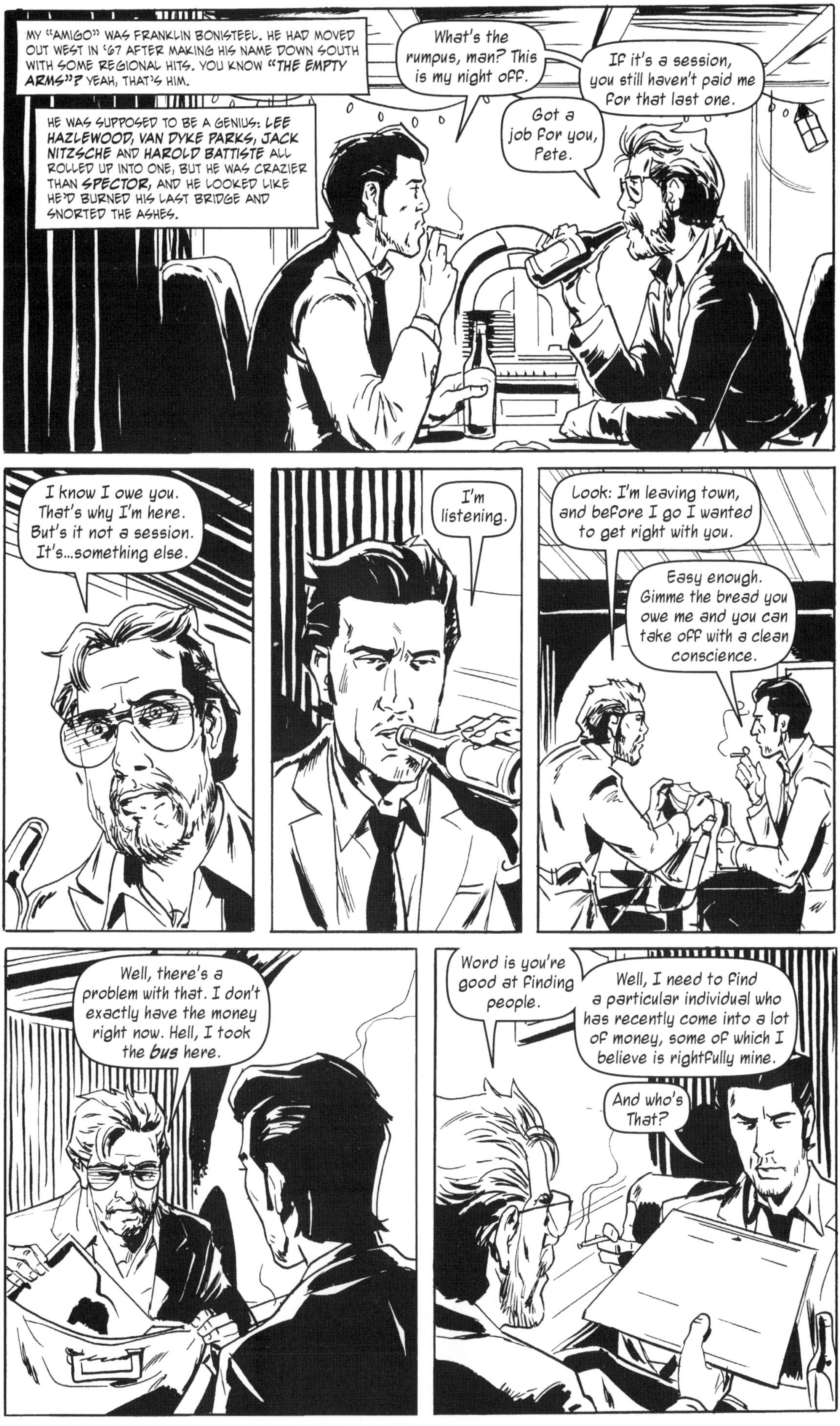
MY "AMIGO" WAS FRANKLIN BONISTEEL. HE HAD MOVED OUT WEST IN '67 AFTER MAKING HIS NAME DOWN SOUTH WITH SOME REGIONAL HITS. YOU KNOW **"THE EMPTY ARMS"?** YEAH, THAT'S HIM.
HE WAS SUPPOSED TO BE A GENIUS: **LEE HAZLEWOOD, VAN DYKE PARKS, JACK NITZSCHE** AND **HAROLD BATTISTE** ALL ROLLED UP INTO ONE, BUT HE WAS CRAZIER THAN **SPECTOR,** AND HE LOOKED LIKE HE'D BURNED HIS LAST BRIDGE AND SNORTED THE ASHES.
What's the rumpus, man? This is my night off.
Got a job for you, Pete.
If it's a session, you still haven't paid me for that last one.
I know I owe you. That's why I'm here. But's it not a session. It's...something else.
I'm listening.
Look: I'm leaving town, and before I go I wanted to get right with you.
Easy enough. Gimme the bread you owe me and you can take off with a clean conscience.
Well, there's a problem with that. I don't exactly have the money right now. Hell, I took the *bus* here.
Word is you're good at finding people.
Well, I need to find a particular individual who has recently come into a lot of money, some of which I believe is rightfully mine.
And who's That?

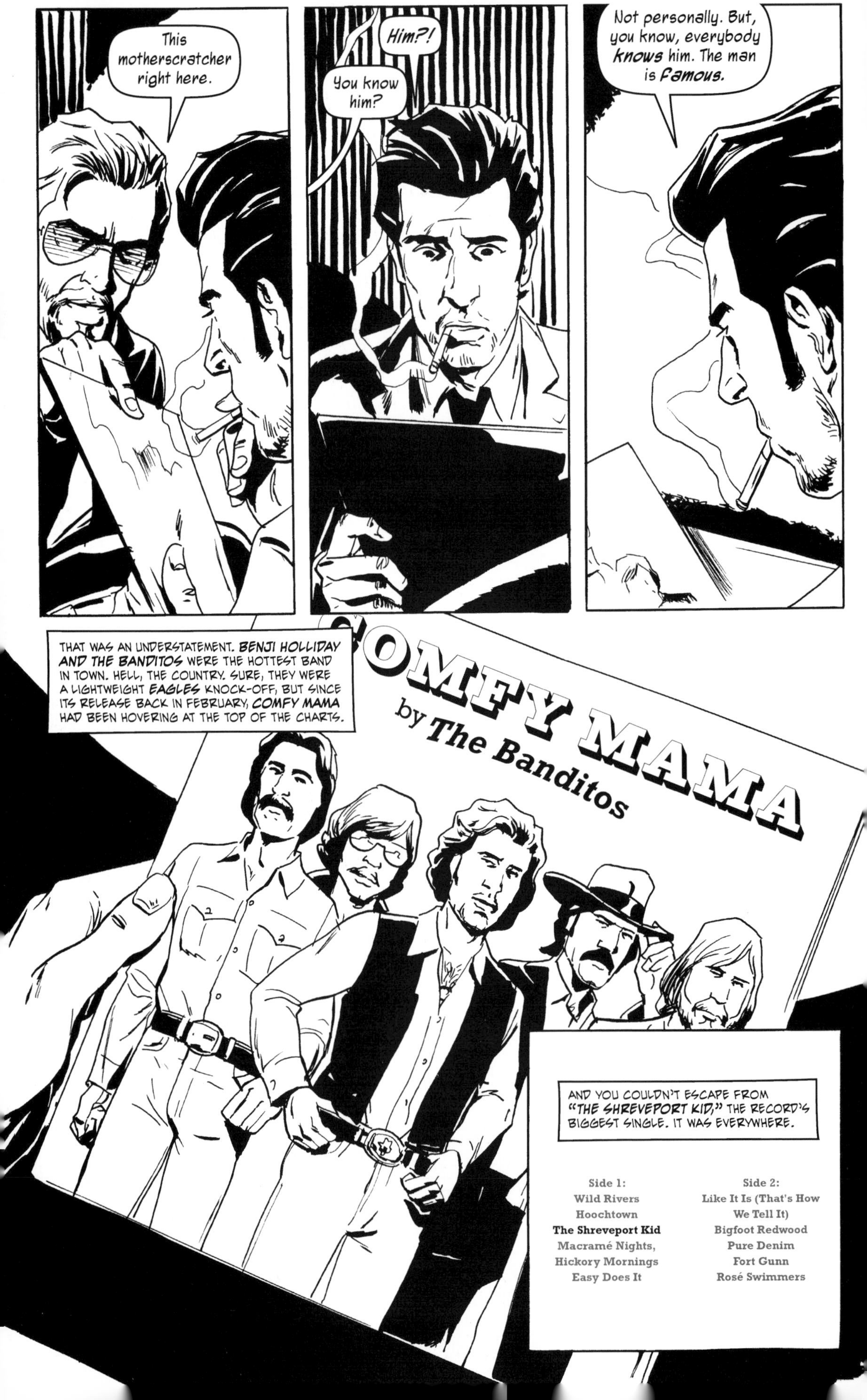

This motherscratcher right here.
Him?!
You know him?
Not personally. But, you know, everybody *knows* him. The man is *famous.*
THAT WAS AN UNDERSTATEMENT. ***BENJI HOLLIDAY AND THE BANDITOS*** WERE THE HOTTEST BAND IN TOWN. HELL, THE COUNTRY. SURE, THEY WERE A LIGHTWEIGHT ***EAGLES*** KNOCK-OFF, BUT SINCE ITS RELEASE BACK IN FEBRUARY, ***COMFY MAMA*** HAD BEEN HOVERING AT THE TOP OF THE CHARTS.
COMFY MAMA
by The Banditos
AND YOU COULDN'T ESCAPE FROM ***"THE SHREVEPORT KID,"*** THE RECORD'S BIGGEST SINGLE. IT WAS EVERYWHERE.
Side 1:
Wild Rivers
Hoochtown
The Shreveport Kid
Macramé Nights,
Hickory Mornings
Easy Does It
Side 2:
Like It Is (That's How
We Tell It)
Bigfoot Redwood
Pure Denim
Fort Gunn
Rosé Swimmers

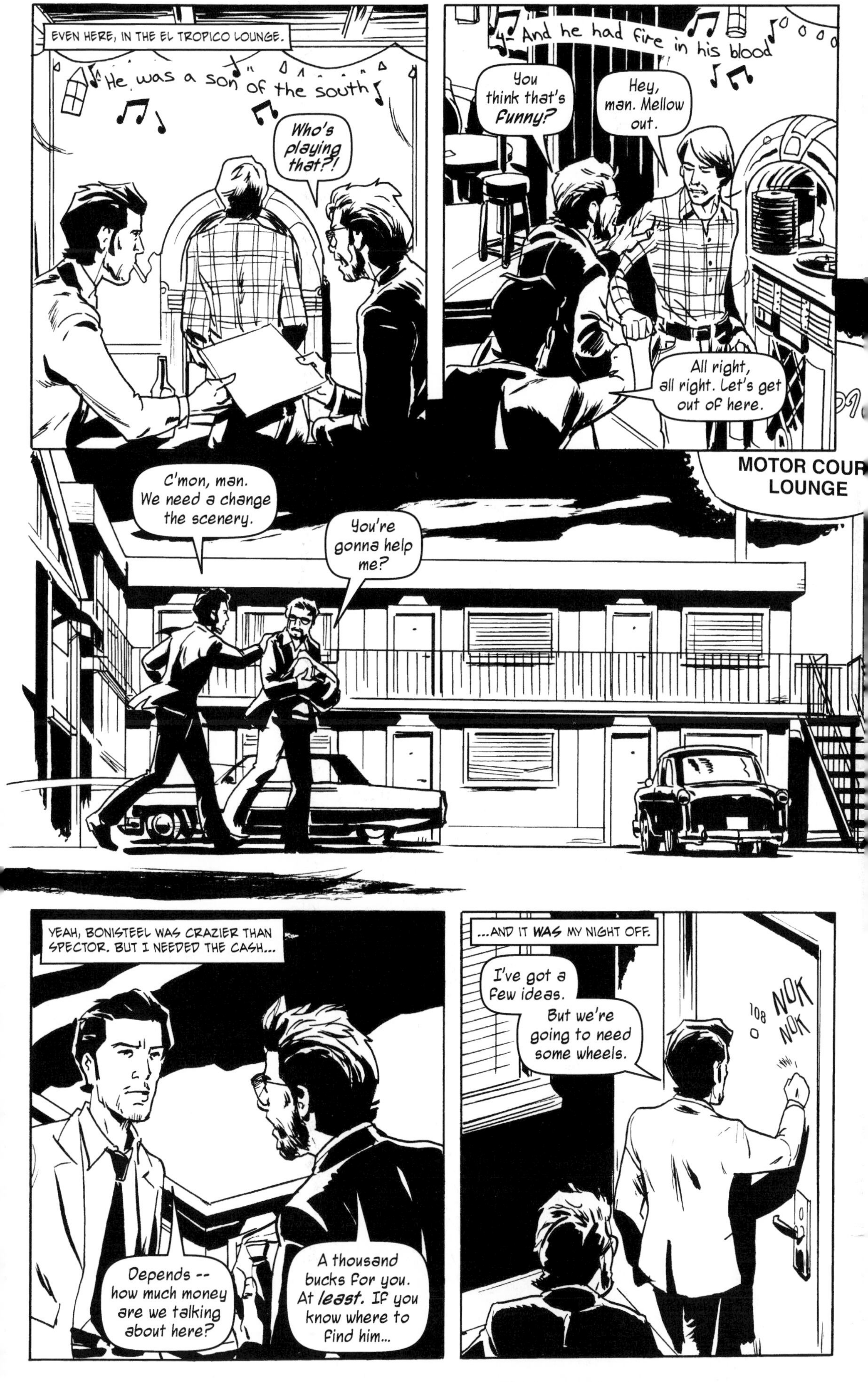
EVEN HERE, IN THE EL TROPICO LOUNGE.
He was a son of the south
Who's playing that?!
And he had fire in his blood
You think that's *funny?*
Hey, man. Mellow out.
All right, all right. Let's get out of here.
MOTOR COUR
LOUNGE
C'mon, man. We need a change the scenery.
You're gonna help me?
YEAH, BONISTEEL WAS CRAZIER THAN SPECTOR. BUT I NEEDED THE CASH...
Depends -- how much money are we talking about here?
A thousand bucks for you. At *least.* If you know where to find him...
...AND IT *WAS* MY NIGHT OFF.
I've got a few ideas.
But we're going to need some wheels.
108
NOK
NOK

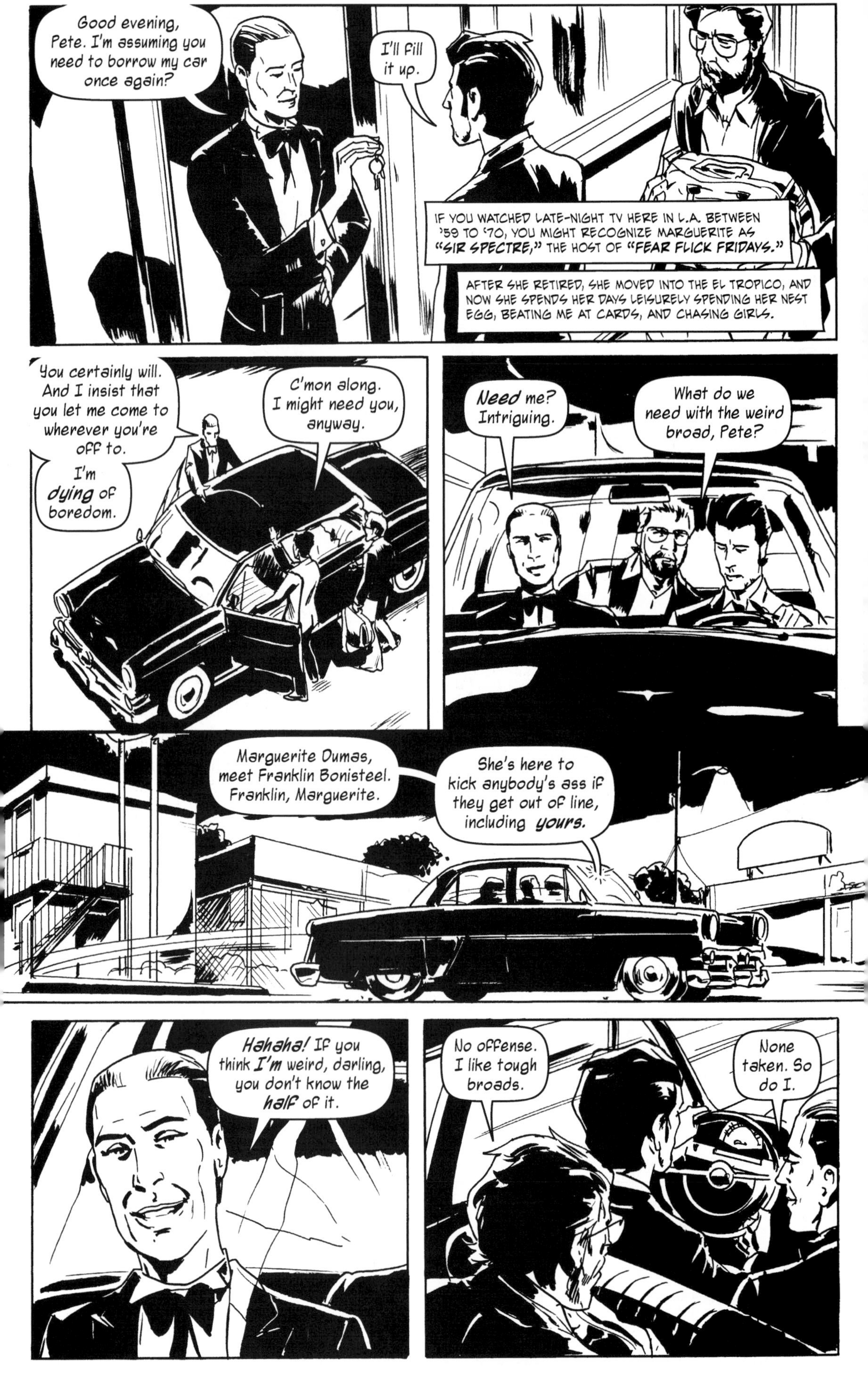
Good evening, Pete. I'm assuming you need to borrow my car once again?
I'll fill it up.
IF YOU WATCHED LATE-NIGHT TV HERE IN L.A. BETWEEN '59 TO '70, YOU MIGHT RECOGNIZE MARGUERITE AS "SIR SPECTRE," THE HOST OF "FEAR FLICK FRIDAYS."
AFTER SHE RETIRED, SHE MOVED INTO THE EL TROPICO, AND NOW SHE SPENDS HER DAYS LEISURELY SPENDING HER NEST EGG, BEATING ME AT CARDS, AND CHASING GIRLS.
You certainly will. And I insist that you let me come to wherever you're off to.
I'm dying of boredom.
C'mon along. I might need you, anyway.
Need me? Intriguing.
What do we need with the weird broad, Pete?
Marguerite Dumas, meet Franklin Bonisteel. Franklin, Marguerite.
She's here to kick anybody's ass if they get out of line, including yours.
Hahaha! If you think I'm weird, darling, you don't know the half of it.
No offense. I like tough broads.
None taken. So do I.

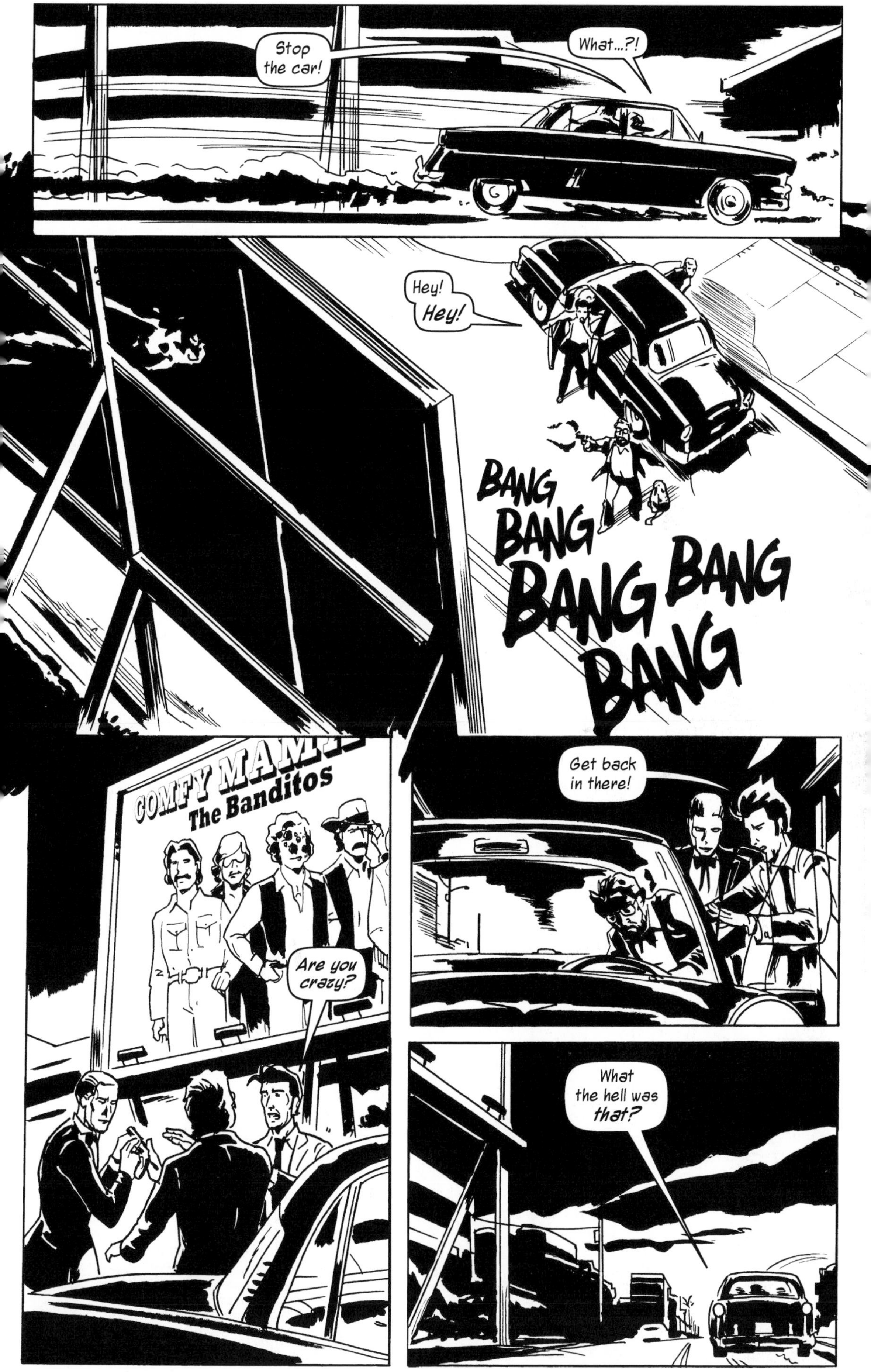
Stop the car!
What...?!
Hey! Hey!
BANG BANG BANG BANG BANG
COMFY MAMI
The Banditos
Are you crazy?
Get back in there!
What the hell was that?

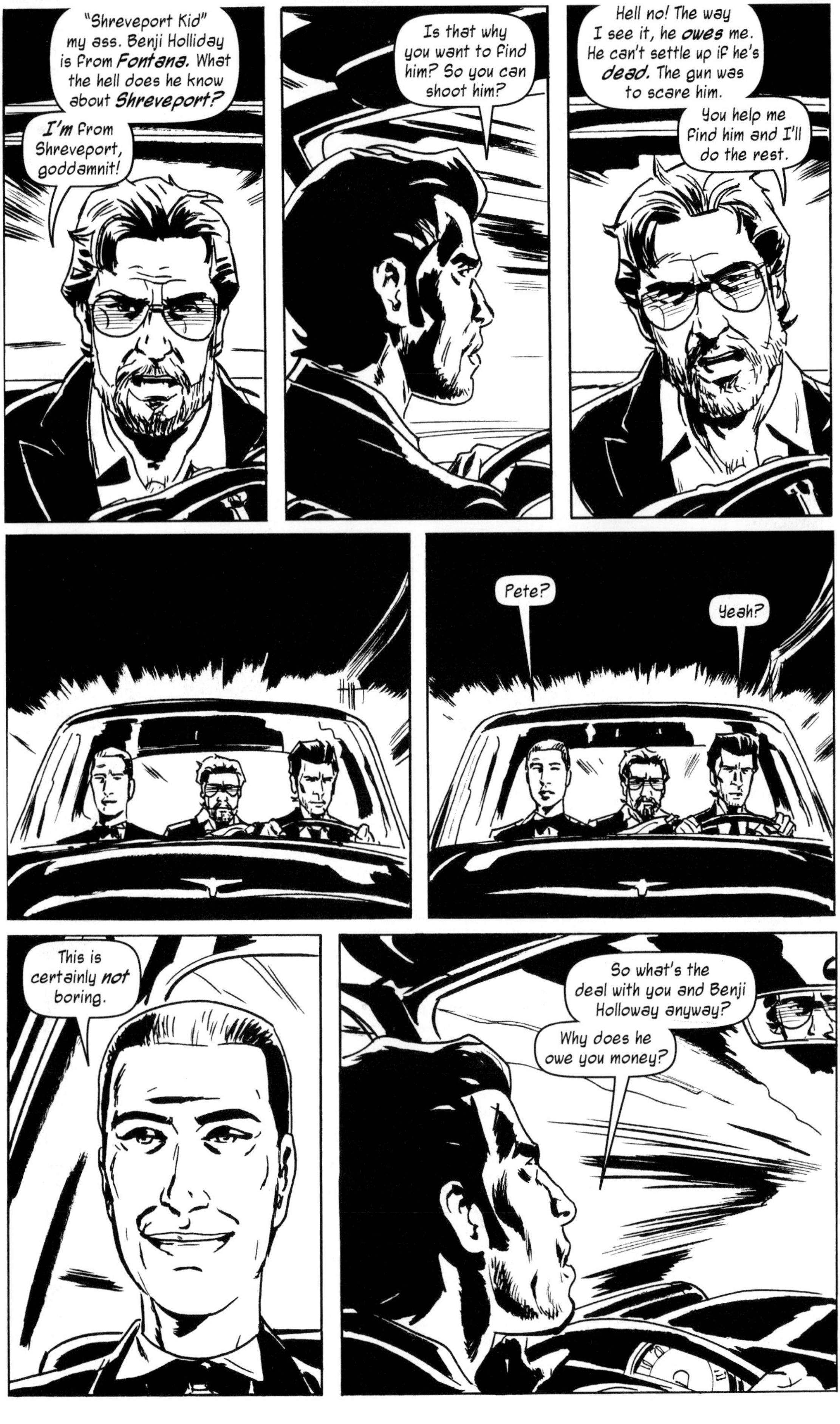
"Shreveport Kid" my ass. Benji Holliday is from Fontana. What the hell does he know about Shreveport?
I'm from Shreveport, goddamnit!
Is that why you want to find him? So you can shoot him?
Hell no! The way I see it, he owes me. He can't settle up if he's dead. The gun was to scare him.
You help me find him and I'll do the rest.
Pete?
Yeah?
This is certainly not boring.
So what's the deal with you and Benji Holloway anyway?
Why does he owe you money?

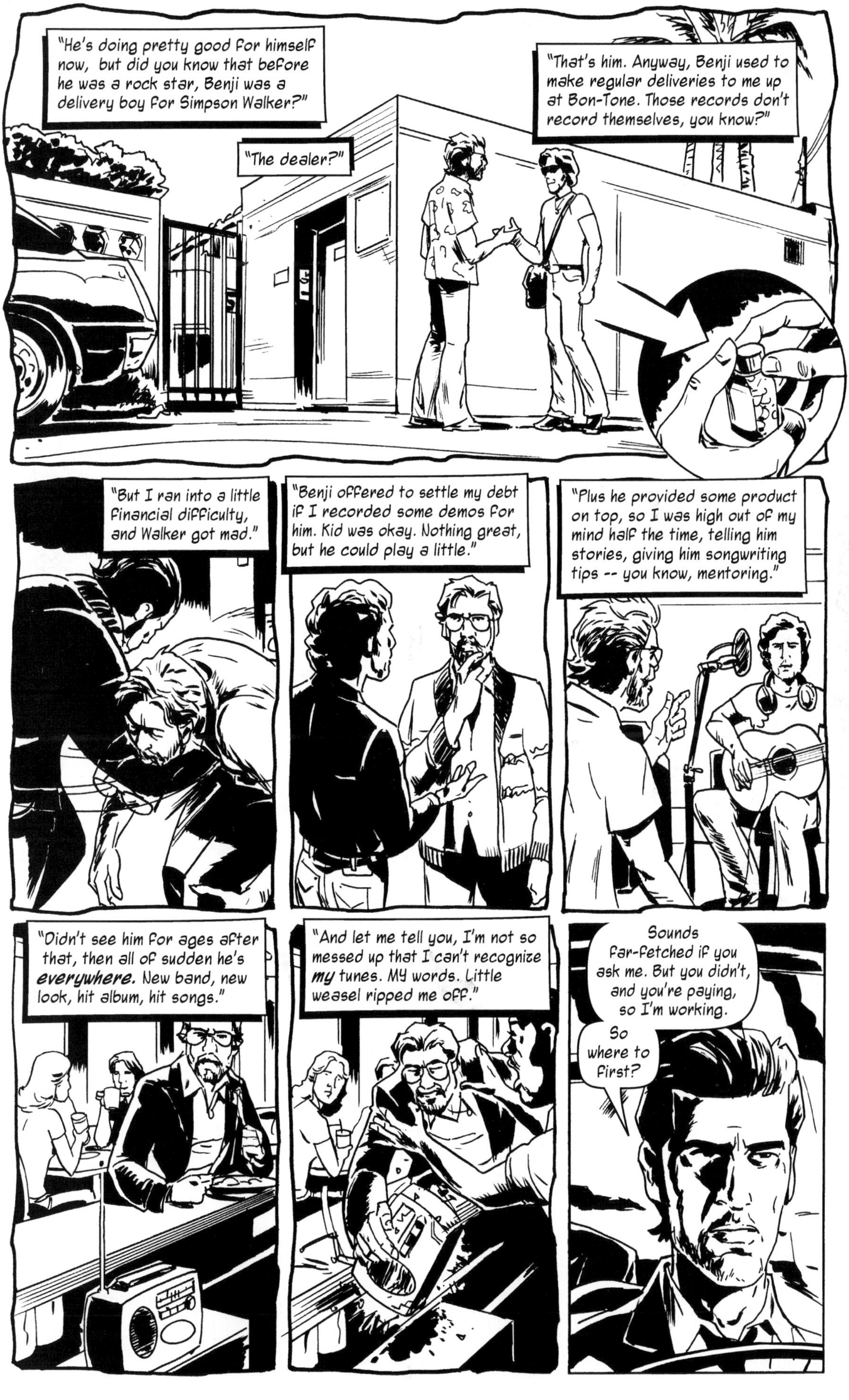
"He's doing pretty good for himself now, but did you know that before he was a rock star, Benji was a delivery boy for Simpson Walker?"
"The dealer?"
"That's him. Anyway, Benji used to make regular deliveries to me up at Bon-Tone. Those records don't record themselves, you know?"
"But I ran into a little financial difficulty, and Walker got mad."
"Benji offered to settle my debt if I recorded some demos for him. Kid was okay. Nothing great, but he could play a little."
"Plus he provided some product on top, so I was high out of my mind half the time, telling him stories, giving him songwriting tips -- you know, mentoring."
"Didn't see him for ages after that, then all of sudden he's ***everywhere.*** New band, new look, hit album, hit songs."
"And let me tell you, I'm not so messed up that I can't recognize ***my*** tunes. MY words. Little weasel ripped me off."
Sounds far-fetched if you ask me. But you didn't, and you're paying, so I'm working.
So where to first?

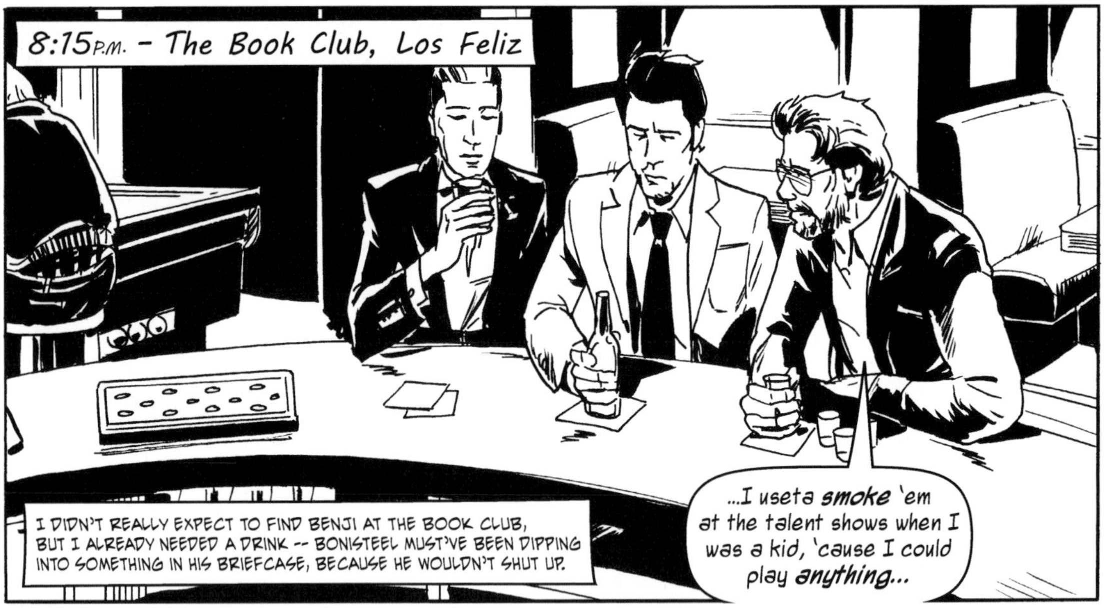
8:15P.M. – The Book Club, Los Feliz
I DIDN'T REALLY EXPECT TO FIND BENJI AT THE BOOK CLUB, BUT I ALREADY NEEDED A DRINK -- BONISTEEL MUST'VE BEEN DIPPING INTO SOMETHING IN HIS BRIEFCASE, BECAUSE HE WOULDN'T SHUT UP.
...I useta *smoke* 'em at the talent shows when I was a kid, 'cause I could play *anything*...

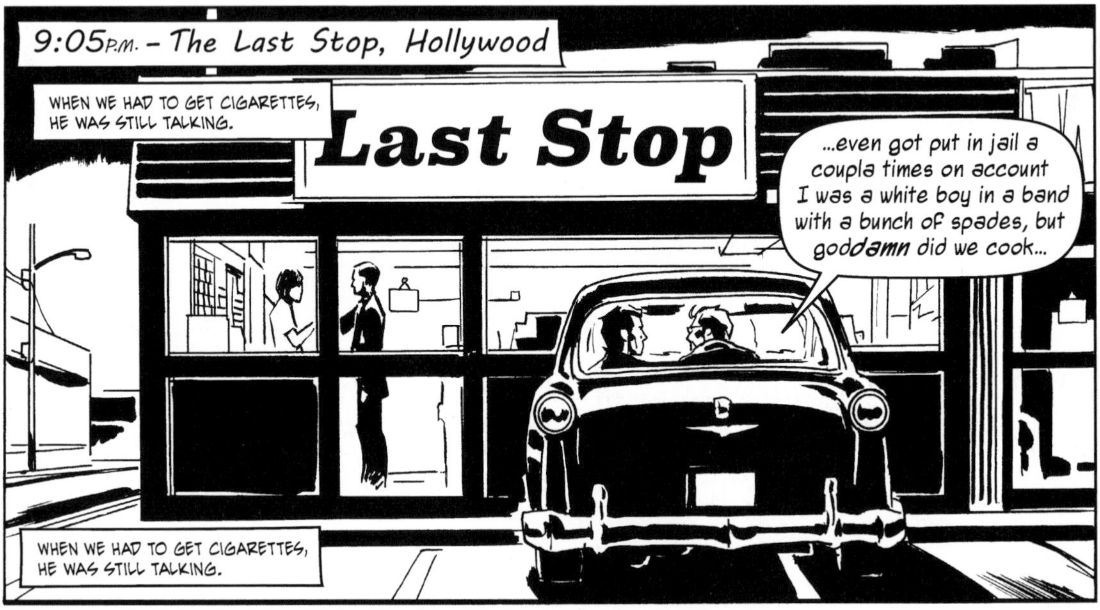
9:05P.M. – The Last Stop, Hollywood
WHEN WE HAD TO GET CIGARETTES, HE WAS STILL TALKING.
Last Stop
...even got put in jail a coupla times on account I was a white boy in a band with a bunch of spades, but god*damn* did we cook...
WHEN WE HAD TO GET CIGARETTES, HE WAS STILL TALKING.

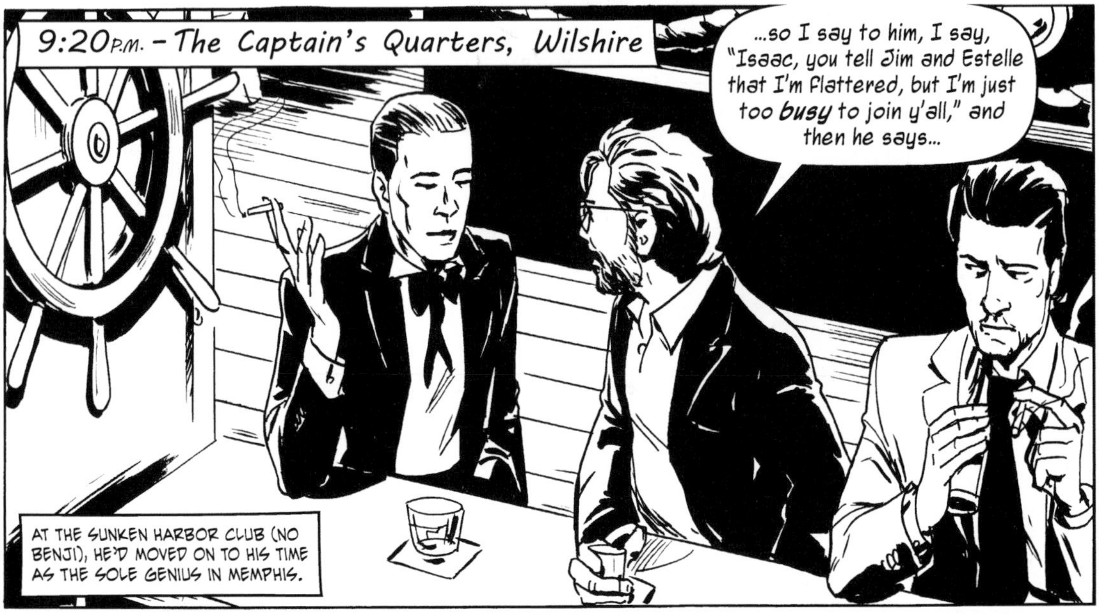
9:20P.M. – The Captain's Quarters, Wilshire
...so I say to him, I say, "Isaac, you tell Jim and Estelle that I'm flattered, but I'm just too *busy* to join y'all," and then he says...
AT THE SUNKEN HARBOR CLUB (NO BENJI), HE'D MOVED ON TO HIS TIME AS THE SOLE GENIUS IN MEMPHIS.

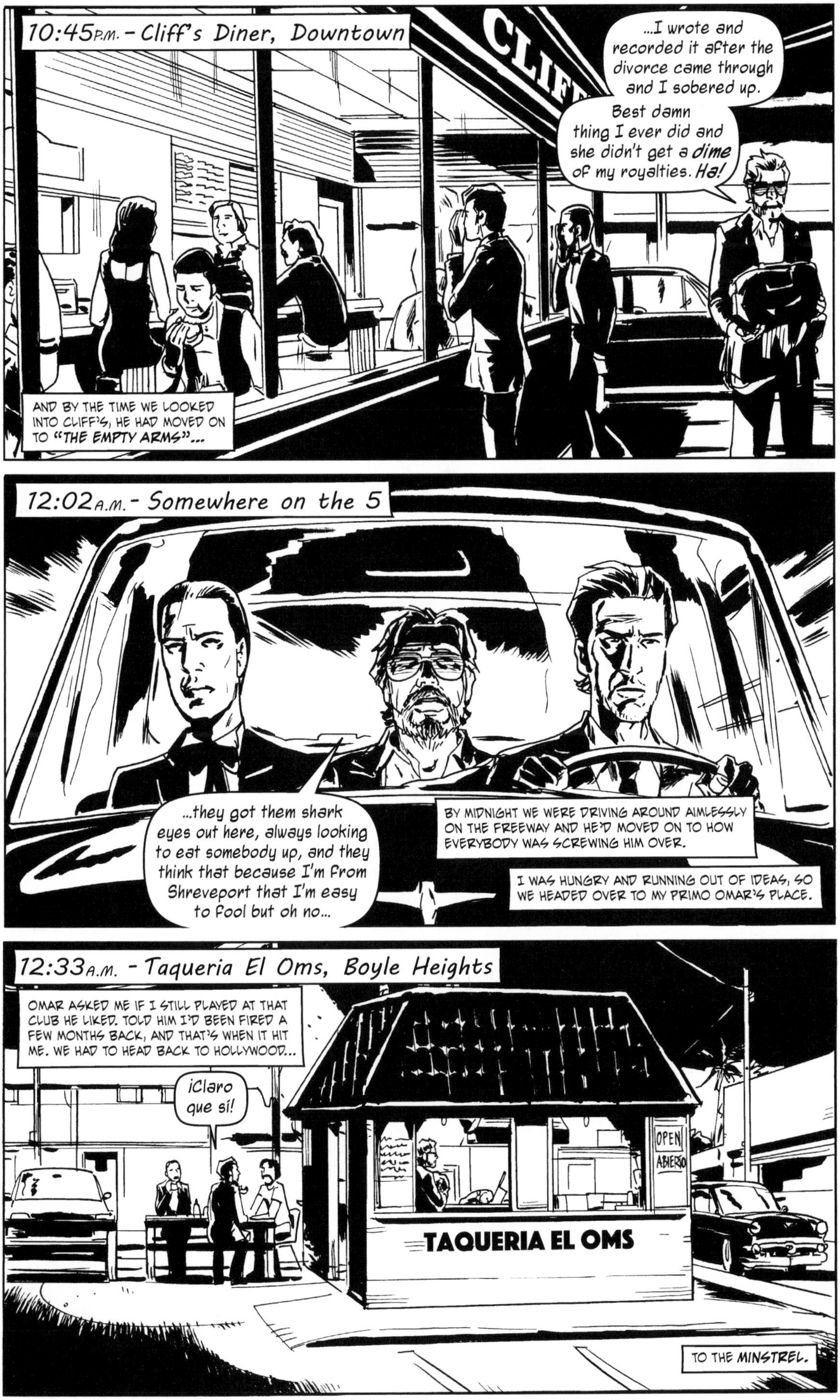
10:45P.M. - Cliff's Diner, Downtown
CLIFF
...I wrote and recorded it after the divorce came through and I sobered up.
Best damn thing I ever did and she didn't get a *dime* of my royalties. *Ha!*
AND BY THE TIME WE LOOKED INTO CLIFF'S, HE HAD MOVED ON TO **"THE EMPTY ARMS"...**
12:02A.M. - Somewhere on the 5
...they got them shark eyes out here, always looking to eat somebody up, and they think that because I'm from Shreveport that I'm easy to fool but oh no...
BY MIDNIGHT WE WERE DRIVING AROUND AIMLESSLY ON THE FREEWAY AND HE'D MOVED ON TO HOW EVERYBODY WAS SCREWING HIM OVER.
I WAS HUNGRY AND RUNNING OUT OF IDEAS, SO WE HEADED OVER TO MY PRIMO OMAR'S PLACE.
12:33A.M. - Taqueria El Oms, Boyle Heights
OMAR ASKED ME IF I STILL PLAYED AT THAT CLUB HE LIKED. TOLD HIM I'D BEEN FIRED A FEW MONTHS BACK, AND THAT'S WHEN IT HIT ME. WE HAD TO HEAD BACK TO HOLLYWOOD...
¡Claro que sí!
OPEN
ABIERTO
TAQUERIA EL OMS
TO THE ***MINSTREL.***

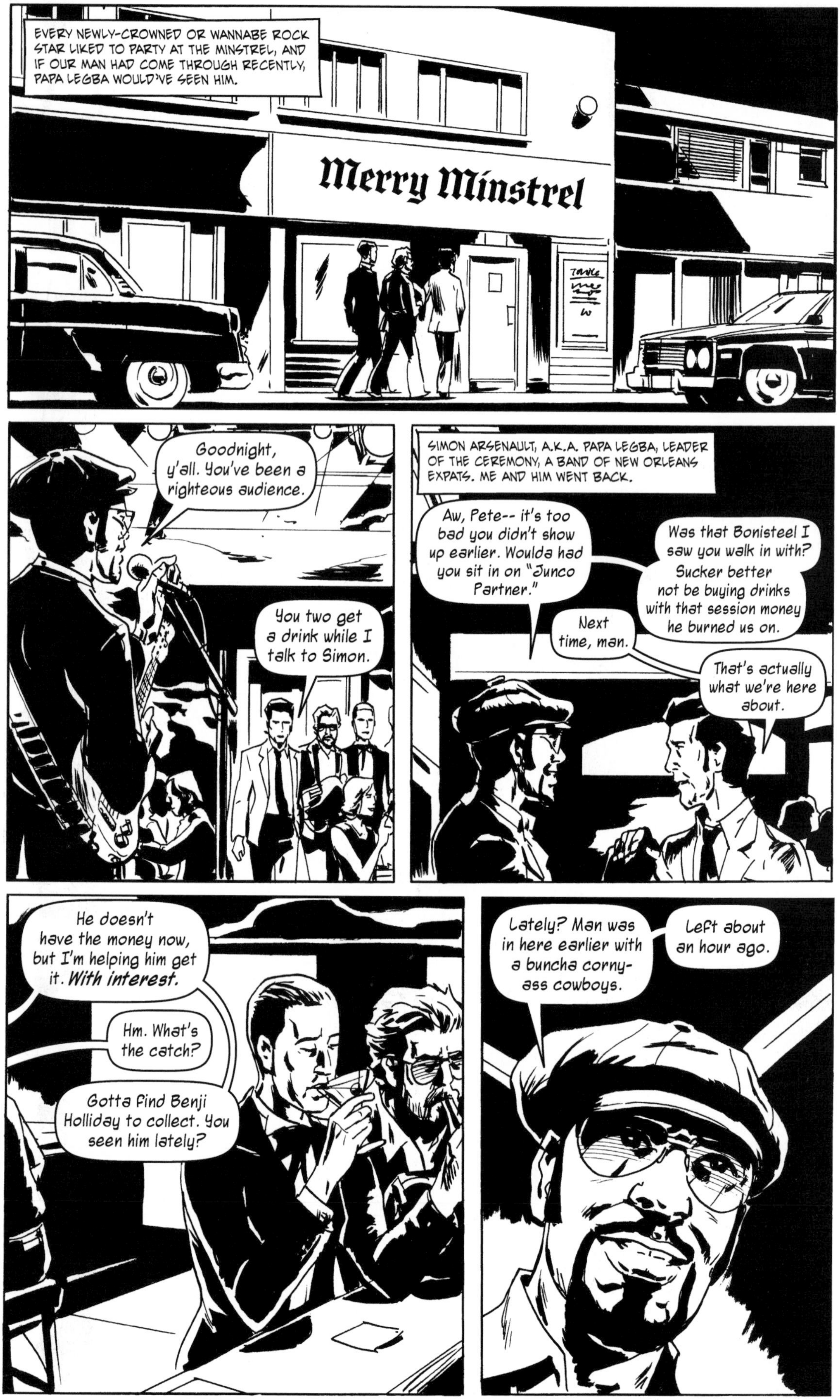
EVERY NEWLY-CROWNED OR WANNABE ROCK STAR LIKED TO PARTY AT THE MINSTREL, AND IF OUR MAN HAD COME THROUGH RECENTLY, PAPA LEGBA WOULD'VE SEEN HIM.
Merry Minstrel
Goodnight, y'all. You've been a righteous audience.
You two get a drink while I talk to Simon.
SIMON ARSENAULT, A.K.A. PAPA LEGBA, LEADER OF THE CEREMONY, A BAND OF NEW ORLEANS EXPATS. ME AND HIM WENT BACK.
Aw, Pete-- it's too bad you didn't show up earlier. Woulda had you sit in on "Junco Partner."
Next time, man.
Was that Bonisteel I saw you walk in with? Sucker better not be buying drinks with that session money he burned us on.
That's actually what we're here about.
He doesn't have the money now, but I'm helping him get it. *With interest.*
Hm. What's the catch?
Gotta find Benji Holliday to collect. You seen him lately?
Lately? Man was in here earlier with a buncha corny-ass cowboys.
Left about an hour ago.

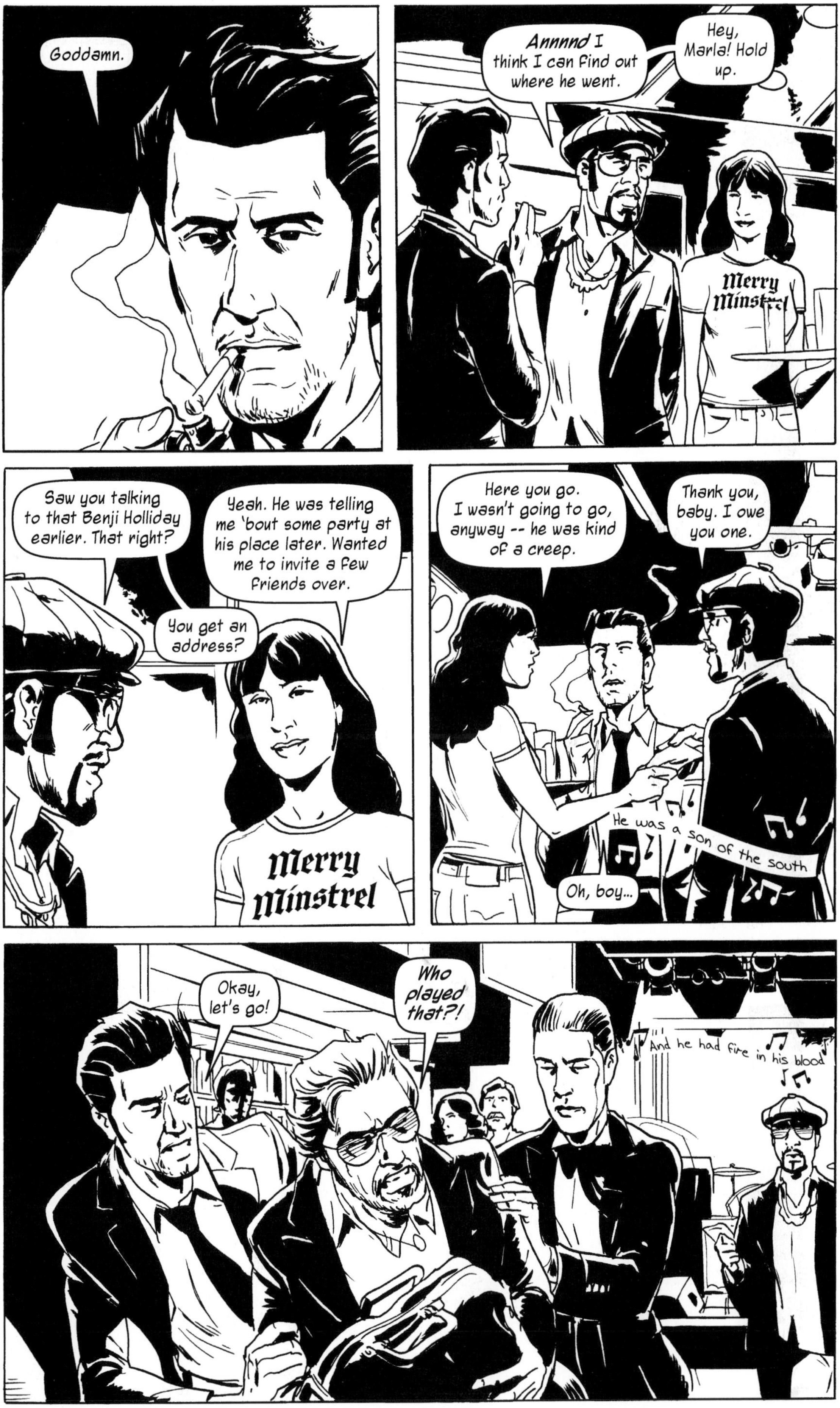
Goddamn.
Annnnd I think I can find out where he went.
Hey, Marla! Hold up.
Merry Minstrel
Saw you talking to that Benji Holliday earlier. That right?
Yeah. He was telling me 'bout some party at his place later. Wanted me to invite a few friends over.
You get an address?
Merry Minstrel
Here you go. I wasn't going to go, anyway -- he was kind of a creep.
Thank you, baby. I owe you one.
He was a son of the south
Oh, boy...
Okay, let's go!
Who played that?!
And he had fire in his blood

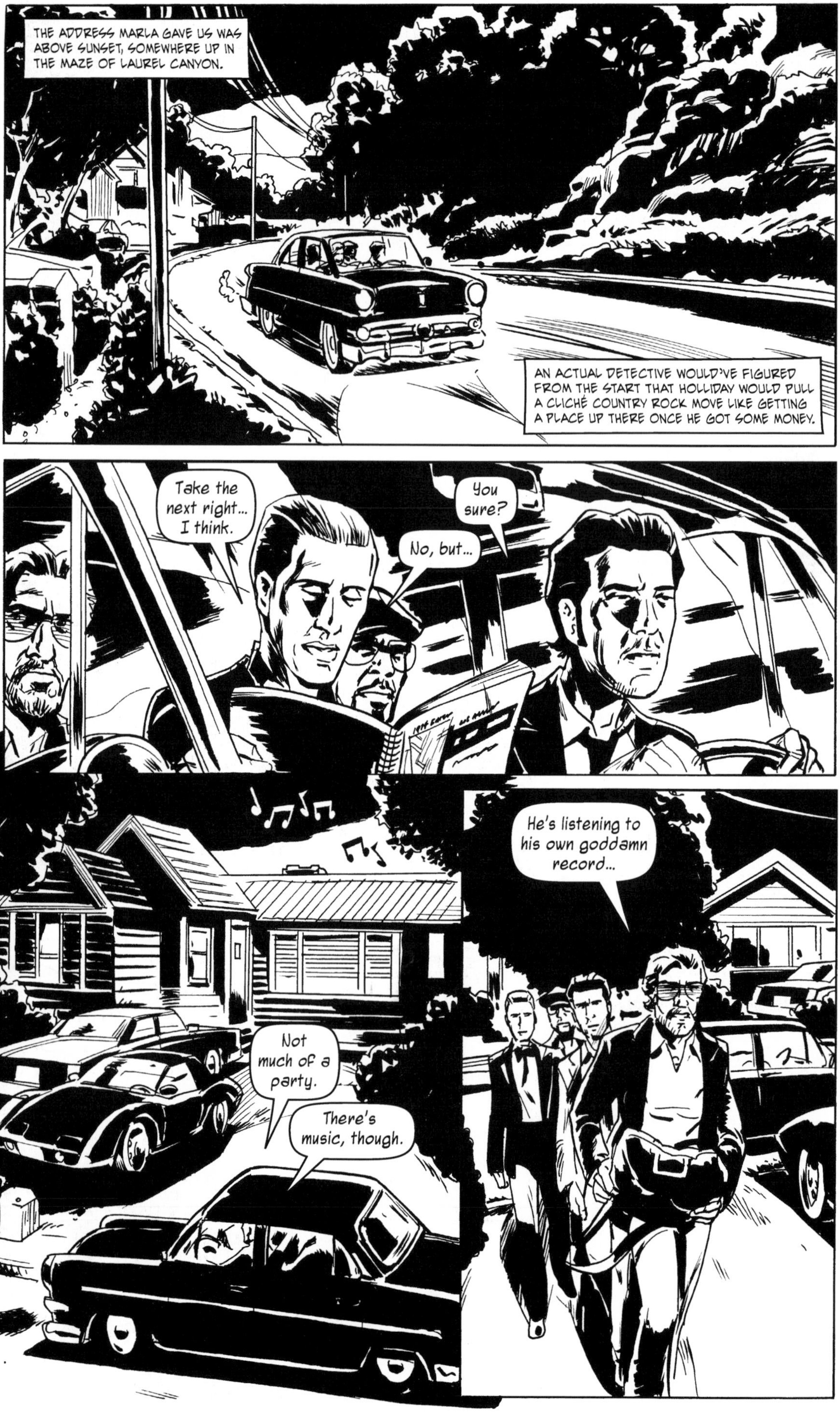
THE ADDRESS MARLA GAVE US WAS ABOVE SUNSET, SOMEWHERE UP IN THE MAZE OF LAUREL CANYON.
AN ACTUAL DETECTIVE WOULD'VE FIGURED FROM THE START THAT HOLLIDAY WOULD PULL A CLICHÉ COUNTRY ROCK MOVE LIKE GETTING A PLACE UP THERE ONCE HE GOT SOME MONEY.
Take the next right... I think.
You sure?
No, but...
Not much of a party.
There's music, though.
He's listening to his own goddamn record...

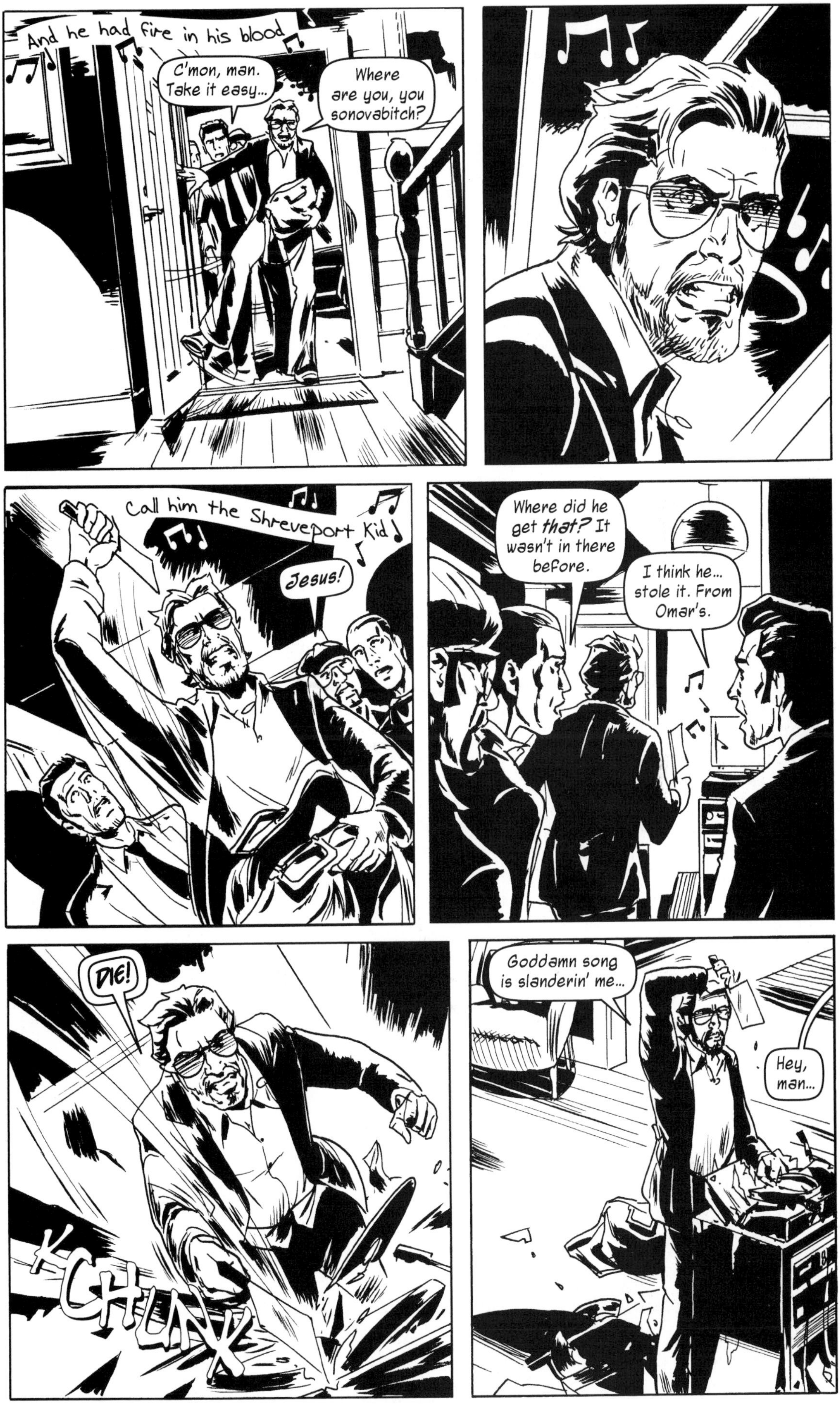
And he had fire in his blood
C'mon, man. Take it easy...
Where are you, you sonovabitch?
Call him the Shreveport Kid
Jesus!
Where did he get that? It wasn't in there before.
I think he... stole it. From Omar's.
DIE!
KCHUNK
Goddamn song is slanderin' me...
Hey, man...

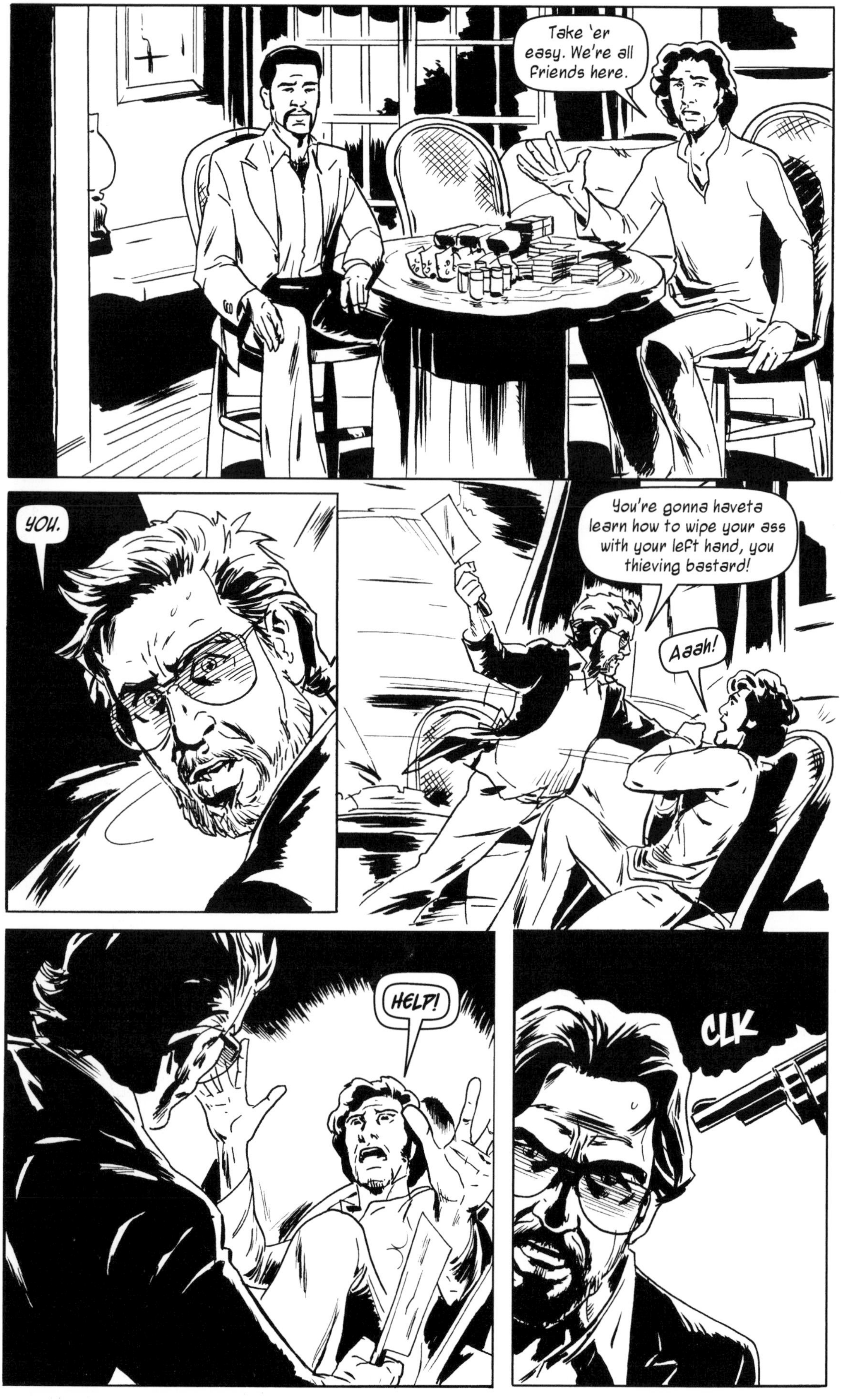

Take 'er easy. We're all friends here.
YOU.
You're gonna haveta learn how to wipe your ass with your left hand, you thieving bastard!
Aaah!
HELP!
CLK

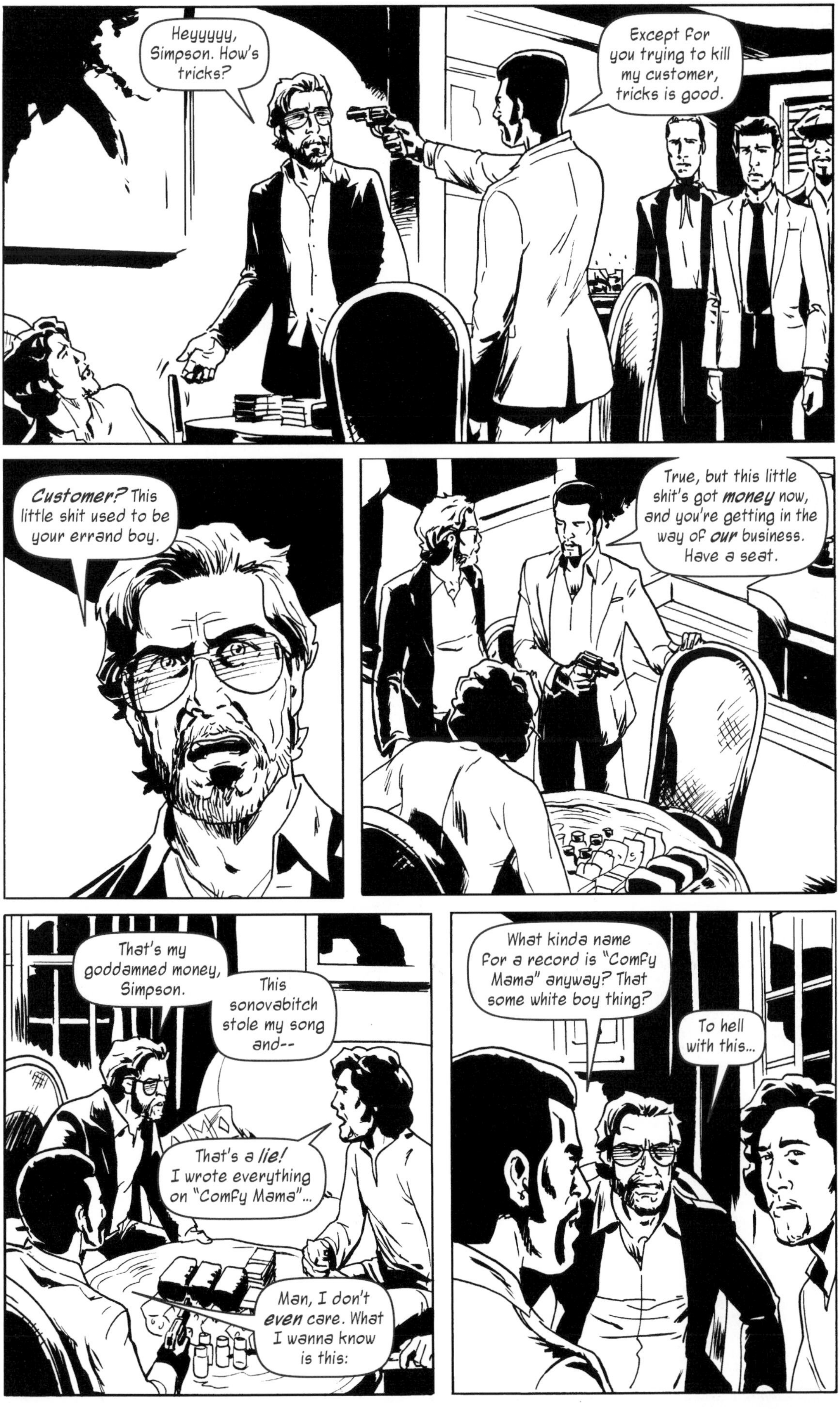
Heyyyyy, Simpson. How's tricks?
Except for you trying to kill my customer, tricks is good.
Customer? This little shit used to be your errand boy.
True, but this little shit's got money now, and you're getting in the way of our business. Have a seat.
That's my goddamned money, Simpson.
This sonovabitch stole my song and--
That's a lie! I wrote everything on "Comfy Mama"...
Man, I don't even care. What I wanna know is this:
What kinda name for a record is "Comfy Mama" anyway? That some white boy thing?
To hell with this...

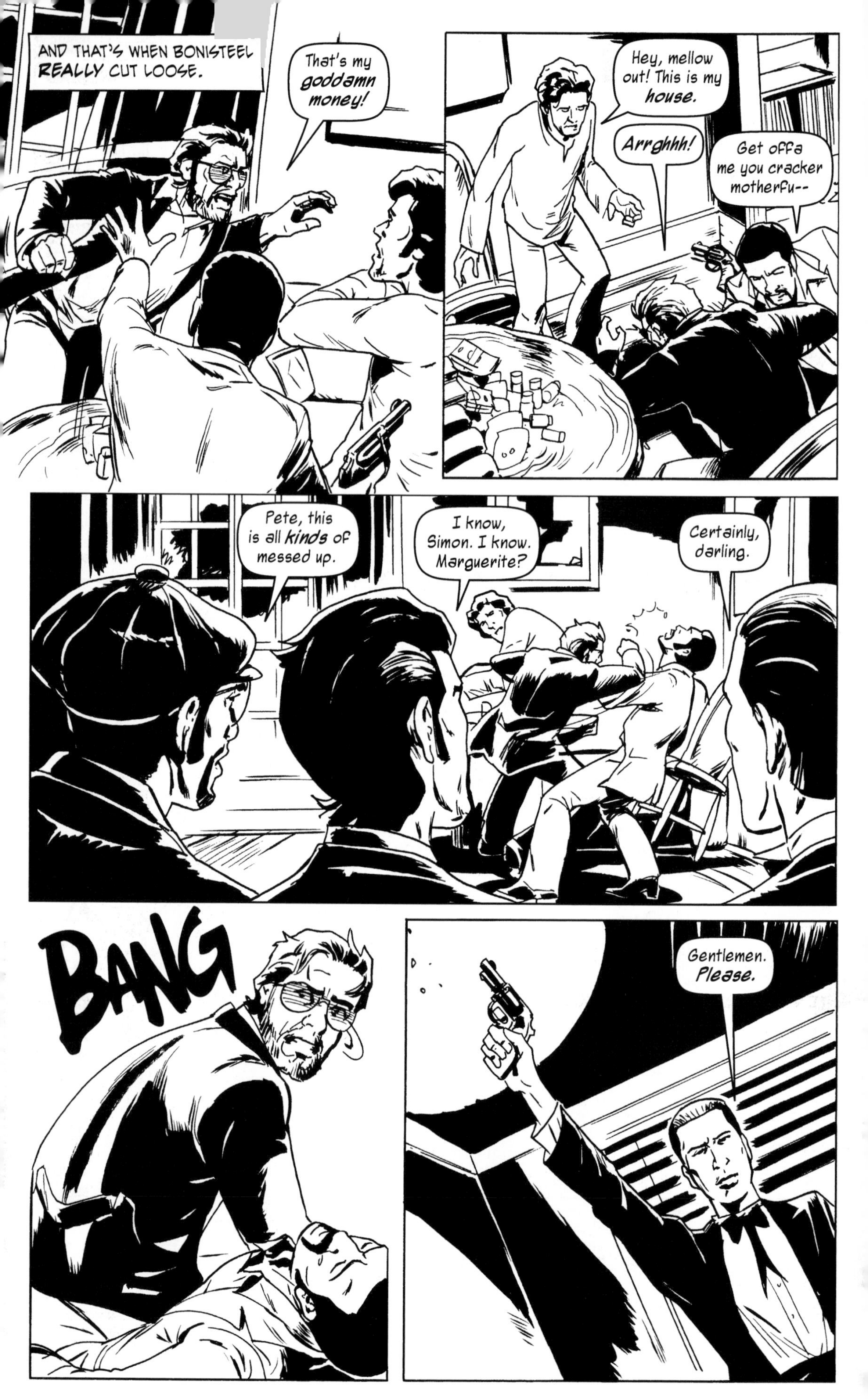
AND THAT'S WHEN BONISTEEL REALLY CUT LOOSE.
That's my goddamn money!
Hey, mellow out! This is my house.
Arrghhh!
Get offa me you cracker motherfu--
Pete, this is all kinds of messed up.
I know, Simon. I know. Marguerite?
Certainly, darling.
BANG
Gentlemen. Please.

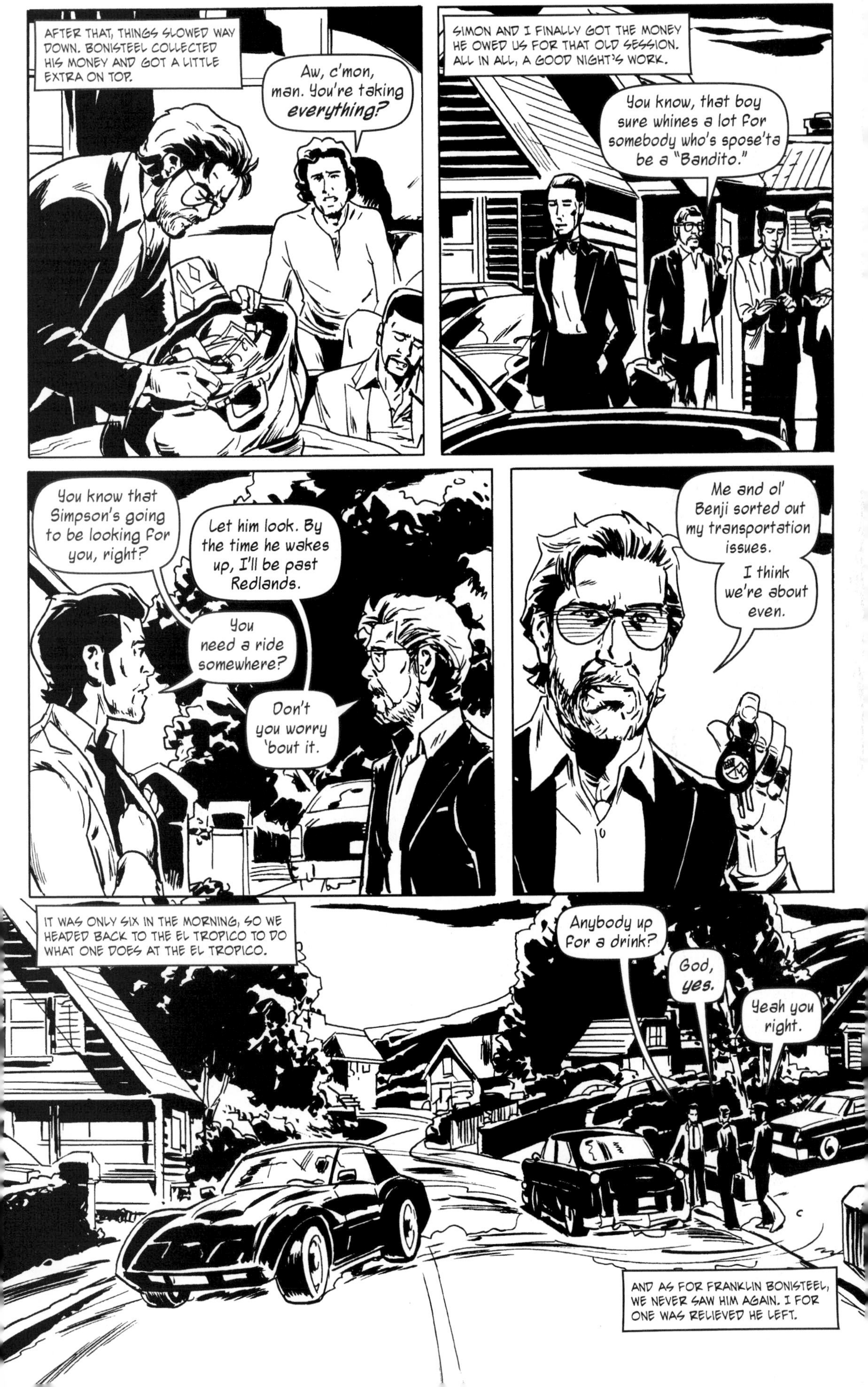
AFTER THAT, THINGS SLOWED WAY DOWN. BONISTEEL COLLECTED HIS MONEY AND GOT A LITTLE EXTRA ON TOP.
Aw, c'mon, man. You're taking *everything?*
SIMON AND I FINALLY GOT THE MONEY HE OWED US FOR THAT OLD SESSION. ALL IN ALL, A GOOD NIGHT'S WORK.
You know, that boy sure whines a lot for somebody who's spose'ta be a "Bandito."
You know that Simpson's going to be looking for you, right?
Let him look. By the time he wakes up, I'll be past Redlands.
You need a ride somewhere?
Don't you worry 'bout it.
Me and ol' Benji sorted out my transportation issues.
I think we're about even.
IT WAS ONLY SIX IN THE MORNING, SO WE HEADED BACK TO THE EL TROPICO TO DO WHAT ONE DOES AT THE EL TROPICO.
Anybody up for a drink?
God, *yes.*
Yeah you right.
AND AS FOR FRANKLIN BONISTEEL, WE NEVER SAW HIM AGAIN. I FOR ONE WAS RELIEVED HE LEFT.

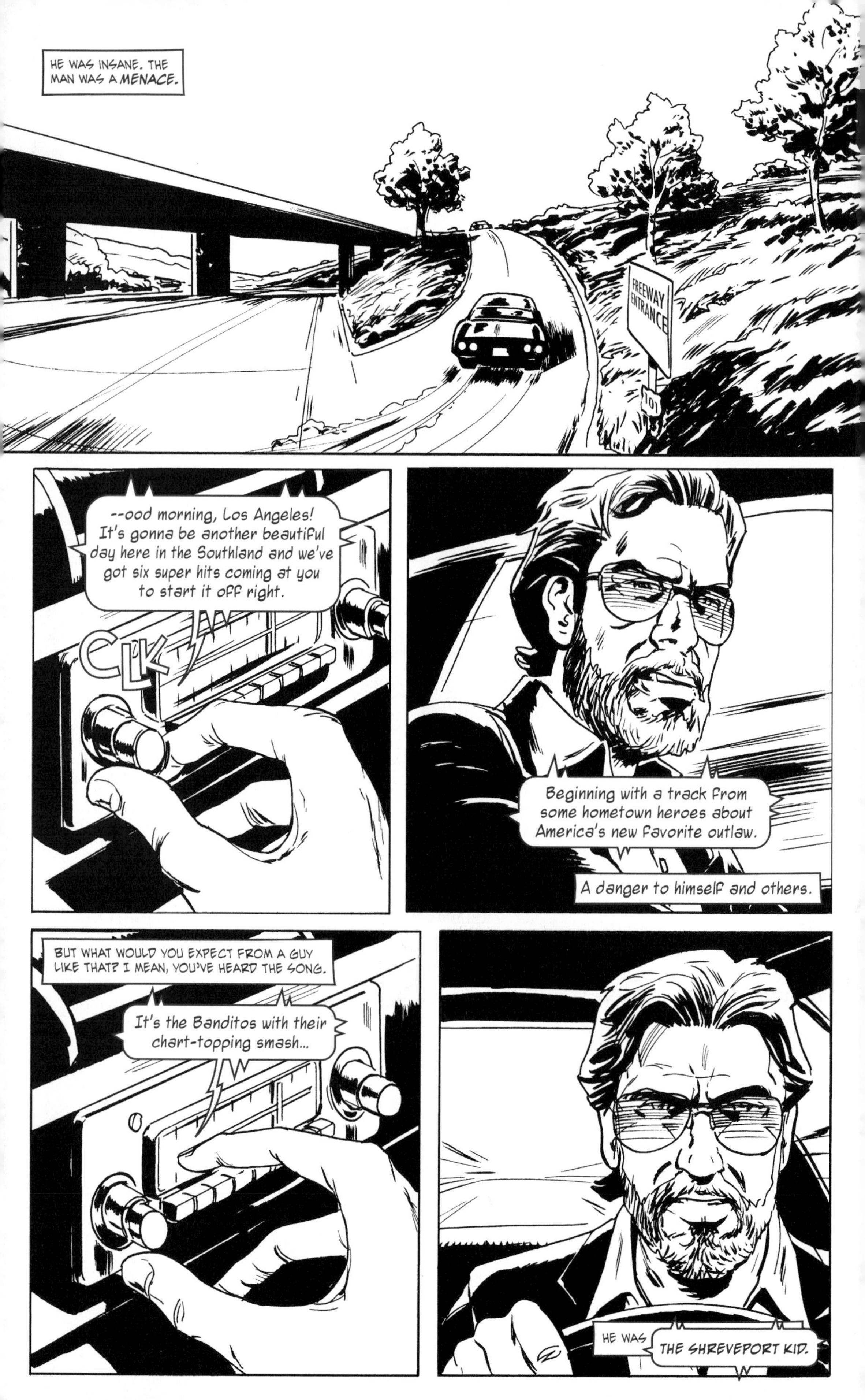
HE WAS INSANE. THE MAN WAS A MENACE.
FREEWAY ENTRANCE
101
--ood morning, Los Angeles! It's gonna be another beautiful day here in the Southland and we've got six super hits coming at you to start it off right.
CLK
Beginning with a track from some hometown heroes about America's new favorite outlaw.
A danger to himself and others.
BUT WHAT WOULD YOU EXPECT FROM A GUY LIKE THAT? I MEAN, YOU'VE HEARD THE SONG.
It's the Banditos with their chart-topping smash...
HE WAS
THE SHREVEPORT KID.

SHOUT OUTS DUE: PAUL REINWAND, CHRIS HUNT KENDRA WELLS AND FRED STRESING, DAN AUERBACH AND EVERYBODY AT EASY EYE, ROBERT FINLEY, LEFTY PARKER, JAMES WEBER, JOE KILE, RYAN, WILL, MAX, JUSTIN AND THE REST OF THE CREW AT EUCLID RECORDS, MAC TAYLOR, BOB MECOY, ANDRES VERA-MARTINEZ, PRESTON LONG, JACKY MORGAN, WADE HAMMETT, PETE RELIC, JOHN PATTERSON, PAUL CULLUM, ST. JOHN FRIZELL, STEVE BURNS, CLARK COLLIS, JASON ADAMS, MIKE CAVALLARO, RON WIMBERLY, DEAN HASPIEL, NICK BERTOZZI, NATE DOYLE, WARREN PLEECE, JESSICA ABEL, JAY BABCOCK, ARIK ROPER, SRIDHAR AND JOSH, ALEX PAPPADEMAS, JOE GROSS, EVIE NAGY, SEAN HOWE, AND ESPECIALLY CHARLIE OLSEN, WHO NEVER, EVER GIVES UP.

--GABE SORIA

I HAVE TO THANK JOSH FRANKEL AND SRIDHAR REDDY OF Z2 COMICS AND WRITER GABE SORIA FOR BRINGING ME ONTO THIS PROJECT, THAT I HAVE COME TO LOVE SO MUCH.

MY FRIEND, MY BROTHER, MY TEACHER-PAUL POPE WHO BOLSTERED MY CONFIDENCE AND HELPED ME MOVE PAST MY INSECURITIES TO REACH NEW HEIGHTS WHILE WORKING ON MB.

MY MOM, BETH SWEIG WHO HAS ALWAYS BEEN THERE FOR ME THROUGH THICK AND THIN, AND CONVINCED ME TO HOLD ON A LITTLE LONGER WHEN I WAS READY TO GIVE UP ON COMICS NOT LONG AGO, AND TO BELIEVE IN MYSELF AND MY WORK.

--CHRIS HUNT